What's Wrong with your Rights?

'The centralisation of State power is the hallmark of the present Government. Roger Cook and Tim Tate vividly describe the gap between the freedoms which are cherished in theory – and the assaults made on them in practice. Their book should be read – and used – by everyone concerned about civil rights. Eternal vigilance is *still* part of the price of liberty!'

Rt. Hon. Neil Kinnock, MP

'I see the 1990s as the decade when the rights of our citizens will be fully recognised, restored and strengthened by written statute. Sadly, the 1980s will undoubtedly be remembered for the years when individual freedom was eroded and weakened.

What's Wrong With Your Rights? represents an accurate and far-sighted account of the situation now. It also illustrates quite dramatically how the State has leapt forward and also often stepped back some way when considering the rights of the individual. . . . It successfully identifies areas where the law needs changing to benefit our citizens.'

Paddy Ashdown, MP

Roger Cook is Britain's best-known investigative reporter. He has presented hard-hitting *exposés* of crime, incompetence and bureaucratic bungling on radio and television for more than eighteen years. *Checkpoint*, the legendary BBC radio investigative series he created, ran from 1973 to 1985, and he now leads Central Television's investigative series, *The Cook Report*. He is married, with one young daughter.

Tim Tate is a freelance investigative journalist. He has worked with Roger Cook since 1982, finding and researching investigations for *Checkpoint* and *The Cook Report*. He is married with five young children.

What's Wrong with your Rights?

Roger Cook and Tim Tate

Methuen · Mandarin

A Mandarin Paperback

WHAT'S WRONG WITH YOUR RIGHTS?

First published in Great Britain 1988
by Methuen London Ltd
This edition published 1989
by Methuen · Mandarin
Michelin House, 81 Fulham Road, London SW3 6RB

Copyright © 1988, 1989 Roger Cook and Tim Tate

Printed in Great Britain
by Cox & Wyman Ltd, Reading

British Library Cataloguing in Publication Data
   Cook, Roger
      What's wrong with your rights?
      1. Great Britain. Civil rights. Law
      I. Title   II. Tate, Tim
      344.102'85

ISBN 7493-0023-X

This book is sold subject to the condition
that it shall not, by way of trade or otherwise,
be lent, resold, hired out, or otherwise circulated
in any form of binding or cover other than that
in which it is published and without a similar condition
being imposed on the subsequent purchaser.

Contents

Introduction ix

1 No Fault or Flaw? 1
2 An Englishman's Home 74
3 A Free Country? 93
4 The Source of all Discontents 119
5 Masters and Servants 163
6 Citizens in Uniform 226
7 And Justice For All 282

Index 285

Introduction

'I know my rights' and 'It's a free country, isn't it?' Two of the comforting things we all say when faced with a major problem at work, at home, anywhere. But do you, and is it?

This book is to help put you on your guard. In almost every aspect of life you have rights and freedoms – and responsibilities. There are pitfalls and hidden traps lying behind all of them. Many handbooks are on the market listing what rights you have in theory, and how to go about enforcing them – in theory again. This book is different, different because we have spent a good deal of time and energy (in Roger's case more than twenty years) trying to see people get those rights, and all too often finding theory depressingly different from practice. Of course, remedies do exist for many of the problems outlined in this book (though for just as many others they do not), but most of them came to our attention precisely because those remedies did not work.

No one is immune. Again and again those who proclaim that 'it could never happen to me' find that it can – and does. In some cases existing rights are being eroded. Freedoms are being circumscribed. Safety nets are being dismantled. Responsibilities are often ill-defined.

Efforts are of course constantly made to improve the quality of life, to revise repressive or archaic legislation. But the process is deadly slow and cumbersome; vested interests are protected to the last. New legislation often makes things worse rather than better, while instilling a renewed – and yet more dangerous – complacency amongst rulers and the ruled.

The problem goes even deeper than that, however. Our system of law – hailed by lawyers and politicians as the envy of the world – rarely bestows on us actual rights. We, unlike many Western democracies, have no written constitution to define the basic powers of the State and our own unassailable freedoms.

Instead we have that typically English phenomenon, the compromise. Ask any lawyer if we have a constitution, and the answer will be an unequivocal 'yes'; ask him where it is, and whether you can have a quick look, you'll get a prevarication. Just because, he or she will explain, our constitution isn't there in black and white for all to see doesn't make it any the worse; rather, it makes it more flexible, more responsive to an ever-changing world. This is almost certainly the only time your lawyer will advise you to accept a vague and unwritten contract which the other party to it hasn't signed. And be in no doubt, written or not, our constitution is the most important contract you will ever get tied up in. So what does it say?

Rather than listing what basic rights you and the State have under the constitution, there is a rough-and-ready concept that anything is lawful unless Parliament forbids it by statute or the courts have established it to be illegal over many years (such rules being known as the common law). It is, perhaps, a fair guide to the way this country is run that the rights of its citizens have never been written down, evolving instead by a process of elimination.

There have of course been attempts through the centuries to create a written constitution, or bill of rights. The latest, in February 1987, would have incorporated the terms of the European Convention on Human Rights into English law (instead of the present position which requires English courts to throw out a case before the European Commission on Human Rights may consider it). It was far from perfect as a means of safeguarding citizens' rights, but it was certainly better than nothing. Significantly, perhaps, it was a private member's bill. More significantly still, it failed to clear its first parliamentary hurdle: fewer than a hundred MPs bothered to turn up and support it and as a result the bill had to be abandoned. Nothing illustrates better the total disregard that our elected representatives have for the civil rights of their electorate than this sad and pathetic spectacle.

Even when Parliament does take action on our behalf, however, we should temper gratitude with caution, because it is often on those comparatively few occasions when rights are handed out that the trouble starts. It is all very well for Parliament to give us rights (such as they are), but unless we are able to enforce them they become no more than a series of well-meant marks on a piece of paper. All too often the whole shaky foundation rests upon that peculiarly British – and mythical – belief in everyone 'playing the game'. This is where the legal machinery and profession are vital – and, as you will read, so often found lacking – in protecting the public.

This book is not exhaustive. Nor is it a civil liberties handbook. It is based around case histories that are sadly all too typical: for every one included there will be literally dozens of others. Above all, this book is a warning of the dangers and defects, the injustices and idiocies, of the very laws passed on our behalf and in our name. We must constantly be on our guard. There is little or no political capital – and certainly no votes – to be made out of the issue of personal rights. For this reason our masters and mistresses in Parliament are frequently less protective of their electorate than they should be. It is no exaggeration to say that we are under attack from every side.

One man's civil rights, after all, are only another man's inconvenience – and all too often that 'other man' turns out to be the representative of government, business, law or the police.

The sheer weight of evidence that our legal system is crumbling and inadequate may at times appear depressing; we have deliberately not tried to lessen that gloom. Instead, we put forward at the end of this book a series of unified suggestions to create a new framework within which the rights of every citizen – rich and poor, rulers and ruled – could, we believe, be sensibly safeguarded.

Roger Cook and Tim Tate

Warning

On 22 November 1988, the government published its long-awaited White Paper on a replacement for the widely discredited Official Secrets Act. Stung by the repeated humiliations heaped upon it in courtrooms round the world during the Spycatcher debacle, the Home Office had promised a less draconian measure.

In fact what emerged was, in some ways, more savage, even more of a catch-all, than before. Not merely did the government propose to close once and for all the loophole by which Peter Wright had made public MI5's illegal plot to topple the Wilson government, but to make almost any disclosure of official information (however minor) an absolute offence. For the first time a defence that disclosure was in the public interest was specifically ruled out.

Three areas of information would be specifically protected: any disclosures by members of the security services, any information about the interception of communications, and several categories of data received from foreign governments.

Many of the cases cited in this book fall squarely within these restrictions. If the White paper enters law unaltered this book would be illegal. Nor do the restrictions apply only to matters of spying or (genuine) national security. Many of the innocent and ordinary people you will read about in the following pages have been painfully caught up in the machinery of the State:

- Madeleine Haigh, who wrote a letter to her local newspaper and became a target for Special Branch surveillance.
- Jan Martin, whose career was almost destroyed by totally unfounded 'intelligence' from a European government.
- Annie Trotter, from Kirriemuir, whom the police wrongly branded a criminal.
- The authors of an official, but unpublished, government investigation into diet-related diseases.
- The pesticides researchers who uncovered deficiencies in the safety tests on a government-approved weedkiller.
- Clive Ponting, the high-flying civil servant whose Whitehall career ended when he helped Parliament uncover a web of deception spun by the Ministry of Defence during the *Belgrano* affair.

Ponting was acquitted of breaking the old Official Secrets Act after he pleaded that his actions had been in the public interest. His story, like countless others featured in this book (and elsewhere) would be circumscribed by the proposed legislation. Such stories could not be reported fully, perhaps depriving the victims of redress, and certainly preventing journalists from fulfilling their proper task of keeping a watchful and critical eye on the workings of our democracy.

ONE

No Fault or Flaw?

'The Law is the true embodiment
Of everything that's excellent.
It has no kind of fault or flaw,
And I, My Lords, embody the law.'

The Lord Chancellor's song from
Iolanthe, W. S. Gilbert

As a nation we like to believe that we have the finest legal system in the world: a bastion of impartial and universal justice, a tried and tested machine the envy of other, less well-equipped, nations. Whether such a claim has any value or is in any way provable is open to doubt, but what is beyond doubt is that our law machine can be neither impartial nor universal in the way it treats us.

Or is it beyond doubt? When Gilbert satirised the office of Lord Chancellor a century ago, he couldn't have imagined that the real-life successors to that office would stubbornly cling to such a doctrine of infallibility. But they, and many others, still do.

In 1982 Lord Hailsham, then Lord Chancellor, declared at the annual conference of the Law Society: 'Lawyers and other members of the professions serve the public by [a] . . . practice involving a considerable degree of self-denial, and a habit of disinterested professional judgement.'

In this chapter we will examine those professions which man and maintain our system of justice and see to what extent they serve us, themselves or the system itself.

A little history

English law first took some sort of formal shape in 1066 with the Norman Conquest and the gradual regularisation of earlier rudimentary local laws. Over the next three centuries full-time judges were introduced, the jury system was created and the traditions of trying cases by ordeal and compurgation (swearing an oath without stumbling or hesitation) replaced by the makings of our 'modern' system. From the beginning there was little doubt about the law's leaning or allegiance: the judges were Kings' judges and the law chiefly concerned with the protection of property and the maintenance of the *status quo* – both of which are, of course, important and necessary duties of any legal system.

The argument against our present law machine is that, while it has developed an immense range of protective legislation and case law with regard to those duties, it has largely ignored the need for similar protection to be given to the ordinary citizen. Such protection as there is has only been granted after a long struggle, and does not amount to a real tradition of public interest law. Perhaps we shouldn't be too surprised by this; lawyers, after all, have to earn a living and the big money is to be found with those who have something to defend – the owners of property.

Before we embark upon our examination of the component parts of our legal system and what they are supposed to do, let us call our first witness. Miss Betty Burke Hayward was, in a small way, an owner of property – a small but pleasant flat in West London. Miss Hayward's story is one to keep in mind; it is as chilling an example of what is wrong with all aspects of our system as can be imagined.

Early in 1967 Miss Hayward, the head of remedial teaching at a London school, scraped together enough money to buy a ninety-eight-year lease on a flat in London's West End. Four years later, she decided to let it out for twelve months while she took a working holiday abroad, and set about finding a tenant.

It wasn't until the end of February 1972 that Miss Hayward found the right person. Her estate agents recommended the Vicomte de Borenden, a French aristocrat, war hero and man of the world: gracious, grand and apparently wealthy. The flat, he said, was just the *pied à terre* he was looking for in London; he normally lived at l'Hôtel George Cinq in Paris, but since he was about to become chairman of a London publishing house, he needed a base in town. A deal was quickly struck.

Within nine months Miss Hayward had served nearly a week's imprisonment for contempt of court, forfeited her lease, lost all her savings, was being sued for debt and was forced to go back to court simply to obtain the few remaining clothes and possessions she had left behind when taken to Holloway prison. Incredibly, Miss Hayward had done nothing at all to justify this ordeal. She was simply a victim of all the worst faults of our system combining in the same place at the same time. Although hers is an extreme case, it serves as an awful warning of the flaws and faults in our law machine.

Fessenden Charles Rex Morley-Morley, Vicomte de Borenden, company chairman, war hero and sometime resident of l'Hôtel George Cinq, had been born plain Rex Morley, the son of a warehouseman, in Auckland, New Zealand in 1902. But the young Rex evidently had a taste for the high life and began travelling the world, collecting – by his own account – a string of company directorships, a clutch of war service medals, and the gratitude of several governments.

The version of his life held on file at Scotland Yard reveals a rather different picture: he had excited the interest of the Fraud Squad for several years prior to meeting Betty Hayward, he had been made bankrupt – twice, he had four fraud convictions to his several names and was about to face seventeen further fraud charges at the very moment he took possession of Miss Hayward's flat.

Not, of course, that she knew any of that; she had no reason to suspect that he was anything other than an ideal tenant. 'But by the end of the year I had received only two rent cheques and in fact was totally penniless, unable to pay my own rent and quite desperate. He had even persuaded me to lend him more than £1,000 of my savings.'

Finally, at her wits' end, she visited the Fraud Squad, who explained that she'd been had. At roughly the same time, Morley–Morley obtained an injunction – without Miss Hayward's knowledge – banning her from entering her own flat. He did so quite simply by lying convincingly to a judge, who apparently never thought to check the truth of the 'Vicomte's' claim to the flat. Then, on 3 September 1973, eighteen months after he moved into her flat, Morley-Morley telephoned Miss Hayward at her digs.

It was, he told her, all over; he had conned her, and he was sorry. The police had charged him with fraud, but he was now going into hospital for an operation and would she like her flat back?

Betty Hayward was delighted and immediately moved back into her home. But she'd been conned again, and within days Morley-Morley's solicitor, Anthony S. Feldman, applied successfully to have her committed to prison for breaking the original injunction not to re-enter her flat.

In doing so Feldman had badly deceived the court. He knew full well that Morley-Morley was facing both criminal fraud charges and proceedings in the civil courts. He should also have known – that had the judge known about these proceedings, or about Morley-Morley's undischarged bankruptcy, he would never have sent Miss Hayward to prison. But Feldman kept quiet and Miss Hayward spent four unforgettable days and nights in Holloway.

> I was carted off and the first morning was spent in the reception wing, together with terrifying drug addicts and the spillage from the magistrates' courts who in the course of the morning are brought into Holloway and dried out. Conditions were just as horrific as they have been described over and over again – one of the prison officers was totally sadistic. When I was released from prison it was just with the clothes I stood up in, not a penny in the world and nothing to return to.

The effects of four days in the hothouse conditions of a womens' prison on a middle-aged spinster who has already been through eighteen months of trauma aren't hard to imagine. But Betty Hayward struggled on.

She decided to sue Morley-Morley and Feldman. Suing a solicitor is never easy, however, and in Betty Hayward's case it was made almost impossible when solicitors repeatedly declined to act for her and she was regularly refused legal aid. Finally, on Friday, 19 December 1975, with Miss Hayward acting for herself, the case came before Lord Denning, then Master of the Rolls.

Lord Denning was impressed. Morley-Morley, alias Vicomte de Borenden, was a thorough-going confidence trickster, he said, and should pay compensation for his original misdemeanours and for having Miss Hayward imprisoned. But there was a snag. 'I'm afraid that that order may not be of much avail to her,' Lord Denning said, 'because the Vicomte de Borenden, or Mr Morley, is on social security. He has no money at all.'

As for Anthony Feldman, Lord Denning was far from satisfied with his behaviour. He ordered that the solicitor be brought before him to explain just why he hadn't felt obliged to reveal his client's background and forthcoming court appearance. Lord Denning also asked the Law Society to grant legal aid to Miss Hayward. Neither of Lord Denning's requests were met. Even though he was the most important civil judge in the land, his remarks were never acted upon. So Miss Hayward continued to be refused legal aid, and Feldman was never brought to court to explain himself. Meanwhile, Miss Hayward was ruined.

It was to take her until 1983 to find a solicitor who would believe her story and who managed to get her a limited amount of legal aid. But by then it was too late. Morley-Morley had died and Feldman was out of danger simply because the time that had elapsed prevented any action against him.

In effect [Miss Hayward says] this has been like having spent ten years in prison – except more painful; my life savings, my work, about which I cared very deeply and which I tried to be good at, being denied me. My family believed me to be a guilty party and have ostracised me. I have been frightened – extremely frightened – and my whole faith in everything which I previously – perhaps naively – believed, has been totally undermined.

Just what was it, then, that Betty Hayward had believed in? She had thought what we all want to think: that English law dispenses justice. But she had found that the law itself can't protect the innocent from those who choose to ignore it; that the judiciary can be at times blind and unquestioning, and at other times conveniently ignored; that lawyers can be both mendacious and craven; that the courts can exclude the weak and helpless from their protection; that prisons can remain Victorian hellhouses closed to the few concerned eyes watching from the outside.

She had also found that the financial safety net established to help those unable to pay for legal representation has huge, gaping holes in it. And she would later learn another lesson about the people whose job it is to pay compensation to the victims of our law machine – a lesson we'll come to further on in this chapter.

But first we must examine the component parts of our system of justice – the judiciary and courts, solicitors and barristers, juries, compensation, law-breakers, and the law itself.

We shall start at the top, with the judiciary.

The judges

Our laws are made by Parliament (or that is to say our *written* laws are made by Parliament – the rag-bag of unwritten 'common law' is based on the decisions of earlier judges) and in theory our judges cannot alter statutes or common law.

In practice they do both, by interpreting what the actual words of a law or a judgement might really mean, a process they call 'distinguishing'. Some judges are more adventurous in this area than others – Lord Denning being the foremost adventurer in recent history. Judges are allowed a good deal of latitude in exercising their discretion; and that, in turn, means that the way they think and are trained to behave – and their social, educational and political backgrounds – are very important factors. Which is why many non-lawyers (and even some lawyers) view the shallow and exclusive pool from which our judges are drawn with a good deal of alarm.

There are at any given time roughly 420 part-time judges, known as recorders, plus a further 550 assistant recorders; 370 circuit (junior) judges; 77 High Court (senior) judges; and 11 Law Lords, who, together with the Lord Chancellor, form the highest court in the land in the House of Lords.

Four out of five full-time professional judges have had public-school educations, and two-thirds are graduates from Oxford and Cambridge. With few exceptions full-time judges are selected by an arcane procedure from the ranks of practising barristers, and since it is very difficult indeed to survive the first years of practice at the bar without a private income – 'pupils' are paid little or no money by their 'masters' – it follows that most barristers, and therefore almost all judges, have well-off families to support them.

This is not, of course, necessarily a bad thing. But the traditions and confines of a barrister's life make for even further separation from the lives of those for whom they act and, later in their careers, whom they will sentence. It is a common criticism – and one not without foundation – that our judiciary is by and large ignorant of the strains and pressures faced by most of their 'clients'.

On 26 May 1915, the then Master of the Rolls (the most senior civil judge outside the Lords), Lord Cozens-Hardy, wrote to Lord Buckmaster about the latter's appointment as Lord Chancellor. 'There is,' he said, 'one matter which I ought to mention. All the judges, without exception, are members of the Athenaeum [a

London gentlemen's club] and I presume you will wish to be a member. If so, may I have the pleasure of proposing you?'

More than seventy years later, little has changed. Judges belong to one or two 'legal' clubs in the environs of St James's and circuit judges live in no little splendour in a network of fine houses (known prosaically as judges' lodgings) when sitting in courts around the country. Similarly, most of the potential judges of the future, London barristers, practise from a warren of medieval Inns of Court, and must by tradition – strictly enforced – 'dine in' a set number of evenings every year.

It all sounds, at first hearing, a cosy and harmless tradition. But the attitudes such traditions breed in our judicial minds can be far from cosy, as a Miss Ward, a student at Bradford Teacher Training College was to discover.

By 1972 what sociologists are pleased to call the 'sexual revolution', and politicians prefer to label 'the permissive society', was well-established. It had long ceased to be regarded as a mortal sin for young unmarried men and women to sleep together. But Bradford College retained a rule which forbade women students from entertaining men in their hall-of-residence rooms. Miss Ward (together, it should be said, with a large section of the college population) chose to ignore the rules. The college principal found out and advised Miss Ward to move into other, less choosy, lodgings – which she duly did. Then, the college's governing body decided to make an example of Miss Ward, though the rules prevented them from disciplining any student unless the principal asked them to – which she did not. Undeterred, the governors simply changed the rule and expelled the unfortunate Miss Ward.

The ensuing case reached the Court of Appeal and Lord Denning. He wasn't worried that the governors had acted as judge and jury in their own favour, despite a long-held principle of natural justice forbidding this to happen, nor by the retrospective aspect of their decision under the new rules (normally retrospective laws are not allowed).

Instead, he upheld the expulsion (and with it the ending of Miss Ward's chosen career). 'I expect,' he explained, 'the governors and the staff all thought she was quite an unsuitable person . . . She would never make a teacher. No parent would knowingly entrust their child to her care.'

If Lord Denning held such a romantic view of young ladies and their virtue (a quality unexpected, perhaps, in a man who had, a decade earlier, conducted an enquiry into the Profumo sex scandal), some of his judicial colleagues are a good deal less chivalrous. Judge Michael Argyle, for example, once freed an attempted rapist with these ringing words: 'You come from Derbyshire, which is my part of the world. Now off you go.'

Or then again, Judge Brian Gibbens had the following words to say while summing up in the case of a man who, while drunk, had had sex with his friend's seven-year-old daughter: 'It strikes me, without belittling the offence, as one of the kind of accidents which happen in life to almost anyone, although of a wholly different kind.'

At least there was some public disquiet when circuit judge Bertie Richards let a businessman off with a fine for raping a seventeen-year-old girl. The victim had been hitchhiking home alone and late at night, so she was obviously, decided the judge, 'guilty of a great deal of contributory negligence'. But although this caused a storm of public protest, the judicial profession was apparently unconcerned. Sir Melford Stevenson, a retired High Court judge, weighed in on the controversy thus: 'It is the height of imprudence for any girl to hitchhike at night. She is in the true sense asking for it.'

The task of keeping the judiciary in line falls to the Lord Chancellor. Did he promptly discipline or dismiss Mr Justice Richards? Not a bit of it. He merely issued a gentle rebuke by dissociating himself from Richards's comments.

The Lord Chancellor took a similarly tolerant view of another of Judge Gibbens's opinions, this time (and only a matter of weeks after considering sex with a child an accident) delivered to those present in an attempted suicide case: 'I wish these people would show more efficiency about their overdoses. How much trouble they would save.'

Only once, in fact, did Hailsham publicly rebuke a judge. In January 1984 Recorder Simon Goldstein made the mistake of criticising Woolworths' management for prosecuting a seventy-seven-year-old widow for a piece of petty shoplifting. Hailsham, reproved Goldstein for his 'insolence'. Certainly there is no evidence of any complaints by the public resulting in a judge being hauled over the coals – a fact which is perhaps not surprising since there is no such thing as a judicial complaints board. Lord Hailsham acknowledged that such a body might be a helpful tool in dealing with public complaints about the judiciary – but did no more. Even a proposal to give the prosecution a right of appeal against lenient sentences has been watered down – and, as we write, is by no means certain to become law.

Perhaps the real problem lies in the fact that there is no real training for the bench. Unlike other countries in Europe (notably France), judges do not make up a separate profession, nor do we have a judicial training school. Instead, those selected for the bench receive, on average, three and a half days' training – plus, of course, the lifetime of experience they have had as a practising barrister.

Critics of the present educational system point to the success of an American national judicial education programme which deals with, amongst other things, changing social values, economic realities and attempts to iron out sexual stereotypes and biases. But the major flaw in legal administration is the patronage and power wielded by the Lord Chancellor. He alone appoints High Court and circuit judges, recorders, and stipendiary and lay magistrates.

Appointments to the higher courts are made by the Queen on the recommendation of the Prime Minister – who in turn receives recommendations from the Lord Chancellor. All these appointments are carried out in secret, and the system for choosing those who will sit in judgement on their fellow men is unknown, save for the fact that the Lord Chancellor takes soundings from other senior members of the judiciary and the bar.

As if that were not remarkable enough, we should not forget that the office of Lord Chancellor is in many ways the strangest in the entire British constitution.

In one man are combined three separate (and, one might have thought, wildly conflicting) roles. He is: a senior member of the Cabinet and head of a government office, the Lord Chancellor's Department; a judge who may sit in any court including the House of Lords, the highest court in the land; an officer of Parliament as Speaker of the House of Lords.

For none of these roles is he accountable to the House of Commons, and all too frequently any attempt to criticise his role or office within that House is viewed as a dangerous attack on the constitution. Instead, every day that Parliament meets, the Lord Chancellor parades through the heavily carpeted corridors in full-bottomed horse-hair wig, ruff, and knee-breeches, before perching uncomfortably on the Woolsack.

He has little to do, since the House of Lords, unlike the Commons, rarely needs keeping in order. It is, in short, a waste of his time. Critics of the system – including those from within, like Lord Tony Gifford, QC – want to replace the Lord Chancellor's office with a fully fledged Ministry of Justice.

> It is one thing to perpetuate ancient rituals in order to attract the tourists. But it is not acceptable for an important government position to become encrusted by traditions which have lost their meaning. Like other areas of essential social provision, justice should be the responsibility of a minister accountable to the House of Commons, who should not necessarily be a lawyer. The Minister of Education is not required to be a teacher, nor the Health Minister a doctor.

Either way, Lord Gifford argues, 'the Minister of Justice should not have the right to sit as a judge. It is contradictory to the concept of an independent judiciary that a Cabinet minister should sit in the highest courts in the land.' (Tony Gifford, *Where's the Justice?*, Penguin, 1986.)

Lord Gifford is, of course, a Labour peer, and thus sees the law rather differently from the majority of senior practitioners. In particular, he sees the law as an 'essential social provision', rather than the traditional view that law and justice is a profitable business for lawyers.

His belief in the need for a Ministry of Justice is shared by other lawyers, however. A clearly defined department with clearly stated rules for appointments and disciplining judges (plus responsibility for overseeing the entire legal system – a responsibility at present stretched across three government departments) might not be open to the sort of criticism levelled at the Lord Chancellor's Department over, for example, the choice of Sir John Donaldson as successor to Lord Denning as Master of the Rolls in 1982.

Donaldson, rightly or wrongly, had a reputation as a politician of the same hue as Hailsham which dated from his days as a local councillor and from his presidency of the National Industrial Relations Court. The court was created by Edward Heath's 1971 Industrial Relations Act and was despised universally by the unions. Donaldson's reputation wasn't helped when, in 1982, he gave private advice to the Conservative government on how the judiciary could be used more effectively to control industrial relations.

Even more importantly, however, a Ministry of Justice with an allied training, selection and promotion arm for judges and magistrates could put an end to the iniquitous system whereby lawyers are afraid to speak out for fear of being blacklisted from judicial office by the Lord Chancellor, and where judges can find themselves dismissed apparently on a whim.

We will see in Chapter 3 what happened to one, Judge James Pickles, when he dared to air his views in public. Judge Pickles risked dismissal, despite an admission by Sir John Donaldson himself that there is a real need for some formalised machinery to enable judges to speak out in the public interest.

The treatment of Manus Nunan is even more alarming. Nunan was made a recorder in 1978. The appointment was renewed in 1981, and was due to be renewed again at the end of 1984. Early that year Nunan asked to be considered for a permanent, full-time judge's job. The Lord Chancellor's Department gave every indication of taking the request seriously. Nunan had, after all, averaged fifty days a year on the bench and no conviction of his had ever been upset by a higher court, nor had any notice of appeal alleging misconduct ever been filed.

On 10 September he was invited to meet Thomas Legg, the civil servant in charge of judicial appointments at the Lord Chancellor's London headquarters in Page Street. Legg, according to Nunan's notes (the accuracy of which has been agreed by the Lord Chancellor's Department), told him: 'Your reputation professionally is of the highest. You are a pillar of the northern circuit. And of course we regard you as a person of the highest integrity.' On the debit side, said Legg, Nunan was 'a bit unpredictable, impatient and theatrical'.

Nunan accepted the criticism – though he told Legg that he thought impatience could be an asset on the bench in dealing with the notorious delays in the system. In turn Legg promised to try to arrange more sittings in London. On 11 October Legg wrote to Nunan explaining that problems of cost ruled out any more London sittings, but that he would be be back in touch shortly about renewing Nunan's post as a recorder in the provinces.

Letters of renewal were issued to recorders at the end of October 1984. One-third of the total number of part-time judges were involved in this process of re-selection. All but one – Manus Nunan – were re-appointed. Legg wrote him a curt note to the effect that Lord Hailsham had decided against him. There was no explanation.

The letter came as a bombshell, and Nunan quickly wrote asking for a reason why he had been so summarily sacked – particularly in view of Legg's comments at their meeting. At first Legg disputed Nunan's version of their meeting, and added that Hailsham's decision was also taken 'in the light . . . of further extensive consultations thereafter.'

There had been a stenographer present at the September meeting, so Nunan asked to see a transcript of his conversation with Legg. He also suggested that any adverse report on his conduct should be shown in confidence to a neutral figure – he suggested any judge the Lord Chancellor cared to choose – and that if the judge then assured him that there were serious criticisms he would concede defeat. Both requests were summarily refused. Instead, Legg wrote to say that Hailsham's office had made further enquiries during October and November, and had put these together with 'substantial adverse reports' from chief clerks in a number of courts plus 'a significant number of circuit judges as well as others.'

All of this was news to Nunan. Surprised and deeply hurt that his colleagues should feel like this, he approached a string of senior judges on the northern circuit – including those in Manchester and Liverpool where he sat most often – and both of the presiding northern circuit judges. All, he claims, denied making any criticism of him and were as mystified as he was by his sacking.

Nunan went on to double-check that complaints hadn't been made by barristers on the circuit. The leader of the northern bar – the channel for any complaints against a judge or recorder – was so surprised that he wrote to Hailsham's office for an explanation. He got the same response – there had been various unsourced and unspecific complaints about Nunan. To date no one has told Manus Nunan what he allegedly did wrong, nor who says so.

In the absence of any official explanation, Nunan began searching for his own. On 11 October Legg had written to him indicating that his post would be renewed; by the end of the month Hailsham had decided to sack him. What had happened in the intervening three weeks?

On 12 October 1984 the Grand Hotel in Brighton exploded. The bomb, planted by the Provisional IRA, was intended to kill Margaret Thatcher and the leaders of the Tory Cabinet in Brighton for the party conference. Manus Nunan is an Irish citizen.

The possibility that a senior member of the government could allow himself to be swayed into taking revenge on an Irish lawyer by an act of terrorism took Nunan's breath away. It was surely incredible? Or was it? Some colleagues now share his view, including a QC, and a recorder on his old circuit has accused Hailsham of a petulant decision and his department of a cover-up. 'All the evidence,' says Nunan, 'points in one direction, however horrific and unbelievable that direction may be.'

Nunan broke a self-imposed eighteen-month silence to discuss the case in public in June 1986. A month later the Attorney General (less senior than the Lord Chancellor) – announced in response to a request from the Bar Council that Hailsham would reconsider his decision and that Nunan would get a proper explanation of the original sacking.

A meeting was finally fixed for 26 September 1986 – nearly two years after Hailsham removed Nunan from the bench. The transcript which Nunan has made available shows just how alarmingly unjust and unjudicial the Lord Chancellor is empowered to be. Hailsham began by saying that he would give 'as much detail as is appropriate' about his original decision. Nunan quickly found out that his view of what was appropriate differed significantly from Hailsham's.

Would the Lord Chancellor say who were the mysterious sources of complaint? No, the Lord Chancellor wouldn't. Could he provide transcripts of the cases in which he was supposed to have given cause for complaint? No, he couldn't – and what's more it was not really up to him to give reasons for the sacking. It was up to Nunan to prove that he was suitable. 'It's no good harping back and saying that I have got to provide instances and so on,' Hailsham explained. 'You have got to persuade me that you are up to snuff.'

And so it went on. Hailsham gave a little ground: his sources included judges, presiding judges and senior barristers. They all said that Nunan was 'lowering the standard' of courts in which he sat and, worse, was considered 'something of a joke' – but more than that he couldn't, or wouldn't, say. 'I cannot be able [sic] to produce anything more than the effect you produced on the people whom I consulted.'

But, said Nunan, none of these judges could have been in his court – not one of them. So how could they pass judgement on him? Hailsham refused to be drawn any further, but in a subsequent letter he said that it all came down to 'tone and atmosphere, professional personality and total performance' – in all of which departments his sources apparently said Nunan had been found wanting. He did admit, however, that Nunan hadn't actually been guilty of any misdemeanour he could put his finger on; nor had any of his judgements been overturned.

While Nunan was considering those few details that Hailsham had been prepared to divulge, Judge Pickles began taking an interest. He found few judges willing to be quoted on the touchy subject of judicial appointments, but court clerks – many of whom sat in cases where Nunan was involved – were almost unanimous in praising him. One said: 'When we were stuck for a judge we always suggested Mr Nunan. He had a brusque manner and took short notes and got the backs up of some barristers at times, but he was efficient at getting through the work.'

The chief clerk at the same court confirmed this view: 'We were very willing to have Mr Nunan and used to ring and ask for him.'

Nunan's suspicion that Hailsham allowed the Brighton bombing to influence him is surely wide of the mark. It is just as likely that those barristers irritated with his style had the ear of the Lord Chancellor. The problem is that under the present secret system of electing and disciplining judges the true facts are concealed behind the omnipotent figure of the Lord Chancellor. Both Nunan and Pickles are highly critical of the methods of hiring and firing the judiciary, and of the legal profession's ability to stand up to the Lord Chancellor.

'The trouble,' Nunan believes, 'is that judges and barristers are unwilling to press this case or enquire too deeply because they are all terrified of the Lord Chancellor's Department. It is like an oriental court, wielding absolute power. I can see the fear in their eyes. It is a ghastly sight.'

Pickles takes a robust view of his relationship with the Lord Chancellor: 'I am answerable to the public. I do not work for the government, I work for the public, and if I feel there are facts it should know I will not be stifled.' (Lest it be thought that Judge Pickles is some kind of fiery judicial revolutionary, we should perhaps note that he long since abandoned his Labour Party membership, and one of his most vehement public speeches prominently featured criticism of Lord Whitelaw for the latter's 'soft' approach to sentencing.)

Lord Hailsham himself took a more relaxed view: the man with 2,500 judicial appointments in his gift said of the process in June 1986: 'The system is almost as foolproof as it could be made.' It was not a view shared by an increasing number of lawyers and academics. Even Hailsham's own Advisory Committee on Legal Aid had warned in its 1985 report that 'the lack of clear ministerial responsibility and direction for legal services is a chronic problem'.

Eventually Hailsham conceded the principle. By the end of 1986 – a year of unprecedented criticism from all sides – he admitted that his disciplinary powers over the judiciary should be vested elsewhere, and that the problem was of his own making since he drafted the 1971 Courts Act which gave him those powers – but failed to establish any procedure for using it. 'The section is impossible to operate. I should have been less slap-happy. I never thought I would have to use it.'

Having neatly defined the problem, and even laid the blame at his own doorstep, Hailsham then failed to suggest any solution – despite promptings from the Chairman of the Bar Council, Peter Scott, QC. Scott suggested that the profession should examine the case for a judicial appointments board, though cynics say that the close involvement of the profession in such an examination is likely to produce the answer best suited to its own needs rather than that of justice and the consumer.

The real answer, as Lord Gifford and others repeatedly point out, is a proper Ministry of Justice, equipped to argue effectively in Cabinet for sufficient funds to meet the needs of today's legal machine. Perhaps then, for example, enough circuit judges might be created to keep up with the growing backlog of criminal cases in the Crown courts. (Hailsham, to his credit, managed to boost numbers by 10 per cent over two years – but still faced an uphill struggle for more judges.) Gifford has even suggested a workable form of words for the enabling Act:

> It shall be the duty of the Minister of Justice to promote the establishment in England and Wales of comprehensive legal services designed to secure that the people of England and Wales receive such advice and assistance as may be effective and

necessary for them to obtain justice under the law for the redress of their grievances.

Those with a long memory may notice a distinct – and deliberate – similarity with the wording of the 1946 National Health Service Act – a potentially useful model for a future national legal service. And just as the NHS Act enabled both doctors and patients to obtain treatment under its provisions, so would a Ministry of Justice Act protect the rights and interests of its judges as well as those who come before them.

The need for our judiciary to have the same type of employment protection as the rest of us was brought home rather forcefully in 1981 to Jean Thompson. Dr Thompson, then aged fifty-five, was a senior lecturer at Leeds College of Higher Education. She was also a magistrate.

The magistrates

Jean Thompson had been appointed to the bench as a lay magistrate (the other sort being professional or 'stipendiary' magistrates) in 1976, by which time she had been a widow for seven years.

In 1979 she began going out with another magistrate from Leeds who had been separated from his wife for more than eighteen months. To be on the safe side they both talked over their relationship with the chief clerk of the Leeds bench, who told them that what they did in private was their own affair but advised them not to sit together in the same cases – advice which they duly followed. The clerk also suggested that they might care to be discreet, since if there was 'any scandal affecting the bench your places will be in jeopardy'.

The couple were extremely discreet and Jean Thompson added to her existing reputation as a caring and hard-working magistrate by taking as many voluntary refresher courses as possible. Then, in 1981, both were abruptly asked to resign by the head of their bench because of their relationship. They refused. Someone – certainly not Jean Thompson or her friend – promptly leaked the story to the press. The couple spent the next few days behind their respective front doors hiding from an ever-growing posse of reporters.

At which point Lord Hailsham – once again, as Lord Chancellor, responsible for the hiring and firing of all magistrates – summarily sacked them. When at last he granted them an interview – the closest to an appeal against dismissal that magistrates are allowed – Hailsham explained that they had been dismissed for bringing the bench into disrepute through the newspaper publicity – a turnaround that Jean Thompson found truly Kafka-esque.

> This interview was very painful and it really honestly seemed as if the case was pre-decided. The gist of the accusation seemed to be that there had been all this scandal – the newspapers were thrown across the desk to us – and how could we then justify being kept on the bench; that was the expression. This was despite the fact that the newspaper articles were nothing to do with us and indeed added quite considerably to our pain.
>
> We hoped to have some sort of fair hearing, having acted as magistrates and being trained fairly adequately to look at both sides of the question. We didn't feel that this occurred. We weren't even allowed to have our lawyers present for most of the interview.
>
> If this can happen to two respected magistrates, hard-working and committed to the job, God help the defendant!

In fact the 26,000 magistrates in England and Wales are the only 'judges' the vast majority of defendants will ever meet. Justices of the Peace, as magistrates are more traditionally known, deal with 97 per cent of all criminal cases. In theory their courts are the people's courts – administered by part-time lay benches for the benefit of the community they serve and represent.

Yet their appointment – as with that of judges – is controlled by a mysterious and unaccountable network of highly secretive committees reporting only to the Lord Chancellor in London.

Critics of the system – including both sitting and dismissed magistrates, those that have come before magistrate's courts and those who make their living in them – claim that this protection from public scrutiny leads to dramatic regional variations in the dispensing of justice, to a loss of confidence in the magistracy and a potential for corruption. Put simply, the selection of magistrates is crucial to good justice. Good selection will produce good justice, partial selection will produce partial justice and secret selection will produce secretive, partial and unjust decision-making. Whoever controls appointments to a local bench controls the quality of justice in that town.

Ole Hansen, solicitor, law lecturer and former director of the Legal Action Group (a respected group of 'insiders' campaigning on all legal issues) sums it up: 'Magistrates' benches are meant to represent the community. If you have an unrepresentative bench you run the risk of bad justice, unfair decisions and an inability to grasp the problems of those who come before you.'

Before we document the 'bad justice' often dispensed in magistrates' courts we need to examine their origins to understand how our confused and confusing system came about.

The first justices or keepers of the peace (that, of course, being the King's peace) were appointed in the twelfth century by Richard the Lionheart. For the next 150 years they acted as an embryo police force before acquiring a judicial function from the 1361 Justices of the Peace Act (an Act, we should note, still in use in their courts today). This confusion of thief-taking and magistracy continued until the founding of the modern police force in the mid-nineteenth century – although not all magistrates have accepted this division of responsibility.

In the early stages of a case which would come to be known as R. v. Bingham Justices, the chairman of the local bench summed up thus:

> Quite the most unpleasant cases that we have to decide are those where the evidence is a direct conflict between a police officer and a member of the public. My principle in such cases has always been to believe the evidence of the police officer, and therefore we find the case proved.

The verdict was ultimately quashed by the appeal court judges who kept faith with that basic tenet of English law that the police have to prove a person guilty beyond all reasonable doubt, rather than the accused having to prove his innocence.

However, judging from their attitudes and behaviour displayed in court, many magistrates think the same as the bench chairman in 'Bingham', although most are perhaps more discreet about saying so. If so – and we will examine the track record of our JPs later on – the root cause is likely to be found in their selection.

The modern system of magistrates' courts stems from a 1948

Royal Commission-backed reforming Act. It set up a series of local advisory committees, of which there are now ninety-six, to recommend to the Lord Chancellor suitable candidates for the bench. The official booklet on the appointment of JPs is typically short on details of the qualities needed:

> The first and most important consideration in selecting Justices of the Peace is that they should be personally suitable in character, integrity and understanding for the important work which they have to perform, and that they should be generally recognised as such by those amongst whom they live and work. Under no circumstances will the Lord Chancellor appoint anyone as a reward for past services of any kind.

More helpful are the comments of Sir Thomas Skyrme, a former Secretary of Commissions in the Lord Chancellor's Department who dealt with appointment policy:

> The declared policy of each Lord Chancellor since 1945 has been to make sure that every bench is a microcosm of the local community, and this amounts to seeing that in every petty sessional division there are at least some justices from each of the principal political and social groups in the area, and that the Bench is not dominated by any one group. [*The Changing Image of the Magistracy*, Macmillan, 1979.]

And Lord Hailsham himself told the Magistrates Association in October 1984: 'There is, I verily believe, no people's court on either side of the Iron Curtain or anywhere in the world which is as representative of the responsible elements in society as the lay bench of England and Wales.'

Sadly, the official rhetoric is often utterly divorced from reality. Advisory committees not only make their selection in secret but keep their own existence and membership a closely guarded secret. Of the ninety-six advisory committees only two have voluntarily published the names of their members, whilst one other has had disclosure forced upon it. In many cases the full membership is known only to the full-time committee clerk (also clerk to the bench) and to the committee chairman. Not even fellow JPs may know the identities of the other members.

The theory behind the secrecy is that it protects committees from lobbying or 'persistent importuning' by those with a burning ambition to sit on the bench. It is a theory that is, at the very least, open to question. In February 1983 the Attorney General told Parliament that the Lord Chancellor's Department was not aware of any problems facing those committees which had come out of the magisterial closet: 'No comments or effects, adverse or otherwise, have come to the notice of the Lord Chancellor.'

Dr Douglas Acres, leading light of the Magistrates Association, experienced JP and a member of the Essex advisory committee which went public some years ago, is somewhat less bland.

> It has always struck me as anomalous that in Britain, where we are so concerned for justice and courts to be seen to be public, the selection of magistrates should be a secret affair. I have never been subjected to any undue influences since we published our committee members' names, and anyway I take the view that if you are going to be doing this job you should be able to resist such pressures.

But aren't the antics of the selection committees just another manifestation of that traditional British obsession – secrecy for its own sake? And if so, isn't it all just harmless ritual? Sadly not.

Secret selection often means bad and unrepresentative selection. Warrington bench provides a telling example. The town boasts 180,000 people and is neatly divided into two separate areas by the presence of a canal. The inner section houses the bulk of the population; the outer section is notable for its more genteel suburbs. The inner section has forty magistrates; the outer, less populous section has seventy.

The local council is Labour-controlled – there are two Labour councillors for every one Conservative councillor. Two Labour-held wards have populations of 13,000 – and not one magistrate lives there. In three much smaller Conservative-held wards live thirty-nine of the town's 110 JPs.

Put simply, the population of the more prosperous outer suburbs is half the size of that in the inner section, yet produces three times the number of magistrates. Warrington bench has simultaneously earned the statistical prize for being amongst the meanest courts in the country when doling out legal aid (a 23 per cent refusal rate) and similarly for refusing 18 per cent of all applications for bail made to it. Nearby St Helens has a 1 per cent rate for identical applications.

Solicitors in Warrington also claim that the bench imposes extremely high fines, which causes non-payment by those already on supplementary benefit – which in turn provokes the bench to jail them. Local lawyers allege that the JPs are therefore operating what amounts to an unofficial deferred-sentencing policy. The bench's sentencing policy itself exceeds the Magistrates Association guidelines in no fewer than fourteen separate areas.

The Lord Chancellor's Department says that the make-up of the bench is fairly typical. Doug Hoyle, the town's MP, puts it rather differently. 'I'm not just concerned,' he says, 'I'm angry about it.' Because the identity of the advisory committee is kept secret we do not know the attitudes or political persuasions of those who pick JPs. We do, however, know that in the summer of 1986 almost one quarter of those on the Warrington bench lived within a mile of Warrington Golf Club.

Bail is a closely defined matter of right for most defendants appearing before the bench. None the less, Warrington and other benches may often ride roughshod over these rights – especially, as we shall see later, when local feelings run high or situations are tense. But in the matter of legal aid magistrates have much more discretion.

The test, or rule of thumb, used in deciding whether to grant legal aid is notoriously subjective: according to the 1974 Legal Aid Act it should be granted when 'it appears desirable to do so in the interests of justice'. It is on such subjective tests that the background and prejudices of magistrates come into play. Nor is Warrington an isolated example. In 1985 the national average refusal rate was 11 per cent. But defendants facing the justices of Long Ashton in Avon were refused legal aid in 30 per cent of all cases.

Similarly, Newcastle had a refusal rate of 20 per cent, compared with only a 5 per cent rate in the neighbouring Gateshead district. There is little relevant difference between 'interests of justice' in Gateshead and 'interests of justice' in Newcastle, and quite why such huge variations occur has never been explained or justified. But one thing is certain: these disparities turn applying for legal aid (and therefore the quality of the accused's defence) into a grim legal lottery.

There is, thankfully, a right to have refusal of legal aid by JPs reviewed by one of a series of regional Criminal Legal Aid Committees (although as yet it does not apply to those defendants charged with summary offences – those which can only be tried by magistrates). And the figures issued by the committees give a good indication of how often legal aid is unjustly refused by magistrates; in 1985, for example, they granted legal aid in 70 per cent of the cases which they reviewed.

Inevitably, of course, the committees themselves mirror the habits of the courts they are supposed to be reviewing. In 1985 London East committee refused only 14 per cent of review cases, whereas its next-door-neighbour London West refused 55 per cent – all of which merely goes to strengthen the need for a clearly defined set of criteria in granting criminal legal aid.

Even if such criteria were introduced, however, rogue benches might simply ignore them. Bail applications, as we have said, are governed by just such a strict set of rules. Bail is regarded as a right not lightly denied a defendant because to do so is to keep him in jail for an offence he may not have committeed. (There are also very sound financial and practical reasons for not putting more remand prisoners than necessary into our already overcrowded prisons.) So the 1976 Bail Act has a general aim that 'the number of persons remanded in custody should be kept to the minimum compatible with the interests of justice', and only allows magistrates to deny bail in the following circumstances:

(1) Assuming that the offence carries a potential prison sentence, bail may be refused if there are *substantial* grounds (i.e. more than mere suspicion) to believe that the defendant would abscond, commit another offence, interfere with witnesses, or that he has previously jumped bail; or if the police haven't had enough time to assess his suitability for bail; or, finally, if he is needed in custody for the preparation of social, welfare, probation and medical reports.

(2) Assuming that the offence does not carry a potential prison sentence, bail may only be refused if the defendant had previously jumped bail and the court believes he will do so again.

Bench-by-bench comparative statistics are not always easy to come by, but wild regional variations and blanket 'bans' do come to light – particularly at times of high local tension such as the inner city riot trials in 1981. The magistrates' magazine, *Justice of the Peace*, has loudly proclaimed that 'the greater the passions, the more important the civil rights of the accused', but defence solicitors like

Gareth Peirce, dealing with the aftermath of the Brixton riots, found that a hollow promise.

> I went to Camberwell Green court because I had been telephoned about two people held there. When I got there I found there were over a hundred people in custody – the duty solicitor couldn't cope.
>
> He was virtually unable to come up out of the cells to deal with the three courts where stipendiary magistrates were sitting. In one of those courts the magistrate said, 'I am not granting bail unless it's an exceptional circumstance.' He had utterly closed his mind before even hearing the defendants.
>
> I sat in court for a while and watched and heard people who couldn't even finish the sentence they were saying. The minute they'd said 'not guilty' they were whipped away to the cells. I finally stood up and asked the magistrate to allow those solicitors in court to represent people under the extended umbrella of the duty solicitor's scheme. I actually physically went and got one woman who had started to say that she had two young children. She was a single parent and she was being taken away to prison – to Holloway – when I got her. I managed to get her bail in a second application.
>
> It was a situation where you were watching magistrates deal with a hundred people who had rights in theory – but none whatever in practice. And this was happening not just in London, not just in one stipendiary magistrates' court, but all over the country.

Similar rough justice was indeed being dished out in 'riot courts' across the country. After those in Nottingham had repeatedly denied defendants access to their solicitors and committed several other infringements of the rules, the local Law Society issued a damning report on their performance. (We should, perhaps, remember that the Law Society is not by nature or inclination a body of hotheaded radicals ready to rush into print at the first sign of trouble.)

Not all magistrates, of course, are so cavalier with the rights of those who come before them. And, as the Magistrates Association is keen to point out, JPs do give up their own time free of charge to sit on the bench. Rogue benches do exist, however, and some magistrates ignore or bend the rules, and do so wholesale. In a sense, Hailsham was right: such problems will occur occasionally in any system, and the network of the magistracy is a cheap and fairly cheerful sort of justice.

Where the system falls down, and where the lie is given to the Lord Chancellor's platitudes, is in the lack of any safety net – a proper public scrutiny to weed out the unjust, the corrupt, the inefficient and the plain wayward. For as long as their selection is carried out in secret, behind doors not just closed to the public but locked and barred to other JPs, the potential for all those weaknesses exists – and as Nottingham, Warrington and many other places like them show, that potential is all too easily translated into reality.

Equally, for as long as responsibility for the disciplining and removal of JPs lies solely in the Lord Chancellor's lap, magistrates like Jean Thompson will continue to feel humiliated in what she describes as a 'kangaroo court'.

The coroners

The office of coroner has existed for almost 800 years, which makes it even older than the office of Justice of the Peace. Medieval coroners existed to seize for their king the estates of those who killed themselves or were deemed by the Crown to have been criminals.

The duties of these 'Keepers of the Pleas of the Crown' were later augmented to summon a local jury (but only to assist with the names of suspects), inspect any dead body and ascertain the cause of death in an age before police forces and forensic science. Many of these original functions have been handed over to professional investigators, but the coroner survives today as a public official appointed and paid for by local councils to certify the medical cause of death and to identify potential health or injury hazards that arise in any particular case. He is, in short, a recorder rather than an enquirer.

Unfortunately, it is precisely an 'enquirer' that is needed in many modern inquests, where major issues of public importance or safety can be involved. This either forces the coroner into an uncomfortable conflict with the system or ensures that those involved receive less than justice. It is a problem that, according to the barrister and campaigner for reform Geoffrey Robertson, requires the coroner 'to behave like Sherlock Holmes presiding over the Star Chamber'. The 200 coroners hold around 25,000 inquests throughout England and Wales every year. In the majority, it is simply a question of recording an obvious verdict – though as we shall see, even those simple cases can cause unnecessary heartache to relatives at a time when they are least able to cope.

There are deaths – probably no more than a dozen a year – which raise wider issues that need a more complex enquiry; most notably these are deaths involving the police, the armed services or some other government agency. It is in these cases, few in number but vital in importance, that the system's shortcomings are dramatically highlighted. In most the coroner's inquest will be the only form of public enquiry into the death.

The death of James Davy in March 1983 was just such a case. Davy was no saint – during an eighteen-year career of petty crime he had notched up seven separate convictions for assaulting police officers. But one of the policemen involved in a fatal struggle with him in the claustrophobic cell block at Coventry's Little Park Street police station, had his own convictions for obstructing the police and failing to stop after an accident. Acting Sergeant Ian Speed later denied thinking of himself as a 'hard man', but admitted that another case of his had been stopped after the jury heard that blood had been found on a confession Speed obtained from the defendant. (No charges have ever been brought against Speed in relation to that incident.) When James Davy was arrested on suspicion of involvement in a gangland killing, the stage was set for a classic confrontation.

Davy died after Sgt Speed and other officers went into his cell to subdue him and stop him swearing, shouting obscenities and banging on the wall. During the struggle Sgt Speed applied a 'standard wrestlers' headlock'. It was subsequently discovered that Davy was unconscious, and he was rushed to hospital. By the time he arrived his heart and breathing had stopped and he had turned blue. Eleven days later his life-support machine was switched off and he died without ever regaining consciousness.

Exactly what happened inside Little Park Street police station will never be quite clear. It may well be, as Sgt Speed claimed, that Davy's death was a complete and tragic mishap. What is beyond doubt is that the subsequent behaviour of the Director of Public Prosecutions, the coroner and the inquest system in general combined to muddy the waters still further.

The DPP announced before the inquest could get under way that he had no intention of prosecuting any of the officers involved in the Davy case. A reasonable and justifiable decision to reach, but because it was announced before the inquest the jury's hands were tied.

Then there was the question of Davy's body. An official post-mortem had been carried out shortly after his death. But, as is common practice and specifically authorised by Coroners' Rules, Davy's family were refused a copy of the pathologist's report. His sister Marie and brother Brian decided to go for the next best option and commission their own autopsy to find out just what injuries Davy had sustained. But by then the body had been allowed to decompose so badly (whilst still under the coroner's jurisdiction) that three-quarters of an inch of mould had grown on the corpse. Not surprisingly, the family's pathologist reported that the body was so severely decomposed that he could not conduct a proper examination.

Next, the Davy family applied for legal aid to be represented at the inquest. They knew now that it would be their only chance to question police officers about their brother's stay in the cells, and that an experienced lawyer would be needed. But legal aid is not available under any circumstances to families involved at inquests. The responsibility for this rests with the Lord Chancellor. Fifteen years ago the Department's own legal aid advisory committee recommended the extension of legal aid to families at inquests, and in 1974 Parliament passed the Legal Aid Act which made provision for inquests to be covered by the scheme. To date, all Lord Chancellors have refused to implement that section of the Act, claiming that coroners' inquests are not real trials and therefore don't need the attendant costs of lawyers to safeguard the reputation of the 'accused'.

Inquests into deaths in custody, particularly when there is already animosity between the police and the victim's family, make a nonsense of that claim. The reputations of the dead man, his relatives, friends and associates, are all called into question and frequently slandered. The same goes for the policemen involved – but then their 'trade union', the Police Federation, will invariably pay for them to be legally advised and represented. This means that families face the choice of being hopelessly outgunned by police lawyers, or of desperately seeking a way to pay their own lawyers' bills. A fair fight it is not. And those legal costs can be huge. Lawyers' fees for the Blair Peach or Jimmy Kelly cases – both deaths involving the police and major questions of public importance – topped the £20,000 mark for their respective families.

The Davy family faced an agonising choice – to sell all their belongings, use their savings and borrow the thousands of pounds necessary to pay for lawyers, or to go into court alone against the ranks of police-retained solicitors and barristers. The choice was made harder by the decision of the coroner to deny them access to relevant police statements and evidence from the enquiry into their brother's death. Unless they had legal advice they knew they would be walking blindfold into a judicial ambush.

In the end they were saved by a spectacular act of legal charity. Gareth Peirce agreed to act as their solicitor free of charge. It was a sacrifice she had become used to. By 1984 she had devoted months of her time, free of charge, to working on six major inquests, including the long-running Deptford fire case in 1981.

> The choices for the families involved are either to find those huge sums of money – and it's very hard to think of people who can do that – or not to be represented at all. Even if those fees were lower and families had to pay only modest remuneration to lawyers, I still believe they ought not to have to find that money themselves, particularly at a time when they will have to pay for expensive funerals and when they will be arguing cases that are of major importance to the whole of society.

The fact that the Davy family had a justifiable cause for concern is confirmed by the jury's first attempt at a verdict. After three weeks of evidence it decided that Davy had died an accidental death, but added a rider that the police in the case had used unreasonable force. In other words, they wanted to find that the police had not intended to kill him but had actually done so by using tactics which should be condemned. But riders of this form are not permitted under Coroners' Rules, and the jury eventually settled for straightforward accidental death.

It is not, however, only the high-profile cases that expose the shortcomings of the ancient system of coroners' courts. Inquest, the group set up to monitor the way the system works, claims that many of the less publicised cases are equally damning. Tony Ward, its joint organiser, says that:

Some people make the mistake of thinking that what is wrong with inquests is only a matter of their inability to deal adequately with a few controversial cases. They think that if you could only get rid of those cases to some other form of enquiry, or have a High Court judge conduct the inquest, then that would be the end of the problem. Unfortunately it's not as simple as that.

Apart from the insoluble problem of how to decide what will be a controversial inquest before it begins, it also overlooks all those thousands of cases which never make the national headlines but which leave families with just as great a sense of injustice as those that do.

Inquest identifies four basic flaws in the system which can prevent families and even coroners' juries from getting at the truth: the denial of legal aid, the refusal of access to police statements taken before the inquest, the limited aim of the inquest itself when it may be the only enquiry ever held, and the almost unfettered powers invested in the coroner himself.

John Cargill discovered those flaws the hard way when his teenage son Ian died in a road accident on 21 October 1982. Ian was a senior aircraftsman with the RAF, stationed at Lyneham in Wiltshire, and his father was assured that the RAF would do all it could to help the family; they even suggested that it wouldn't be necessary for him to attend the inquest.

In fact John Cargill did go. He had begun to feel uneasy when the police investigating the accident refused to let either the RAF or himself see the evidence they had collected. But with the assurance from his son's commanding officer that the service would look after the family – and bearing in mind the cost of engaging their own solicitor – John Cargill went to the hearing alone.

> At first I was allowed to ask questions, though as I hadn't seen the statements I wasn't well enough prepared to question the first witness. But then I realised that there was something wrong with the evidence being given by the second witness, so I started to ask my questions. Shortly afterwards the coroner stopped me, saying that the questions were not helping him reach a verdict, which was all he was there to do.

The third witness at his son's inquest had not even seen the accident but claimed to have seen Ian driving fast and dangerously earlier that evening. But because he had not been allowed to see that witness's statement to the police, John Cargill didn't know until much later that the witness had described the dangerous driver as having blond hair and wearing a uniform and beret. Ian Cargill had dark hair and was dressed in 'civvies'. Although John Cargill wasn't aware of the discrepancy at the time, the police most certainly were. Yet that seemingly crucial piece of evidence was curiously not mentioned during the hearing.

There were other discrepancies too – none of which Mr Cargill was able to pin down until it was too late. In addition, the RAF character witnesses, who had given detailed statements to police about Ian's considerable driving skill and experience and his general level-headedness, were not called. One of the unfettered powers granted to coroners is the sole right to decide which witnesses will appear. (Thus, in one celebrated case in Southwark, South London, the list of witnesses *not* called included a community worker who gave the deceased a vital injection, the police officer who apparently broke nine ribs trying to revive him, and the ambulance driver who conveyed the man to hospital. Not one member of the dead man's family was allowed to give evidence at the inquest.)

The verdict in the Cargill case was accidental death, but couched in such terms as to invite the local press to convict Ian, posthumously, of dangerous driving. John Cargill hadn't wanted to convict anyone of anything; what hurt him most was the slur on his son's name. Ian Cargill, the papers all but declared, had only himself to blame. It seemed to his father, whose witnesses were never called and who only later discovered the discrepancies, that justice had not been done.

> All of this added greatly to the distress my wife and I felt. But I am not just concerned for my son's case, I am angry that this should be allowed to happen at all. I would never have believed such legalised injustice could exist in our country until I actually experienced it.

Coroners' inquests, of course, don't have to operate on the same basic judicial principles as the rest of the system. So, for example, until 1983 the task of selecting a jury was left to a police officer from the district in which the death has occurred (the coroner's officer for any given area will almost certainly be a serving policeman). This has led in, at least, one notorious case in South Wales during 1980 to an extraordinary jury of regulars – all associates of the father of the constable in charge of choosing them, who was himself not merely an ex-policeman, but also the jury's foreman.

Although that case is an extreme example, the same principle applies throughout coroners' inquests. Unlike in other courts, the lawyer for the deceased's relatives is merely, in the words of Mr Justice Comyn, 'a guest of the court'; he has no right to cross-examine witnesses without the coroner's permission, and no right whatsoever to address the jury or sum up the family's case.

Add to this the denial of legal aid, the refusal of access to witness statements and the pathologist's report, and a strict set of verdicts which preclude criticism being attached to any third party involved in the death, and the procedure becomes as injudicial as can be imagined.

Nor does it end there. Some coroners enjoy reputations as 'mavericks' – reputations earned either by browbeating witnesses, taking inexcusable short-cuts, or simply by sheer overbearing arrogance. And such is the independence granted to them that nothing short of extremely costly judicial reviews can stop them.

The behaviour of London coroner Dr Mary McHugh was a case in point. Dr McHugh, who has since retired, decided in 1983 to hold a secret inquest into the death of a British banker, Dennis Skinner. Skinner, who had been based in Moscow, was a part-time spy. Dr McHugh needed no further encouragement – the entire enquiry was to be held in camera.

It was a decision that puzzled Skinner's wife, the legal profession and the Foreign Office. No one (except Dr McHugh), it seemed, wanted a cloak-and-dagger operation. It took several months of complicated legal argument, paid for by the *Observer* newspaper and (perforce) London ratepayers, before the High Court declared that the proceedings should be held in public.

It was not just a case of irritating obstinacy; although local councils are responsible for appointing coroners, they have no other powers to control their behaviour or expenditure. And had it not been for the *Observer* fighting the case through the courts, MPs would never have discovered at the inquest the truth about the Skinner spying affair.

It is time for the system to be reformed. The last major piece of legislation was the 1887 Coroners Act. A hundred years on there is an urgent need to replace inquests with full-blown judicial enquiries, which should be mandatory whenever a question of public interest is involved. (Scotland, which has no inquests, has gone halfway towards this system with Fatal Accident Enquiries. But even these are not foolproof; the decision over whether or not to hold them is at the discretion of the Lord Advocate, and the secrecy surrounding official reports into unexplained deaths there can be even greater than in England and Wales.)

According to barrister Geoffrey Robertson:

> An inquest is not so much an enquiry as an ambush. It takes place after police investigations which have been made available to the coroner. But the coroner is not obliged to show material collected by the police to representatives of the interested parties, and many coroners now habitually, even churlishly, refuse to give lawyers a sight of the evidence available to them.
>
> This means that lawyers are sometimes unprepared for the evidence which the coroner decides to call. It means, too, that at inquests where police misconduct is alleged, the police lawyers will have exclusive access to statements taken by police officers, and so have an unfair advantage.

And if that imbalance can outwit an experienced barrister, what chance for the layman, alone and unrepresented because legal aid is not available? The inquest system must be brought into the twentieth century to meet the needs and difficulties of modern society.

One of the factors which allow us to remain complacent about our ignorance of coroners' courts injustices is the comforting feeling that in many cases there is a jury, a panel of randomly selected citizens watching out for the interests of people against State. As we have seen, that can be a dangerously misleading complacence – inquest juries are not necessarily selected at random.

Perhaps more worrying still is the power of the coroner to decide whether or not to call a jury in a particular case. The death of Blair Peach at the hands of an unidentified police officer in 1979 would seem an obvious case for a jury to be empanelled. Yet it took several months of legal argument and the costs of a High Court hearing before the family was able to force the coroner to have a jury. Costs, of course, that came on top of the family's (who had no legal aid) inquest bills.

If an inquest jury can be little more than a muzzled paper tiger, what of the real thing – the twelve good men and true who sit in judgement in most serious criminal cases?

The jury

All serious criminal trials today – except where the accused pleads guilty – are heard by a judge and jury. The English judicial system operates on the basis of a separation of powers. The judge is there to decide on questions of law (what exactly the statute or offence means or requires); while the jury has to decide on questions of fact – whether the defendant has really broken the terms of the law which the judge has outlined to them.

The idea is that twelve men and women, who have no prior knowledge of the case, the defendant or the witnesses, listen to the evidence and give a dispassionate verdict. It is a concept of which we are justly proud, and one which we use as a yardstick of judicial fairness to measure against other countries' systems.

Lord Devlin, a former High Court judge and Law Lord, described trial by jury in 1956 as a protection against tyranny. 'It is more than an instrument of justice,' he said, 'and more than one wheel of the constitution. It is the lamp that shows that freedom lives.'

It may come as something of a surprise, therefore, to discover that although juries were first introduced after Pope Innocent III banned trial by ordeal or battle in 1215, the modern democratised jury system, in which anyone over the age of eighteen (except lunatics, members of the House of Lords, and those with a serious criminal record) can serve, was only introduced sixteen years after Lord Devlin's paean of praise to the concept – and yet is already under attack.

Medieval trial juries were composed of men who knew the accused and decided cases on what they knew of his character and the prevailing local circumstances. They did not have to trouble themselves with listening to witnesses, since these were not introduced into court for several hundred years. And it was not until the eighteenth century that the jury began to take on a shape which we would recognise today.

At that stage the principle began to become established that juries should not be a party to, or be aware of, the facts of a case before being called on to try it. It is no coincidence that authority's love-hate relationship with the jury system began almost immediately. For while the worst of the tyrants and despots who ruled the country had, by the eighteenth century, succumbed to some form of parliamentary democracy, the statute book was still packed with harsh and oppressive laws.

Once a jury with a measure of independence became the arbiter of the accused's guilt, it began to reject the worst of these laws by refusing to convict (often in the face of relatively clear-cut evidence). This happened throughout the decades when stealing goods of above a nominal value was a hanging offence; juries regularly returned verdicts of guilty, but at just below the level where the offence became a capital one. Similarly, London juries earned a reputation for unwillingess to convict on any matter affecting civil and intellectual liberties in the period from around 1690 to 1794.

This period is neatly delineated by two famous trials. In 1690 two Quakers, William Penn and William Mead, were tried at the Old Bailey for holding a 'conspiratorial gathering'. The jurors infuriated both judge and Crown by acquitting Mead and failing to make up their minds about Penn. The judge proceeded to rant, bully and threaten them, before ordering them to be locked up for the night 'without meat, drink, fire and tobacco'.

The court recorder informed them that: 'We shall have a verdict by the help of God or you shall starve for it.' When, three nights later, they acquitted Penn they were fined and imprisoned until the fines were paid. Four jurors refused to pay and were locked up for several months until the Chief Justice declared 'the right of juries to give their verdict by their conscience', and released them.

The Penn case was the first of the major battles between the Crown and what it saw as 'perverse juries'. It was a case, as we shall see, that was to have uncomfortable echoes 314 years later.

The climax of the era of the independent jury came in 1794 when three campaigners for reform, the leaders of the London Reform Societies, were acquitted of high treason by a London jury. A Crown campaign against reformers was stopped in its tracks, and the path cleared for the fundamental electoral and penal reforms of the nineteenth century.

It was in order to deal with the independent juries in these reform trials (and simultaneously with those refusing to convict writers and publishers of anti-government, seditious leaflets) that the Crown began its long and sordid history of tampering with juries. First it introduced 'special verdicts', reached by the judge without the help of a jury; then, after the 1792 Libel Act effectively stopped that, 'special juries' were introduced.

'Special juries' were drawn from a limited and well scrutinised panel of forty-eight men whom the prosecution believed, often with good reason, could be trusted to convict. In a considerable number of cases the 'special jurors' became well known to the Crown and many were paid for their services so long as they continued to convict.

These packed juries were widespread – if far from popular. The reformer Jeremy Bentham wrote in 1821 that the packing of juries was 'a regular, quietly established and quietly suffered system. Not only is the yoke already about our necks, but our necks are already fashioned to it.' ('Elements in the Art of Packing.')

Gradually the special jury fell out of favour, with a series of landmark trials coinciding with a greater professionalism on the part of the newly formed police in detecting and presenting evidence in court. Finally, the 1949 Juries Act sounded its death knell. The notion of twelve good men (and later women) and true, chosen at random, coming to a fair decision for no other reason than that their individual prejudices are likely to cancel each other out, was born. Inevitably, governments have been trying to strangle it ever since. And although the 'special jury' of the nineteenth century was ultimately abolished in 1972, the packing of juries continues in secret and on a much greater scale to this day.

Even before the modern jury system was created in 1949, the government set up mechanisms to subvert it, by drawing up secret guidelines for jury vetting – a polite modern euphemism for jury packing.

Then, in 1967, the centuries-old safeguard of a unanimous verdict in jury trials was abolished by the Criminal Justice Act. Thereafter a defendant could be convicted on a 10–2 majority verdict. This makes a logical mockery of the theory of English criminal justice that the case must be proved beyond all reasonable doubt. Now the reasonable doubt of two of the jury can be conveniently discounted.

The reason given for the introduction of majority verdicts was that the unamimous-verdict rule made it easier for professional criminals to intimidate jurors and ensure an acquittal. This seemingly reasonable argument is regularly used to defend official subversion of the jury system. Yet there has never been any coherent evidence that such intimidation either exists on any real scale, or that majority verdicts reduced its impact. Instead, subsequent jury laws made it impossible for anyone other than the Crown to know what, if anything, had been said or done to, by or on behalf of any jury member.

Two further modifications were made to the jury system in 1973. (Ironically, juries had received their final democratisation only a year earlier with the removal of a property qualification for potential jurors.) In January 1973, defence barristers were banned from asking potential jurors questions aimed at revealing any bias against the defendants. The issue had arisen in the 'Angry Brigade' trial, when the judge allowed the defence to ask jurors such questions as what papers they read, and whether they were members of a political party. The barristers felt it vital in a case carrying heavy political overtones to be able to question and have excluded politically biased jurors.

Perhaps reasonably, senior judges did not approve, feeling that the independence of juries was at stake. A 'practice direction' was then issued to all judges banning future questioning. (Such a direction does not need to be made in consultation with government or Parliament; it is an unchallengeable power vested in our top judges.) The direction declared: 'A jury consists of twelve individuals chosen at random. It is contrary to established practice for jurors to be excused on more general grounds such as race, religion or political beliefs or occupation.' This would have been fine, had it applied equally to the prosecution as well as the defence.

For any trial a large pool of potential jurors is summoned. Most of them will either be assigned to a different trial beginning at the same court on the same day, or will be sent home. The process by which the final twelve jurors for a case are selected is known as challenging; as the potential juror is about to be sworn in either side in the case can object to him or her.

In English courts both the prosecution and the defence have always had the right to challenge a juror 'for cause'; they have to explain to the court their objection. But to do that requires some form of knowledge. The past two decades of jury trials have witnessed a concerted campaign to deny any such knowledge to the defence, whilst at the same time building up by lawful or unlawful means the prosecution's file of information on jurors.

The removal of the defence's right to question jurors in 1973 was the first stage in the campaign. Later that year jurors' occupations were removed from the list of their names and addresses which is provided to both sides in any trial. Lord Hailsham, then in his first period of office as Lord Chancellor, feared that defence barristers were using the knowledge of jurors' jobs to decide on whether to make a challenge. The right to challenge jurors and have them removed was being 'abused', he said, in cases with political connotations.

Furthermore, since the 1971 Courts Act had given him overall control of jury panels he did not have to consult Parliament as to its views, but simply to make an executive order. He did so even though the very sections of the Act which gave him the power seemed to oppose, at least in principle, the move: Section 32(2) pronounces that 'a party to proceedings . . . shall be entitled to reasonable facilities for inspecting the panel'.

Meanwhile, as we shall see, files dealing with very much more than a potential juror's occupation were being passed to the prosecution to aid them in their challenges. It is hard to understand why what is considered an abuse for the defence becomes acceptable for the prosecution.

Having effectively destroyed the defence's ability to challenge for cause, the next move was to attack its parallel historical right, the peremptory challenge.

The right to challenge jurors and have them removed without giving any reasons dates back to the days when a defendant would know personally all the jurors who had been called together to try him, and he could object to those whom he knew to be unfairly prejudiced. By 1977 the right of peremptory challenge had been reduced from thirty-five challenges to just seven. The Criminal Law Act of that year cut it back to three and the present government has removed it altogether.

But what, meanwhile, of the prosecution? It had lost the right to peremptory challenge in 1307 – the theory being that the defence should be put on a better footing since the jurors would make a decision that could hang the defendant or imprison him for many years. A statute in 1307 ruled that the Crown could only challenge for cause '. . . if they that sue for the King will challenge any of those jurors, they shall assign a cause certain, and the truth of the same challenge shall be inquired of according to the custom of the court'.

The statute-makers of 1307 reckoned without the inventiveness of lawyers. Even when, 300 years later, the legal authority Sir Edward Coke thought that the statute had been effective and 'the King is now restrained', he underestimated the Crown's desire to pack a jury. The phrase 'the custom of the court' was used to allow peremptory challenging to go on as before, but under a different name. Despite the fact that the 1307 statute still remains law today, prosecution counsel can reject a juror without giving reasons through the simple device of asking him to 'stand by for the Crown'. This ensures that he goes to the end of the jury panel and will only be called if there are no more potential jurors remaining.

At first the prosecution attempted some measure of self-restraint by claiming that it was a convention of the bar that the stand-by power was rarely, if ever, used. Today that scarcely applies, and the peremptory challenge for the prosecution is increasingly being used. (In one case revolving around picketing rights the Crown stood by six potential jurors.) If, then, the intention of the 1977 reduction of defence peremptory challenges, or for that matter their proposed removal altogether, was to put both sides on an equal footing it failed miserably – the defence can only use the challenge three times in any one case. As we write, the prosecution right is statutorily unlimited, though the government announced in November 1987 that it would in future only allow prosecution challenges with the prior permission of the Attorney General.

The 1977 Criminal Law Act made one further significant assault on jury trials: it removed a substantial number of offences from the Crown courts (where juries sit) and sent them instead to the magistrates' courts. Ostensibly the reason was overcrowding in Crown courts. In 1973 Lord Hailsham set up a committee to recommend ways of reducing the length of time defendants spent on remand waiting for their trial to start. He and Robert Carr, then Home Secretary, gave the committee the apparently innocuous brief of 'investigating the distribution of criminal business'.

Hailsham and Carr then proceeded to pick a committee well stacked with magistrates and magistrates' clerks. To nobody's great surprise – but to the undisguised delight of the police, who know it is far easier to obtain convictions in magistrates' courts – the James Committee proposed removing the right to a jury trial in roughly 8,000 cases per year. But, the committee insisted, it wasn't simply a question of cost-cutting or expediency:

> We have not regarded as our main objective the finding of a
> means of relieving the Crown Court of work. We have
> approached the issue from the standpoint of principle . . . The
> demand made on the Crown Court by the volume of business
> and the considerable expense of trial in the Crown Court are
> important factors to be taken into account, but they are not the
> only factors.

The 'principles' upon which the committee reached this view are hard to understand. Historically, defendants have had the right to have cases affecting their reputation, livelihood and freedom decided by their peers. One of the James Committee recommendations was for the removal of that right in public-order offences such as threatening or insulting behaviour, and some cases of theft where the goods stolen were worth less than £20. Both these categories of offences are amongst the most frequently heard cases up and down the country, and they both have serious potential effects on the defendant's standing in his or her community.

Fortunately, a majority of MPs agreed that this was undesirable, and in the debate on the bill voted down the theft proposal; but the bulk of the James Committee recommendations (including those confining public-order cases to magistrates' courts) survived to become law in the 1977 Act.

The results were quickly seen. Later that year a group of Asian workers went on strike at the factory of a company called Grunwick. The dispute became long-running and bitter. At one stage tens of thousands of people, including several MPs, went to support the strikers on the picket line; more than 500 were arrested and charged with a variety of public-order offences.

Before the new law took effect the defendants would have had (and would certainly have exercised) the right to have their cases heard by a jury. In a large number of the hearings the sole evidence was provided by the police – a factor which has traditionally influenced juries – and was noticeably weak on details. None the less, many of the defendants were convicted. According to the National Council for Civil Liberties, the 1977 Act was the thin end of a highly unjust wedge, and it drew attention to an earlier assault on juries:

> For those who are concerned to protect the institution of the jury
> in criminal cases there is a lesson in the decline of juries in civil

cases. The removal of most of their business has meant that today juries sit in only a handful of civil cases. There are many who would like to see the role of juries in criminal trials similarly eroded. The re-allocation of offences from juries to magistrates is a major step in that direction. [NCCL, *Justice Deserted*, 1979.]

The shifting of trials from one court to another is historically far from new. In the eighteenth century cases of riot and treason were taken away from ordinary juries and handed over to special commissions where the Crown had control over the selection of juries; convictions were noticeably easier to come by before these commission juries.

Similarly, delays in hearing cases (resulting in lengthy remand periods) have become a shameful tradition of English legal practice in the past three decades. The Criminal Law Act of 1977 appears to have made little impact on the problem; a decade later the Lord Chancellor's Department again announced plans to ease the pressure on Crown courts. This time the proposed solution is to remove the right of any defendant remanded in custody to appear before a court every eight days and apply for bail.

The eight-day rule is a vital safeguard of a remand prisoner's rights and safety – particularly now that the Home Office admits to prisoners' families that it doesn't always know exactly which prison houses a particular remanded defendant. It also has the virtue of highlighting any physical abuse a prisoner may have received whilst on remand – a far from unusual phenomenon in our overcrowded and tense jails.

(If reducing the right to jury trial and abolishing weekly remand appearances don't solve the problem, the Lord Chancellor's Department could try attacking one of the root causes of delays in criminal hearings – the short working day of the average judge. Most Crown court hearings don't start until 10 a.m., and habitually adjourn at 4.30 p.m. Given at least an hour off for the judicial luncheon, many judges only actually sit for five and a half hours a day. This, combined with antiquated and time-consuming court rituals and procedures, adds to the log-jam of pending trials caused by the increasing crime-rate.)

So why all the fuss? Why has government after government pursued the jury with such vigour, determined to control its make-up and powers? On 17 April 1986 the Prime Minister explained.

Answering questions in the Commons, Mrs Thatcher said she found the acquittal rate in jury trials 'very disquieting'. It was, she thought, too high – a problem not unconnected with the defence's right of peremptory challenge. Quite simply, the Prime Minister and her legions of backbench MPs, policemen and judges object to juries who decline to do meekly as the prosecution ask and convict enough defendants.

That these defendants might actually have been innocent, or that the police case against them might be unconvincing (due to lack of evidence or inept presentation), doesn't appear to occur to the jury's critics. What makes the attempts to control these 'perverse' juries even more ludicrous is the government's own statistics.

There is a mere 1 per cent difference in the acquittal rate between cases where the defence has used peremptory challenges and those where it has not. According to Home Office figures for 1985, the former had an acquittal rate of 46 per cent compared to the latter's 45 per cent.

Sir Robert Mark, then Commissioner of the Metropolitan Police, encapsulated the argument in 1973. He insisted that the jury system was faulty because it resulted in the acquittal of too many guilty defendants. In Sir Robert's words these acquittals were 'failures' – and 'the failure rate is too high'. He didn't explain why he believed that in such cases the jury had got it wrong rather than the police; in his view it was a simple matter of too many perverse verdicts.

Sir Robert addressed his remarks to the public at large. Judge Alan King-Hamilton was more specific. In the so-called 'Persons Unknown' anarchist trial of 1979 he ordered the jurors to stay behind after they had acquitted all the defendants. He then subjected them to a humiliating tirade on their performance. They had, he said, been 'remarkably merciful in the face of the evidence' (for which we should read that evidence which Judge King-Hamilton chose to believe) and he 'prayed to God that none of you ever have reason to regret it'. He then insisted they come into court the next day to hear the final defendant in the case plead guilty – an act of spite which wasted another day of their time, and was presumably designed to punish them for reaching the 'wrong' verdict.

The jury was understandably annoyed. Four of its members wrote to the Lord Chancellor to complain. There is no record of any response from the Lord Chancellor's Department. One of the jurors then explained their thinking during the trial.

We went through all the evidence very carefully. We thought about it, we talked about it, and in the end we decided the police hadn't proved their case.

I still think about it from time to time and I'm still convinced that we were right. The judge behaved incredibly. I was quite appalled. He made us look stupid. But the jury's verdict has got to be the final one. The judge might not like it, but it's not up to him.

Lord Devlin, the former Law Lord, agrees. In 1978 he firmly rejected the argument that high acquittal rates in Crown courts are the result of perverse verdicts by biased juries.

Perversity is just a lawyer's word for a jury which applies its own standards instead of those recommended by lawyers. The smear of perversity is applied by judges but erased by time. It is not the disobedient jurors whom history has reprobated, but the judges who called them perverse.

However, there have been occasions when juries use their powers to acquit as a means of drawing attention to what Lord Devlin went on to describe as 'harsh and oppressive laws'. On those occasions the jury is acting as a final line of defence – an insurance policy that laws passed by Parliament conform to the ordinary person's idea of what is fair and just. 'If there is a law which the juryman constantly shows by his verdicts that he dislikes, it is worth examining the law to see if there is anything wrong with it, rather than the juryman.'

The sedition and other civil-liberty trials of the eighteenth century, and the nineteenth-century game laws which made poaching a capital offence, exemplify this tradition. In similar fashion a jury at the Old Bailey in 1985 declined to convict the former civil servant Clive Ponting on secrets charges, despite a ruling from the judge that the defence case was invalid in law. The jury appears to have felt it wrong to send Ponting to jail for upholding the right of Parliament to know that government ministers were not being wholly truthful.

Nor is it true to say that juries abuse their role in support of some left-wing utopian dream of how government or the courts should operate. In cases where a law has become more progressive than public opinion – for example the Race Relations Act – juries will often decline to convict people charged under it. It is a regular and bitter complaint of those on the political left that juries are reluctant to convict defendants accused of incitement to racial hatred. Yet no one seriously suggests that the jury system should be radically overhauled or undermined to ensure convictions.

Even if we accept that all the amendments, modifications and restrictions in the various jury laws of the 1960s and 1970s were aimed at safeguarding the interests of justice – and that would surely be the most perverse of conclusions – there is one final piece of evidence which is difficult to ignore: jury vetting.

On 5 September 1978 the case of R. *v.* Aubrey, Berry and Campbell opened at Court Number 1 at the Old Bailey. The charges could hardly have been more serious: all three were accused of breaking sections 1 and 2 of the Official Secrets Act, and all three faced the possibility of life imprisonment if convicted. But their trial was to have a deeper significance – for the first time the public would learn how juries were secretly vetted, in their name, to weed out potential 'subversives'.

Aubrey and Campbell were journalists; Berry was a former army corporal who had worked for Signals Intelligence, Britain's secretive electronic eavesdropping network.

Berry had become disillusioned with the way SigInt behaved, and on 18 February 1977 had talked at length to Aubrey and Campbell about his former employers. Special Branch officers arrested them as they left Berry's flat, and eventually charged them with spying under the draconian section 1 of the Act. It was the first – and, to date, last – time a journalist has ever been so accused.

When the jurors filed in one by one to take their seats on that autumn morning in 1978 none of them knew that they had been individually and secretly assessed as to their 'loyalty' and checked for 'extreme political beliefs' by the Special Branch, the same police department which was mounting the prosecution. Nor were any of the defence lawyers aware that six weeks previously the vetting process had been ordered by the Home Office.

It was during a chance conversation with a court usher that one of the barristers discovered that the prosecution had asked for – and been granted – an advance list of the eighty-two-member jury panel from which the trial jury would be selected. The entire process had been conducted in secret, as was the subsequent exclusion of eleven of those original eighty-two jurors from court. The defence barrister,

Lord Hutchinson, QC, raised the matter in court. John Leonard, QC, counsel for the Crown, said that jury vetting had taken place and that 'anyone who is known to be disloyal would obviously be disqualified'.

In the event, he added, the Crown had not had any objection to anyone on the list – but he failed to explain what had happened to the missing eleven, nor what constituted 'disloyalty'. The judge, Mr Justice Willis, ruled that the procedure was perfectly proper 'in a case like this'. The Crown, it appeared, didn't want anyone on the jury who might be an opponent of its institutions and policies.

Perhaps that explained the presence, as foreman of the jury, of a former SAS officer – despite the fact that the SAS regiment was clearly named in the trial evidence. Mr Justice Willis seemed unworried by this apparent conflict of loyalties – at least until it was made public on television. Then he discharged the jury and ordered a re-trial with a new (but still vetted) panel.

On 11 October 1978, in the middle of that second trial and amid considerable public debate, the Attorney General, Sam Silkin, made public the guidelines on jury vetting which he had drawn up four years earlier when he discovered that the practice had existed, unregulated, for forty years. (Significantly, perhaps, the guidelines were drawn up in secret by Silkin and the Home Secretary, despite the latter having previously told the Commons that he was unaware of the existence of any system of jury vetting. He didn't seem to feel the need to correct the statement subsequently.) The 1974 guidelines were vague and loosely worded – and they established the principle that police officers could look at Special Branch files to check the political views of potential jurors in cases with 'strong political motives', and that the prosecution could use the resulting information to stand by those jurors without telling anyone why. Perhaps this might be less alarming if the activities and record-keeping of the Special Branch were more open to inspection. A cloak of secrecy surrounds their motives and methods, but what little has emerged (see Chapter 3) is not reassuring.

In the event the original guidelines were superseded in 1980 by a new statement from a new Attorney General, Sir Michael Havers. Perhaps in response to evidence from Northampton that all potential jurors in all trials at its Crown court were systematically vetted to weed out those with a criminal record and those with an 'undesirable' character, Havers had ordered a review of the system.

Under the ensuing guidelines, Havers drew a distinction between terrorist or security-based trials and ordinary criminal cases. In the latter, the only form of vetting authorised, and therefore legal, is a check on the criminal records index to rule out anyone with a disqualifying conviction. (Yet another Juries Act in 1984 ensured that virtually any conviction – even for a minor breach of the peace – may be a disqualification.)

In terrorist trials, or in cases involving security matters (such as official secrets trials), the guidelines allow the Attorney General to authorise a trawl through Special Branch records, and the resulting information to be passed on to the prosecution lawyers. Even if this didn't allow the packing of juries in cases like the Ponting or Sarah Tisdall trials, it fails to take account of two important loopholes.

The first is the nature and method of Special Branch record-keeping. We shall deal in more detail elsewhere with the enormous range of technology used by the State to keep tabs on us, but for jury vetting the process is fairly simple. All criminal records are stored on a central computer database – the Police National Computer (PNC). Special Branch records are held on a separate high-security computer filing system. In theory the two are not linked.

In practice, however, the PNC holds the records of every car owner in the country, as well as holding a number of 'intelligence' and 'suspected persons' records. According to senior police sources, there is a simple warning 'flag' registered against the name of anyone – innocent or otherwise – on any PNC file should the Special Branch have an interest in him or her.

So any legitimate criminal record check in a non-security trial will effectively also include a basic Special Branch check. Of course, any police officer passing on that special Branch information would be acting outside the Attorney General's guidelines.

He would, however, be more likely to receive a commendation than condemnation from his chief constable. Annexed to the Havers' guidelines is a set of instructions from the Association of Chief Police Officers. They contain this telling paragraph:

> When, as a result of any checks of criminal records information is obtained which suggests that, although not disqualified under the terms of the Juries Act, a person may be unsuitable to sit as a member of a particular jury the police or the Director (of Public

Prosecutions) may pass the relevant information to Prosecuting Counsel, who will decide what use to make of it.

In other words: 'if you happen to find out he's a bit dodgy politically just mark the prosecutor's card and leave the rest to us'. Quite how much Sir Michael Havers knew about the internal workings of the PNC is unclear. What is beyond question is that he should either have read the ACPO instructions and seen the danger of over-zealous police officers doing their own political polling of the panel, or recognised that the guidelines are themselves an elaborate fraud.

In 1980 Lord Denning, then Master of the Rolls, had this to say about jury vetting:

> So long as a person is eligible for jury service I cannot think it is right that, behind his back, the police should go through his record so as to enable him to be asked to 'stand by' for the Crown, or to be challenged by the defence. If this sort of thing is to be allowed, what becomes of a man's right to privacy?

Lord Denning ought perhaps to have known that in this country there is no such general right. But his feelings about the jury are understandable – if ignored by policemen and politicians alike. Today's jury is undermined, prevented from airing its opinions in public (section 1 of the 1981 Contempt of Court Act forbids anyone to talk to a juror about anything), and above all vetted. It is just sixteen years since the jury was fully democratised; since then successive governments have been caught rigging juries in order to obtain the verdicts they want.

Legal aid

> The characteristic of all measures for representation of poor people until the end of the Second World War was that they required lawyers to act as a matter of charity without making a charge, or that the fees that might be paid (often on a fixed scale) were inadequate and involved working at a loss. [*Report of the Royal Commission on Legal Services*, 1979.]

Previous sections of this chapter have dealt with the imperfections of the integral parts of the law machine. But even to enter the lottery of litigation means overcoming a formidable financial hurdle; going to court has never been a cheap option.

It was with this in mind that legal aid was created with the Welfare State in the years following the Second World War. The idea was relatively simple: to put the ordinary man or woman on the same legal footing as the rich and powerful, to open the doors of the courts to the whole population. Previously, as the Royal Commission noted, access to law had depended on personal wealth or legal charity.

So, forty years on, how successful is the legal aid system? How far have we come from those days of wealth and charity? Before we examine what legal aid is, and how it works, we need to draw a distinction between the two generic branches of law – civil and criminal. The legal aid system not unnaturally mirrors this distinction, with separate rules for criminal and civil legal aid. In criminal cases the accuser (or prosecutor) is almost invariably the State in the shape of the Crown Prosecution Service, supported by the Director of Public Prosecutions and the police.

Civil law is normally concerned with disputes between individuals, companies or corporations. The State is rarely involved, and the accuser (called the plaintiff) is not backed up by the Crown Prosecution Service, the DPP or the police.

There has been some crude form of criminal legal aid since 1903, when the Poor Prisoners' Defence Act was introduced. Even before then defendants (except those in magistrates' courts) could claim 'dock briefs' – a tradition that allowed them to request any robed barrister to represent them for a nominal fee. The 1903 Act was modified in 1930 to include magistrates' courts, and defined the test for granting aid as whether it was 'desirable in the interests of justice'. That phrase has stayed with us and, as the behaviour of several magistrates' courts confirms, allows huge and indefensible variations in the granting of legal aid by neighbouring benches.

The 1979 Royal Commission had some comforting words to say on the provision of criminal legal aid: 'Nearly all defendants who are charged with serious offences who appear before Crown courts have legal aid for representation. There are criticisms of the adequacy of this service, but there is no doubt that it is generally available.'

Since that report the twenty-four-hour duty-solicitor scheme has been introduced to provide initial free legal advice to people arrested by the police and to extend the existing duty-solicitor cover in magistrates' courts. So, in theory, there should be little room for criticism of the criminal legal aid system.

The reality is a little different. For a start, the twenty-four-hour duty-solicitor service has been plagued with teething troubles over rosters of lawyers and the amount of money set aside to pay their bills. In some areas, these problems persist.

Then there are the rogue benches of JPs who, as we have seen, unjustly refuse legal aid to defendants coming before them. And although there is an appeals procedure, it is both time-consuming and costly. Nor is all criminal legal aid free. In many cases defendants and their families have to pay contributions to the costs of defending themselves – even though they are (until proved otherwise) deemed to be innocent.

The contributions are decided on the size of both a defendant's disposable income and capital. Of course there are many wealthy professional criminals, and it is only reasonable that they should be expected to pay either in full or in part for their legal representation. But the contribution system as it works at present is too cumbersome to be limited to that particular group.

Instead, the moderately poor and those who have deliberately saved money for their retirement face the prospect of paying contributions to the legal aid fund. Those defendants on supplementary benefit or family income supplement – the really poor – are excused from any contribution. But for the rest of us severe means tests come into play.

In 1988 the limits were set at a disposable weekly income of £50, or disposable capital of £3,000. Any defendant who had savings of more than £3,000 could be ordered to contribute to the cost of his defence, and in the case of weekly income, those left with more than £50 per week after paying household and other bills faced the prospect of paying over one quarter of anything they earned above that figure. Contributions can even be required if a defendant is subsequently acquitted.

Two cases, in particular, have shown how arbitrary and unfair this can be. In a 1973 case a man acquitted of helping his son-in-law's illegal entry to the UK was ordered to pay £800 towards his legal costs. Two years later, almost blind and receiving social security, he was sent to prison for non-payment. It was almost as if his contribution order had been used as a punishment – despite his acquittal.

An equally unjust case from 1973 reinforces the point. A Mrs Kilmartin was arrested by Marks and Spencer store detectives. She had been examining a cardigan worth, in those days, £4.87, and had walked to the door of the store, cardigan in hand, to call to her son waiting outside. Mrs Kilmartin had no intention of removing the cardigan without paying for it, but the store detective was not convinced. The case was heard – at Mrs Kilmartin's request – at the Crown court, where she was duly acquitted. She had been refused legal aid because she held a responsible job. But despite her acquittal she was refused her costs out of central funds (some £800) because the judge felt her conduct had brought suspicion on herself. Although not an issue of legal aid contributions in itself, the Kilmartin case highlights the dilemma many innocent people face when forced to pay the costs of defending themselves. Mrs Kilmartin had no right of appeal against the judge's order. She suffered first from depression, then alcoholism. Within eighteen months she died of liver failure. She had paid £400 of the £800 costs.

The reasoning behind contributions is straightforward: cost. The 1986 total legal aid bill was £265 million, an increase of 18 per cent on 1985. Criminal legal aid ate up £80.2 million – 30 per cent of the final tally and a 6 per cent rise on the previous year. But critics of the system find the spiralling cost of legal aid a poor excuse for limitations on its scope. Unlike civil cases, defendants in criminal cases have no choice over whether they go to court. And given the threat of a prison sentence or the loss of job and reputation, defendants facing criminal charges should not feel restrained by cost from engaging a lawyer to help them fight the allegations.

Legal aid solicitors are, however, convinced that many defendants are put off by the prospect of having to pay contributions. Ivan Geffen, a Walsall solicitor and a member of the Legal Aid Practitioners Group, is particularly worried by the lack of any monitoring of the system.

> There are bound to be people to whom legal aid is offered subject to a contribution, who do not pay the contribution and do not have representation. Some of these will face trial at Crown courts. The majority will be dealt with in magistrates' courts.

Needless to say, no one is collecting information regarding the number of people who plead guilty every year, not because they are guilty but because they cannot afford to contest cases.

Geffen and other solicitors like him in the LAPG are increasingly worried by the crumbling legal aid system. And if the criminal legal aid system has huge flaws in it, the position is far, far worse for civil legal aid claimants.

Roberta Tish, LAPG's secretary, ran her own South London legal aid practice, and has first-hand experience of the system's faults and flaws.

The whole object of the legal aid system was to make everybody equal before the law, but unfortunately its present inadequacies make that impossible. Decisions are often arbitrary, decisions are often inconsistent, and those people that very often should get legal aid are the very people that suffer under the present system and don't get it.

There is also a problem in the enormous delays in the granting, or otherwise, of legal aid certificates, and at the other end in solicitors getting paid. The result is that the people who are looking for solicitors willing to do legal aid are finding less and less firms so willing.

There are so many inefficiencies in the present system: it's slow, it's arbitrary, it's unfair and it's unjust. The whole system needs a drastic and urgent overhaul.

In the summer of 1983, Roberta Tish applied for legal aid on behalf of a client, Mrs S., who was involved in complex wardship proceedings over her four young children (because the children have been the subject of care proceedings neither their names nor that of their mother can be used in full). Mrs S. is illiterate; she is also Asian and speaks little or no English. The application for legal aid was turned down and Mrs S. was told to fight the case on her own.

The hearing itself was likely to involve serious allegations about her abilities as a mother, in addition to the complexities of wardship hearings. When Roberta Tish appealed against the denial of legal aid, the Law Society – which until April 1989 handled all applications – turned her down again, but this time cited a completely different, and contradictory, reason for the refusal.

That case is not unusual. The Law Society, known more often to the general public as a trade protection body for solicitors (which role we will examine shortly), has earned itself an unhappy reputation for inefficiency, delay, bloody-mindedness and convenient lapses of memory in its administration of the legal aid fund.

Legal Aid policy is actually the responsibility of the Lord Chancellor's Department. In turn it delegates administration of the fund to the DHSS and a new Legal Aid Board which took over from the Law Society in April 1989. The Board assesses the legal validity of a would-be litigant's case, while the DHSS assesses financial eligibility. But bureaucratic delay has been an unshakeable tradition with paperwork lost or entire files destroyed. The £20 million administration budget was cut in 1988 by £1.8 million but still accounted for almost 8 per cent of the total legal aid budget.

One of London's busiest area offices – Area 1 – highlights the problem. By January 1987 the office, which handles up to 100,000 individual files, had virtually collapsed.

According to the Lord Chancellor's Department review for 1986, it took Area 1 staff an average of 98 days to reach a decision on the legal merits of most applications, a figure which stretched to 121 days for matrimonial cases. These compared with an average 80-day wait in other areas. But worse was to follow. Legal aid rules allow emergency applications for cases which can't wait for months of official deliberation. Typically, these are made by women who have been beaten up by their husbands or lovers, and by tenants illegally evicted by their landlords. In both these cases financial eligibility is checked over the phone, and legal aid granted within a matter of hours to allow the victim's solicitor to apply for an injunction the same day. In January 1987 emergency applications in London Area 1 took up to one month each to be granted. Nine month delays are routine in non emergency applications.

The size and cost of the legal aid bill is a cause of constant concern to the Lord Chancellor's Department, which is perpetually engaged in an unenviable tussle with the Treasury and rival departments for money. The end result is always the same – a squeeze on real-terms spending or on the categories of case that qualify for legal aid.

The common feature of all reviews of legal aid expenditure is an attempted reduction in budget rather than an expansion of scope. This means that the legal aid safety net has large holes in it. Aid is not available, as we have seen, to families at inquests; it is similarly denied to plaintiffs suing for libel (which ensures that the libel courts are the playground for the rich and super-rich only); with very few exceptions (notably the Mental Health Tribunal) it is not available at the many tribunal hearings in England and Wales. There is no logical reason, other than cost, for these exclusions.

Tribunals, in particular, can present complicated legal problems for any would-be litigant, and many are vital to their lives and welfare. Industrial tribunals, for example, typically pit the complainants against employers who have resources and legal advice far beyond their reach. Trade unionists will usually be found legal representatives by their union for such cases, but for the millions of workers who do not belong to a union there is no such assistance. And yet they are often the worst paid and most exploited of all employees.

The same omission applies to social security and pension tribunals which directly affect the livelihood of the claimants who come before them. Benefit law can be complex, and claimants have the right to appeal against tribunal decisions to the Social Security Commissioners. For none of this is legal aid available.

Immigrants refused admission to Britain, or those already here who have been refused permission to extend their stay, have not one but two rights of appeal. Similarly, not only is the law in this field highly involved with a huge history of previous cases to consider, but there is frequently a language barrier to overcome. The only form of legal assistance is through the UK Immigrants Advisory Service, which may be better than nothing but is far from ideal in cases of such vital importance.

The problem has not gone unnoticed: legal pressure groups and trade unions have long campaigned for legal aid to be extended. The Lord Chancellor's own advisory committee on legal aid has added its voice to the campaign. In 1984 it reported: 'There is a need to set up a full system of tribunal assistance now. The need is clearly shown by the research. The failure to act in response to our earlier reports has had its price: people's rights have gone unenforced, their cases unheard.'

Tribunals exist to settle individual cases, one at a time. But what assistance is given to multiple actions – typically test cases on behalf of a large group of victims? In August 1985 the family of Johnnie Kinnear discovered the answer.

Johnnie Kinnear is a severely brain-damaged teenager. His parents, together with 200 other families, claimed that whooping-cough vaccine administered routinely by his GP caused the disability, and began legal action for compensation in 1978. Both the Department of Health and the vaccine manufacturers denied responsibility, and the case developed into public-interest litigation, with the Kinnears being treated as a test case. The Law Society initially granted legal aid and, over the seven years it took to prepare the case, £50,000 of public money was spent. Then, only months before a hearing was due, it withdrew legal aid, claiming that the Kinnear case was outside its scope.

'The legal aid system is thirty-five years old,' June Williams, deputy secretary of the Law Society, explained. 'It is geared to the needs of the individual client. It is not geared to the needs of multiple actions.' In other words, there is no backing or support for public interest litigation in this country.

But even where, as Ms Williams suggested, the legal aid system is geared to the client's needs, it can actually do more harm than good.

There is a relatively unpublicised – though invariably practised – corner of legal aid known as the statutory charge. Essentially it is a device for clawing back legal aid from a litigant who wins his or her case, and as such is a sensible way of balancing the financing of cases against the costs awarded to the winners. So, typically, a man who wins damages from a road accident whilst on legal aid will pay back his publicly funded costs out of the cost element awarded to him by the judge.

On the face of it, then, the statutory charge is a reasonable way of freeing legal aid money for future cases. But there is a darker side, and it crops up at a time when most people are least able to cope: divorce.

Roughly two-thirds of the entire civil legal aid budget goes on matrimonial cases. In the financial year 1985–6 the fund supported nearly a quarter of a million individual divorce or separation cases, and in many of them it would have been the crucial factor in obtaining a fair settlement of a frequently bitter dispute. But the statutory charge can turn that fair settlement into a gross injustice. It will frequently be levied on the 'winnings' – often the matrimonial home – awarded to the wife. Partly because current thinking is to avoid the apportioning of blame, and partly because many judges simply don't understand the workings of the charge, a divorced woman can find herself – having won her case – forced to sell the home she has just been awarded in order to pay back the legal aid fund.

Kathleen Lawton was put in exactly that position in 1981. Her marriage had ended in 1976, but – due in part to her ex-husband's unreliability – it took five more years to sort out the final settlement. Mrs Lawton owned half the equity of the couple's £20,000 house on the outskirts of London, but she had always paid all the bills (including the mortgage) from her own wages, and had rarely received any maintenance for herself or her two children since the marriage broke up.

In July 1981, a final out-of-court settlement was agreed. Mrs Lawton paid her ex-husband £5,000 for his share of the house, and officially gave up all hopes of any maintenance payments. To finance the settlement she took out a £10,000 mortgage.

> I had heard about the statutory charge, but because I had settled out of court there was no award of costs to me; and because I had traded part of my ex-husband's share of the house against maintenance, and paid him the rest into the bargain, I didn't really see how it applied. Nor did I realise how much the Law Society would try to take back.

The final bill Mrs Lawton received from the Law Society came to £9,379. Immediately the Society took a charge over her house – a second mortgage, in effect. Her building society, of course, already had a £10,000 mortgage on the property.

'I had intended to sell the house – it was too big for me and I knew I couldn't have afforded to run it. But suddenly I found I couldn't afford to sell it either.' If Mrs Lawton sold her house, the building society would immediately claim its £10,000. Then the Law Society would rake off its £9,379. She would have no money to re-house herself. And yet Mrs Lawton was the injured party and had in theory 'won' her case. To add insult to injury her husband was let off his contributions after persistent prevarication, and the Law Society even tried to make Mrs Lawton pay them instead.

Nor did it stop there. The Law Society had miscalculated her costs by up to £6,000. But when she tried to challenge the figure she discovered yet another anomaly in the system.

I wrote asking for a breakdown of the bill, and eventually it went
before the taxing master to assess it. [The taxing master is a
court official who evaluates contested legal fees.] But I found that
I wasn't allowed into the hearing because the rules don't allow it.
Although a legally aided person like myself can end up paying
that bill, the rules say that we have no right either to attend the
taxation or voice our opinion on the size of the bill.

Mrs Lawton couldn't believe the law could be so unjust. But her
solicitor confirmed that the legal aid regulations issued by the Lord
Chancellor's Department insist that bills must be assessed 'irrespective of the interest, if any, of the assisted person'. It took Mrs
Lawton, and her solicitor, another four years to persuade the Law
Society that it had got the figure wrong. In January 1985 the Society
reduced Mrs Lawton's bill to £3,854.50.

There have been repeated proposals to make the system fairer. In
1977 the Lord Chancellor's legal aid advisory committee recommended ending the practice of excluding legally aided litigants from
the taxation hearing. And two years later the Royal Commission on
Legal Services suggested removing the matrimonial home from the
scope of the statutory charge.

In 1980 five Law Lords hearing the leading case on the charge,
that of Mrs Mary Hanlon, added their voices to the campaign for
change. Mrs Hanlon had, like Mrs Lawton, sacrificed maintenance
for herself and two teenage daughters in return for the whole of her
£25,000 house in Waltham Cross, London. Because there was an
existing mortgage on the property the actual equity of the house was
just £10,000.

Under existing rules the first £2,500 of any award is free from the
charge. But that was the only crumb of comfort for Mrs Hanlon. As
soon as the award was made the Law Society stepped in with a bill
for £8,000. Mrs Hanlon faced a dilemma: she could not afford the
upkeep of the Waltham Cross house and had planned to sell it and
buy something smaller. Now she could neither afford to sell it, nor
to stay put. When the case reached the Law Lords they reluctantly
upheld the law. The only concession they could make was to inform
the Law Society that it had the discretion to postpone the charge, or
re-impose it on any new house Mrs Hanlon might buy.

The Law Lords were very sympathetic – but at the end of the
day I still owe that money to the Law Society. I have gained

nothing from my divorce, and sacrificed maintenance into the bargain. I honestly feel there has been a gross injustice. I brought up my family without asking the State for any financial help. I went out to work, doing a very demanding job to bring in some money. And yet because I swapped maintenance for a roof over our heads I have been penalised. I feel I have been stabbed in the back.

If the statutory charge is so unfair in its effects in divorce cases how does it survive? According to Ole Hansen, who campaigned for change whilst director of the Legal Action Group, ignorance is the key.

The problem is that many lawyers and judges simply haven't realised how the charge works. They don't understand that unless they make an order for costs against the losing party in contested divorce cases, the winner – often the wife – will have to pay the costs if she has been on legal aid.

The Law Society, which says that it merely administers the rules and can't bend them in the interests of fairness, was so concerned by this judicial ignorance that in 1983 it sent round a circular explaining the regulations. And it is not only inexperienced or junior judges who are at fault.

In 1982 the president of the Family Division of the High Court failed to take the charge into account in the case of a Mrs June Simmons. No order for costs was made and the Law Society promptly claimed legal aid costs of £8,000 from Mrs Simmons's cash settlement of £26,500.

That cash – the proceeds of the sale of the matrimonial home – had been specifically calculated to allow Mrs Simmons to buy a new house. She, like others before her, found herself deep in debt at the start of her new life. Since she earned just £2,600 a year as a part-time secretary, such debts posed an enormous worry. Although the Law Society had the dicretionary power to postpone the charge, according to the Court of Appeal (where Mrs Simmons ended up in 1983), that discretion was not enough to ensure that hardship was avoided.

The Lord Chancellor does not appear to hear or heed these voices.

In July 1983 his department explained why it had shelved the Royal Commission's proposal for change.

> The remit of the Royal Commission on Legal Services in general, and questions relating to the statutory charge in particular, cover broad, difficult and complicated areas; there is room for more than one view as to the best way to proceed. It would be of little help to take action without being confident it would produce worthwhile results.

Campaigners like Ole Hansen wonder how long it will take for the Lord Chancellor to become confident.

> His department has sat on proposals for change of the statutory charge – and similarly for giving legally aided people the right to question the size of their bills at taxation – for far too long. I just wonder how much longer it will take, how many more Hanlons, Lawtons and Simmonses there will have to be before the system is changed. It is difficult to see why it hasn't been done already. I can only put it down to standard bureaucratic inertia.

Inertia and inefficiency are seemingly inescapable parts of the legal system, and it is not only litigants who are affected. Solicitors representing legally aided clients find themselves financially penalised by the system for maintaining it. Ivan Geffen estimated that the fixed rates of pay for legal aid work ensure that solicitors doing those cases earn only 40 per cent of what colleagues undertaking more lucrative work like conveyancing receive.

That might, perhaps, be acceptable, if they didn't have to wait months – in some cases up to a year – for payment from the fund. In 1983 Roberta Tish calculated that she had outstanding bills worth £27,000 – some of which had been owing for twelve months.

The man in overall charge of legal aid at the Law Society in 1983, David Edwards, at first denied Ms Tish's claims. Payments were usually made, he said, within four to six weeks, and any delays were usually the fault of the courts or even solicitors themselves. Later, Edwards conceded that Ms Tish had been right all along.

In May 1988 Roberta Tish's firm went out of business. Ivan Geffen continues by subsidising the system:

Quite apart from being paid less, we are also in the majority of cases unable even to receive payments in respect of out-of-pocket expenses until cases are completed.

If a client comes to me with, for example, a planning appeal, I can ask him for a payment on account of costs and disbursements which is likely to cover the whole of my bill. I am allowed to make arrangements with the client whereby he either pays the whole lot in advance, or he may pay me by instalments. Either way, as I spend money – for example on experts or travel – I use the client's money. I can send him an interim bill whenever I like. Work in progress may therefore cost me very little or nothing.

In legal aid cases the situation is wholly different. I am probably carrying more than £100,000 of unbilled work in my office, entirely relating to legal aid matters. In a very limited number of cases I am allowed by the Law Society to apply for payment on account of costs. This scheme only works once a year, and around about Easter I shall receive what may be no more than 15 per cent of the amount which I claimed.

I have to wait until the cases are completed, my bills taxed (after very long delays) and then submitted to the Law Society before I receive payment. In the great majority of my legally aided civil litigation matters there is simply no system for payments on account of costs whatever.

The effect is, of course, that I am obliged to work as unpaid banker for the legal aid system – while my bank manager tells me how much he is prepared to allow me on overdraft, charges me a three-figure arrangement fee every time I have to re-negotiate and charges me a high rate of interest on whatever I owe the bank.

Although no official scrutiny is given to the problem (there is not even a list of solicitors currently doing legal aid work), the LAPG suggests that many solicitors are increasingly accepting only 'private', fee-paying clients. Of those who continue – often as a matter of principle – to carry out legal aid work, many have had to sign over their house deeds to the bank as security for loans to prop up the legal aid fund.

Responsibility for the crisis facing legal aid practitioners must be shared by the Law Society and the Lord Chancellor's Department.

The LCD has been frequently warned of the system's impending collapse and seems unwilling or unable to solve the problem. In 1986 both the Law Society and the Bar Council had to sue the Lord Chancellor – an unedifying spectacle – for reasonable rates of pay.

The crisis doesn't stop with the practitioners, however. The very nature of the bureaucracy involved in granting legal aid ensures that the public are often ill-served by it at a time when they most need support. In civil cases, applications are considered first on their legal merits by a series of regional committees. The task of those committees is to act as an initial court, judging cases without the benefit of hearing witnesses in person as a normal court would. In 1983, David Edwards explained why his department of the Law Society carried out the screening.

> We get more than a quarter of a million applications for legal aid a year. Over the country as a whole, 84 per cent of all the applications for legal aid are granted; 16 per cent of them are refused. Now it must follow, I think, that some of those cases that are refused might possibly have succeeded. The reason why you have to have a filter is that you're using public money in considerable sums and you must have a filter so that only those cases where there is a reasonable prospect of success are financed by the taxpayer. I must accept that it could be tough luck for some; there isn't a system of perfect justice.

Ann Reed would agree with that verdict. Mrs Reed was once the wife of a property multi-millionaire, living in some style and comfort in the best part of London. Then, quite suddenly, the marriage ended.

> The first I knew of my divorce was on a Monday morning after having breakfast in bed. My husband just told me that when the mail arrived there would be a letter in it for me, asking for a divorce. He told me he wanted me out of the house in four days. I just couldn't believe it. I simply had nowhere to go, so I couldn't leave – I would have been made homeless.

The pressure finally told on Mrs Reed, and her doctor began prescribing extremely powerful anti-depressant drugs to help her cope. She became, in her own words, 'a zombie; sometimes I didn't know where I was, what I was doing. I stumbled around, I fell over. I became very frightened and, coupled with the drugs I was taking, I gradually became unaware of what was going on.'

Mrs Reed was then unfortunate enough to pick a bad solicitor. He failed to keep a watch on the terms of the settlement, failed to ensure that promises were kept, failed even to make her husband put his promises of a flat for Mrs Reed in writing. In the end, and whilst heavily sedated, Mrs Reed signed a settlement that guaranteed her virtually no financial support, and nowhere to live. Her husband, meanwhile, had property in London, Monte Carlo and New York. While he lived in penthouse suites across the world, Mrs Reed ended up in a homeless women's hostel in a seedy part of London's Earl's Court.

It took several years of careful psychiatric treatment to heal the mental scars. Then, with the help and support of a new solicitor and a specialist in the effects of anti-depressant drugs, she applied to the Law Society for legal aid to overturn the unjust settlement.

> I believe I had a right to proper maintenance and a place to live – I put a lot into my marriage. I had the backing of a specialist and testimony from several drug companies about the effects of their products on me. I could also show that my solicitor at the time had since been struck off by the Law Society for mishandling another divorce settlement. I honestly thought I would get legal aid very quickly.

Her specialist doctor, Jack Nabney, agreed. Had he been her doctor at the time of the settlement, Mrs Reed would not have signed any documents.

> She was being treated with huge doses of drugs – with Valium, with Largactil, with Mogadon and many, many more. In no way would a patient of mine be allowed to sign a document while under this dosage of drugs. They are very powerful mind-bending chemicals, so that although a person may be capable of understanding that they are signing a document, they will have no idea what it is they are signing.

Armed with this impressive array of testimonies, Mrs Reed waited for legal aid to be granted. She sought the opinion of a barrister.

His advice was not favourable. Then, with new evidence of double-dealing by her ex-husband during the settlement negotiations, she commissioned a second opinion. This one recommended that the Law Society should grant legal aid to get a new divorce settlement.

But the Law Society refused. It was not prepared to take a risk on losing the case, because courts in general were reluctant to overturn such settlements. And besides, it had all happened long ago...

For Ann Reed it is still happening today.

Betty Hayward knows only too well how that feels. We left Miss Hayward earlier in this chapter at the point in 1983 when she had found a new solicitor, Russell Conway, to take on her case. Conway applied for legal aid and, for the first time in almost a decade, the Law Society granted it. Or rather it granted a limited amount of money – just enough to get counsel's opinion on the merits of her case.

That opinion in 1983 laid bare the official neglect that Miss Hayward had suffered, but concluded that too much time had elapsed for there to be any real prospect of a successful court action. Not the least reason for this was that the con-man Morley-Morley had died during the years in which Betty Hayward had struggled to bring him and his solicitor to court.

So why had the Law Society refused legal aid so often over those years? Partly, it should be said, because they were simply following the strict financial thresholds laid down by the Lord Chancellor's Department. At the time of one of her earliest applications, Betty Hayward had just inherited £2,000 – enough in those days to make her ineligible.

On other occasions, however, the Society seems simply to have lost its patience with what it saw as an erratic, unstable woman; on one occasion it lost not just its patience but its files on the Hayward case. Then again, two separate departments were involved in the matter – legal aid and professional purposes which was responsible for initially examining Miss Hayward's complaint against Morley-Morley's solicitor, Anthony Feldman. The two branches seem rarely, if ever, to have spoken to each other about the case, and files went missing – or were destroyed – between the two. In 1984 neither department had a copy of Lord Denning's judgement and request that Miss Hayward be granted legal aid. At the same time a search of the Society's vaults failed to trace a substantial number of files going back several years.

By the summer of 1984 the Law Society had become sensitive to criticism of its performance. A management study of the way it handled legal aid had been thoroughly critical. At the same time pressure was building up from inside the profession for it to clean up the ever-growing scandal of its complaints procedure. Finally, it agreed to re-consider Miss Hayward's case.

The lawyers

For most of us, solicitors are the most visible and the accessible part of the legal machine – the first point of contact we have with the law. The cases of Betty Hayward and Ann Reed illustrate the fact that lawyers can be either mendacious or careless. But what remedies are open to dissatisfied clients? How easy is it to get recompense for shoddy, negligent or crooked behaviour? And to whom does the dissatisfied client turn?

Most people believe they can ask the Law Society to deal with errant solicitors. It is, after all, the governing body for all solicitors in England and Wales, and it boasts an 'independent' Solicitors' Complaints Bureau.

In fact the truth is shamefully different. In the eyes of the Law Society there are two distinct varieties of complaints about solicitors: allegations of professional misconduct and allegations of negligence. What constitutes professional misconduct is set out in a glossy booklet, and covers such misdemeanours as failing to keep proper accounts, appropriating clients' money and anything which would in general bring the profession into disrepute. Over all of these areas the SCB keeps a watchful eye (its predecessor, the Professional Purposes Department, was known none-too-fondly as 'the Mafia' in some solicitors' offices).

But negligence is another matter altogether, and one which the Society is reluctant to handle. Negligence, according to the SCB, is a matter for the courts to interpret, and until they have done so in any given case neither it nor any other branch of the Law Society can help the dissatisfied client.

The Society also defines negligence in a way which many ordinary people find hard to understand. Fred Whiskin is no exception.

In 1978 he and his wife bought a bungalow on a new estate in

Bromley. Theirs was the end house in a row of four set back off a nearby approach road. But behind their bungalow ran another approach road; it was significantly nearer the Whiskins' home, and before signing the contract Whiskin asked his solicitor to find out whether he had any legal right to use it, since it wasn't clear on the plan whether it was a public or private road.

Whiskin's solicitor was happy to reassure his client that the road wasn't private and that the Whiskins were free to drive along it and park their car on it. Whiskin duly signed his contract.

A year later some new neighbours moved in and told Whiskin that the road was private and he should stop using it. The Whiskins contacted their solicitor, who once again reassured them as to their legal right to drive up and down the road or park indefinitely anywhere they chose. Relations between the Whiskins and their neighbours rapidly deteriorated, and in 1980 the case was set down for a court hearing.

> The builders of the estate told me that I had only a right-of-way on foot over what they called the footpath. I was worried and asked my solicitor whether it was a footpath or a road. He said he was certain it was a road, and I was not to worry. I asked him what would happen if he was wrong – if the court decided it was just a footpath – and he told me that in that event I would be protected by his compulsory insurance policy. This was my guarantee that I wouldn't end up paying thousands of pounds if it turned out he had made a mistake.

Then, quite suddenly, Whiskin's solicitor withdrew from the case. He told the couple that he had taken counsel's opinion and had been advised it would 'not be proper' for him to act on their behalf any more. But by then it was too late for the Whiskins to withdraw from the case. And when the dispute came to court, the judge found against them – with costs. 'To date the costs have been around £6,000. This, of course, is besides all the time I have spent fighting the case personally. To add insult to injury I was informed that I couldn't make a claim against my former solicitor because he was not negligent.'

In fact, the Law Society took the view that Whiskin's solicitor had simply made a mistake – and that didn't add up to negligence. Whiskin found that distinction hard to accept – the more so when he read in a Law Society publication that if a solicitor made a mistake in a conveyancing procedure the house purchaser would be compensated.

> It does seem that the Society is unwilling to live up to its promises. The judge said quite clearly that my solicitor had made a mistake. I have to pay all the legal bills and on top of that my property isn't worth the money I paid for it because it doesn't have any proper approach road.

The Whiskins' case illustrates the problem facing dissatisfied clients. Whiskin followed the prescribed pattern of the complaints procedure – which promptly let him down.

That procedure has come in for so much criticism that the Society has spent the last few years trying to improve its public image. In theory it works like this. The dissatisfied client writes to the Law Society spelling out the reasons for his complaint. If this amounts merely to professional misconduct it is passed to the Solicitors' Complaints Bureau. The SCB will investigate, may hold hearings, and eventually the solicitor may be reprimanded – or in an extreme case struck off.

If the complaint alleges negligence the Society will decline to investigate, but will offer the client an (initially) free interview with a member of its negligence panel. The panel is made up of solicitors with experience of handling complaints against other solicitors, and offers a one-hour free 'diagnostic interview'. If the panel member is satisfied that there has been negligence, he will offer to sue the original solicitor on behalf of the client. But if he does so he will charge his full fees for acting.

Whiskin accepted the initial diagnostic interview – but got no further. In August 1983 he saw Steven E. Henriques of the London firm Bartletts de Reya. Henriques was not encouraging. He summarised his views on paper:

> The story as outlined to us left us full of sympathy with you as an unsuccessful litigant, but we did not feel in all honesty that those who advised you had been negligent. It was to be understood by all litigants that litigation is a hazardous affair and that someone, to his surprise, is going to lose.

Whiskin was far from surprised. In fact, Henriques's letter confirmed his previous view that the Law Society has no real stomach for disciplining its members. He is not alone.

Barry Bowman asked the Law Society to exercise a little control over one of its members in October 1984. Specifically, Bowman wanted their assessment of his solicitor's bill for what amounted to one day's work on a relatively simple commercial conveyance. He had been more than a little shocked to receive a request from Osmond, Gaunt and Rose – a well-established London firm of solicitors – for £3,600.

The bill duly went to the Law Society for their consideration under an assessment scheme called the Remuneration Certificate. On 9 October 1984 the Society approved the bill and granted the certificate. Malcolm Leaf, head of its non-contentious business section, wrote. 'The certificate shows that in the opinion of the Society, after considering the papers, the amount charged in the bill is appropriate.'

Bowman began to investigate. The breakdown of the bill provided by Osmond, Gaunt and Rose showed that the actual work done had cost just £600, that reading and sending forty-nine letters had cost another £490, and that the rest was something called 'the value element'. What he discovered about this made him all the more certain that the Law Society was primarily concerned with its members' interests rather than those of the general public.

> The value element turned out to be perfectly legal. It is a sort of traditional perk enjoyed by solicitors in commercial conveyancing with the Law Society's approval. Under the terms the Society sets out for it, the solicitor can charge a given percentage of the value of the average annual rent of the property concerned. It doesn't represent anything other than pure profiteering – but the Law Society wholeheartedly approves of it.

Bowman also found that he had very little room for manoeuvre. Osmond, Gaunt and Rose had, as is normal, deducted the money from the sale proceeds – though they had as a 'gesture of goodwill' knocked £350 off the final account.

It was this automatic deduction of money that brought Peter and Sylvia Halligey into conflict with their solicitor, and ultimately with the Law Society. The Halligeys had engaged Miss Pauline Twist, of

Neville-Jones and Howie of Poole, Dorset, to act for them in a dispute with a neighbour. The couple became unhappy with Miss Twist's performance and disputed the firm's subsequent bill.

Shortly afterwards, Peter Halligey was forced to sue his former employers for breach of contract. He was extremely reluctant to re-engage Miss Twist, but had no other grudge against Neville-Jones and Howie. He therefore agreed to instruct one of its senior partners from another of its offices. The solicitor he chose, Roger Humble-Smith, was based at Swanage in Dorset. Humble-Smith did a very good job indeed, and secured substantial damages for Peter Halligey.

Unfortunately, not all the damages reached him. Aside from (quite properly) deducting Humble-Smith's fees from the settlement money, Neville-Jones and Howie also deducted Miss Twist's disputed bill of £1,437.50.

> I protested strongly about this. I pointed out that the two matters were entirely unrelated. I then went to the Law Society to complain, and was told the only course of action open to me was to sue the firm. The final words to me from the Law Society man were, 'Don't forget to ask for legal aid'.

Encouraged by the advice, the Halligeys did just that – only to be turned down months later. The Law Society told them that they had no cause for action. But there was always the negligence panel. The Society put them in touch with Steven Henriques at Bartletts de Reya, and the couple sent off their summary of the case. 'We got a letter back saying that they had gone through our letter, but that there was not a single point in it on which they could advise us to take legal action. The letter ended up saying that the writer hoped we would not ask him to go through our papers.'

So much for the negligence panel. In fact, though the Halligeys were not to know, the Law Society had never actually intended the panel to provide a serious complaints service. Just after its inception, Michael Hoyle, head of its professional purposes department, had written to one panel solicitor about a troublesome case:

> You will appreciate that the Negligence Panel was partly set up as a public relations exercise to dispel the argument that no solicitor is prepared to act in proceedings alleging professional

> negligence on the part of another solicitor. This is, of course, the very obvious type of case where, if the member of the public continues to be unrepresented, there could be unfortunate repercussions. I have little doubt that the local profession have good reason for not assisting, and it may well be that there is no evidence that professional negligence existed.

In other words, the negligence panel is at best a piece of window-dressing designed to ward off public criticism.

But what of the commonly held belief that many solicitors are reluctant to sue fellow lawyers? The Halligeys found out the truth very quickly.

> We approached several firms of solicitors about our case, but they all made it clear they didn't want to become involved. In the end my wife's health was completely broken, and we just gave up the fight. We were caught in a sort of Catch 22. The solicitors had our money, and the Law Society told us the only thing was to sue. Then when we tried to sue, it refused us the legal aid money it said we would need and should apply for.

The Halligeys were probably wise to surrender: suing a solicitor can be less of a fight, more of a protracted war – and a war of attrition at that.

Leslie Parsons fired the first salvo in his private war on 26 June 1970. Hostilities were to last for sixteen long and expensive years. Parsons, a Welsh bottler of cockles and mussels, consulted solicitor Glanville Davies on that date. Parsons had previously retained another solicitor, Christopher John Malim, to sue the firm of Mather and Platt Ltd for breach of contract over an onion-peeling machine he had developed.

Malim, a former member of the Law Society's ruling Council, had not been a success – at least not for Parsons. Some time after instructing Malim in 1967, Parsons was surprised to be sent a copy of a letter his solicitor had sent to the defendants in the case. The letter, mistakenly sent out by a secretary, revealed that Malim had secretly met the managing director of the company he was supposed to be suing, had begun to negotiate with the company to defeat his own client, and had named as his price a dozen bottles of best champagne.

Leslie Parsons was far from amused, and consulted Glanville Davies. Davies, by chance, was also a member of the Law Society's Council; he was instructed to sue Malim. Simultaneously, Parsons sent a detailed complaint about his former solicitor to the Law Society. He also instructed Davies to lodge a formal complaint. Davies failed to do so, but Parsons' own letter was received and logged at the Society's headquarters in Chancery Lane. Instead of opening a file and beginning an investigation, however, it simply ignored the complaint. This was to be only the first of a series of similar omissions.

Davies, meanwhile, pursued Mather and Platt Ltd. In 1975 Parsons won the case and was awarded damages of £530,000. Once again he instructed Davies to lodge a complaint about Malim with the Law Society. Once again, Davies failed to do so; but he did deduct £100,000 from the settlement money to meet his own fees. Parsons, who had already paid Davies £48,000, asked for a breakdown of the bill.

It took Davies another eleven months to provide any sort of written account – but even that wasn't itemised, so Parsons had no way of knowing where the final total of £105,000 had been earned or spent. On 6 April 1976 he again asked for a breakdown, but another nine months elapsed before Davies was ordered, in the High Court, to draw up a detailed analysis. The bill was finally ready on 1 September 1977 – more than two years after the Mather and Platt settlement.

Curiously, though, the bill had grown substantially since April 1976. It now amounted to £197,591.40. Solicitors do have the right to charge clients extra for providing a detailed breakdown of a disputed bill – but, even so, Davies appeared to have stretched the point.

Taxing Masters Graham-Green and Berkeley agreed; in two separate hearings the bill was cut down to £67,736.56 – a reduction of almost two-thirds. More was to follow. By September 1980 Davies' bill for work he had done on the case while Parsons had been on legal aid was cut from £8,028.50 to £1,931.50.

All this time, Leslie Parsons had been asking the Law Society to discipline both its wayward solicitors. By 1982 he had made up to a dozen complaints, but was no nearer to achieving anything. In November that year Mr Justice McCowan – in yet another hearing over fees and costs – ruled that Davies had been guilty 'at least of gross and persistent misconduct'.

In December 1982 Parsons served notice on the Society that if they wouldn't deal with Davies, he would; he began private proceedings to have him struck off. Davies simultaneously resigned from the Council. The following month the Council passed a resolution to mark his retirement:

> It was never the ambition of Mr Davies to aspire to the highest office in the Law Society. Perhaps this was due to a less than robust constitution, but also to his innate modesty and the satisfaction he derived from being of service to his profession. All his colleagues will miss a true friend, for to know Glanville Davies is to receive friendship. They greatly regret that reasons of health have compelled him to resign from the Council.

Following that tactless statement, the Society kept silent for the best part of a year. Then, on 24 October 1983, it announced that it would welcome an independent investigation of its handling of the case. What prompted this U-turn was a High Court hearing earlier the same afternoon. The purpose of the case was to hear Parsons' request that Glanville Davies be struck off. Mr Justice Vinelott listened to the evidence, and duly obliged. It had taken eight years, but Parsons had been vindicated.

Independent enquiries into the Law Society's handling of complaints are normally carried out by an employee of the Lord Chancellor's Department called the Lay Observer. He is not a lawyer and is genuinely independent of the Society – though, as we shall see, not all complainants hold him in high esteem.

It was because the Glanville Davies case was so serious, and its ramifications so great, that the Society commissioned its own investigation. A three-man team headed by Philip Ely began work almost immediately, and published its findings in a twenty-two-page report in February 1984. Its key finding was that there had been:

> . . . administrative failures, mistakes, wrong decisions, errors of judgement, failures in communication, high-handedness and insensitivity on a scale that must have done great harm to the Law Society. The whole episode is a disgrace to the Law Society.

> We can find few aspects of the complaint that were handled properly.

Ely couldn't be certain about whether there had been a cover-up, nor whether Davies' position as a Council member had influenced those responsible for handling the complaints against him. But it conceded that he might

> have benefited, not from being a Council member as such, but from being known to the staff and committee members. Davies was well-liked, and we cannot exclude the possibility that in making decisions the fact that Davies was involved may, perhaps unconsciously, have influenced those decisions.

The Law Society immediately wrote a letter of apology to Parsons, and the Council extended its 'sincere regret to the profession for the embarrassment and concern this matter has caused'.

The Lay Observer had, in the meantime, also finished his report. It, too, was far from complimentary about the Law Society – but it was a considerably weaker affair than the Ely report, and managed to leave a lingering – but wholly inaccurate – impression that Parsons had somehow been partly responsible for the past sixteen years' chaos. Simultaneously it expressed sympathy for Davies, whose career, it noted, was in ruins. Parsons and his supporters felt that the Lay Observer had missed several salient points about Davies and his conduct – not least his habit, identified by Mr Justice Vinelott, of writing out fictitious attendance notes of non-existent meetings with Parsons in order to justify spurious bills.

None the less, it was a critical report and, together with the savage indictment of the Ely team, should have been enough to persuade the Society that it owed Parsons a good deal more than an apology.

However, before we come to the Law Society's attitude towards compensation, we must return to the Lay Observer, and the case of Fred Whiskin. He had complained to the then Lay Observer, Major John Allen, about the Society's handling of his original complaint, and the advice given on its behalf by Henriques. Major Allen was not encouraging.

> Having very carefully considered these papers, I have concluded that, in my judgement, the Law Society has acted entirely reasonably in the treatment of your complaint. I am quite unqualified, as a layman, to comment on the advice that Mr Henriques gave you but I am bound to say that it does seem to have been very convincing.

Whiskin was far from convinced. He knew that his original solicitor had first made a mistake and then left him in the lurch prior to a court hearing he had encouraged and arranged. The Law Society had declined to deal with that solicitor and had told him, in effect, that everyone makes mistakes and he would have to pay the bill. It had also conveniently forgotten its own words, in its own magazine, that mistakes, if they happened, would always be compensated. But, in the end, there was nothing Fred Whiskin could do about it.

Major Allen, now retired, was only too willing to admit that his brief excluded more than it included.

> I do get a lot of complaints that I am not able to deal with from members of the public dissatisfied with a solicitor's work and the Law Society's response. Very often it's a legal problem and I have to tell them that they should go and consult a solicitor. But there are a lot of times when I am able to help a lot of people and I think I do so – at least I try, and I think the Law Society does take notice of me.

Surprisingly, it has no legal duty to do so: the Lay Observer's findings are not binding on the Law Society. And critics of the system say that the Lay Observer is too weak a figure – insufficiently trained and with too little back-up – to act as a watchdog with any real teeth.

They concede, however, that he is better than the Society itself. In the wake of the Glanville Davies affair the Law Society attempted to put its house in order. The old professional purposes department was dismantled and a new body, the Solicitors' Complaints Bureau, established to handle allegations of misconduct. The disciplinary process is now supervised by lay members of the SCB, in an attempt to head off criticism of solicitors 'looking after their own'. But how different is the SCB from its predecessor, and what new powers does it have?

The answer is 'not much, and very few' – though as we write there are plans to allow it to reduce contested bills if there is evidence of shoddy work. Many of the old professional purposes department staff have simply been transferred to the SCB. And, of course, any allegation of negligence is still a matter for the courts, not the Law Society.

Further disquiet about the Society's professed new willingess to protect the public from rogue lawyers came swiftly after the Ely Report. Leslie Parsons wrote to the Society asking for compensation – after all, he had been forced to do its job for it. He had been forced by its refusal even to open files on his complaints to go to court to have Davies struck off, and he felt he was entitled to some compensation for the years he had spent on the case.

The Society refused. It told him that although it was the body charged by law with protecting the public (as well as having a parallel role as the trade body for solicitors), it had no duty of care to the general public. And if it had no duty – no responsibility – there was no way it intended to pay up.

Wearily, Parsons prepared to take the case to court. Negotiations stuttered on. Finally, more than a year later, the Society quietly paid an undisclosed amount in an out-of-court settlement.

Betty Hayward was not so lucky. Her new lawyer, Russell Conway, had discovered that the Law Society has a Compensation Fund specifically earmarked for cases where clients have lost money through their lawyer's misdemeanours. Conway felt confident, with the backing of Lord Denning's judgement, that Miss Hayward's financial ruin was due, in a large part, to the antics of Anthony Feldman – solicitor to the late Rex Morley-Morley. He promptly applied to the fund.

It was to take another three years for the Law Society finally to refuse that application. In that time the qualifications for compensation were changed – a clear case of shifting the goalposts while the game was in progress – and Feldman was given the opportunity to put his case to the Society in person. Miss Hayward was not. She is still waiting for justice. 'Had anyone told me fifteen years ago that the conditions which control the law in this country were the same as those which Dickens described in *Bleak House*, I should never have believed them. But nothing has changed.'

Miss Hayward, understandably, saw the law machine differently from Lord Hailsham, then Lord Chancellor. He discerned very real changes – not least in the increasing crime rate, the rising costs of litigation and legal aid, and the pressure for better legal services. In May 1985, around the time that Miss Hayward was fighting her last round with the Law Society, he told the London Criminal Court Solicitors' Association:

> There are constant demands for new expenditures – indeed I sometimes feel that the Lord Chancellor is regarded as some kind of rich uncle with a bottomless purse from which he is expected to go on plucking additional money.
>
> Unfortunately this is not so. For additional resources, Lord Chancellors have to have recourse to the common purse. Law and order have to compete with education, defence, health and social services – indeed all the other areas in which there is also constant and legitimate pressure for more and better provision. I have done my best, and will continue to do my best, to find resources. But there are limits.

We would not argue with the Lord Chancellor's theme, but we will, when we come to the last chapter, suggest that if these limits deny the law's protection to a sizable section of the population, then not only are the limits too tightly drawn but the system itself needs changing. Evidence from, for example, the Legal Aid Practitioners Group suggests that almost 50 per cent of the population do not qualify for free civil legal aid. The 1988 thresholds of £3,000 disposable capital or a disposable weekly income of just £46.15 see to that. On top of that, the sliding scale of contributions for people exceeding those thresholds mean that a further large percentage of the public could never afford to go to court.

Before we leave the law, we should draw attention to a curious anomaly. We have referred throughout this section to solicitors, but there are two branches of the legal profession in England and Wales, and barristers make up the second half. What is more, many of those people who have been induced – often by the archaic laws of audience which deny solicitors the right to speak in the higher courts – to pay the bar's very expensive rates, have come away highly dissatisfied.

It is a common – and justified – complaint, that all too often barristers know nothing of a client or his case until the morning of the court appearance. And in such circumstances it is an exceptional advocate who can do justice to the evidence. We have excluded consideration of this, and of the rights of that client to compensation, for one reason alone. That client has no rights whatsoever. Barristers are legally immune from legal action from clients whom they have represented. There is no legal link between the two.

Under our arcane and archaic system, clients must never directly approach or consult with barristers. These higher beings may only be retained through a solicitor. There are few better symbols of the need for change.

TWO

An Englishman's Home

> 'This is a free country, madam;
> we have a right to share your
> privacy in a public place.'
>
> Peter Ustinov, *Romanoff and Juliet*

Few myths are as cherished as Sir Edward Coke's 400-year-old saw that a man's home is his castle and his refuge. Houses, we believe, are sanctuaries to which we have a right, and to which we can retreat and shut out the world; they are the physical protectors of our established right to privacy, as celebrated (verbally, at least) by judges throughout the past two centuries.

In fact, as Sir Robert Megarry, a former Vice Chancellor (one of the highest judges in the land), recognised in a 1979 case, 'no general right of privacy has been recognised by English law'. And our houses provide little more protection than any other building – public or private.

In this chapter we will examine what rights we have to a roof over our heads (and whether or not it has to be leakproof), what rights we acquire when we get one, and what remedies are available when things go wrong.

The right to a home

There is a widely held belief that local councils have a duty to re-house anyone unfortunate enough to be made homeless, and in certain circumstances that belief is justified.

In 1977, Parliament passed the Housing (Homeless Persons) Act. Its aim was to clear up and clarify the muddled and confusing set of duties and responsibilities imposed on local authorities. Prior to

1977 there was never more than a vague obligation to provide temporary accommodation for the homeless and, because that obligation was split between the housing and the social services departments, homeless families often found themselves caught up in internal wrangling and local council politics.

The new Act, though far from being a straightforward and uncomplicated piece of legislation, did impose a definite legal obligation on councils to re-house the homeless provided that they met certain criteria. A person was defined as being homeless if he (or she) had no accommodation sufficient for himself, his family and dependants (assuming that they normally lived with him). It is not, however, enough just to be homeless as defined by the Act. To be given accommodation the homeless person must also have a 'priority need' – typically having dependent children under sixteen or infirm relatives. Pregnancy or losing previous accommodation through fire, flood or some other disaster also amount to priority needs. But the list effectively excludes one large category of people from the Act's protection – the single homeless, and in particular single homeless men. People in this category have no claim on any local authority housing agency other than assistance and advice on where to find private accommodation. In practice, most councils simply pass on a printed list of local housing associations and accommodation agencies.

In 1985 more than 200,000 households applied for accommodation under the Act. Councils estimate that that figure probably represents around 500,000 people, but just 94,000 households were accepted as having priority needs. The rest joined the growing army of those who never applied, knowing that they didn't meet the criteria for housing. Many of them live in squalid bed-and-breakfast accommodation paid for by the DHSS. By the end of 1984 (the most recent figures available), their numbers had risen to 163,000 – a four-fold increase in just five years. Even some of the priority-need homeless families were put up in this type of accommodation – often overcrowded, frequently a fire risk, and occasionally unfit for human habitation. Government statistics estimate this group at more than 5,400 households, while housing groups and councils (particularly in London) claim that this is a severe underestimate.

Local authorities face an uphill struggle to house the very people that elect them. There are more than 1.2 million people on council-house waiting lists; that number rarely fluctuates to any degree, as housing stock deteriorates or is sold off, and government cash limits preclude the building of new homes on any scale.

Taunton Council owns 8,500 houses, of which 10 per cent have serious structural defects. In 1986 the Council calculated that it had 346 homeless families on its books, yet in 1987 it planned to build just twenty-three new homes. Taunton is not recognised as a particularly unusual or hard-hearted council, but because of the housing crisis it is beginning to interpret the 1977 Act harshly – because it has no money to do otherwise.

Valerie Goodison is on the receiving end of that decision. She and her three young children were forced to camp in the front room of her parents' house because the Council refused to help. Normally Valerie and her husband would qualify under the priority-need criteria; they have, after all, three young children. But there is a loophole: councils have the right to refuse to provide accommodation to families who have made themselves 'intentionally homeless'. The Goodisons – Valerie grew up in Taunton, but had lived in Scotland for several years – moved to the town when Mr Goodison was offered a job there.

He had been unemployed for two years, and jumped at the chance of work. The family moved out of their council house in Scotland and moved south. Taunton Council insist that by simply leaving that house the Goodisons made themselves intentionally homeless. The couple are now split up. Valerie and the children live with her parents, while her husband lives across town in bed-and-breakfast accommodation. When the 1977 Act was passed the Department of the Environment issued a Code of Guidance for handling homeless-persons claims, which says: 'The practice of splitting families is not acceptable, even for short periods.' The code has no legal backing to it – it is purely for the guidance of local authorities.

Even in those cases where a legal challenge can be mounted, the outcome is far from certain. In 1986 the case of Puhlhofer v. London Borough of Hillingdon reached the House of Lords. Mr and Mrs Puhlhofer and their two children lived in one small room in a guesthouse. They were certain that it was quite inadequate and that they should qualify for priority-need housing. The Council refused, and the Law Lords backed their decision. The living conditions might be appalling, the Lords acknowledged, but the room could legally be interpreted as accommodation for the family – who were therefore not entitled to claim the protection of the Act.

The Puhlhofers' predicament is not unusual: thousands of families live in sub-human conditions. Islington Council uses hotels like the Tudor, opposite Paddington station in west London, to house families on its books. At the Tudor a 'double room' can measure ten feet by six feet and include just a single bed and shared bathroom. Breakfast may consist of a cup of tea and two pieces of toast. The hotel's internal walls are damp and have holes in them. One woman resident, designated homeless by the Council after her husband threw her out of their flat, had been told that she could expect to stay there at least a year. She had one eight-month-old daughter and was expecting another. There was nowhere for the child to play; there was scarcely room for her to move.

Other accommodation can be even worse. In December 1981 eight people died when fire swept through a rabbit-warren of rooms in a series of connected bedsitters in London. The landlord insisted that fire precautions were adequate, but a legal action against him has been started. Whether or not he did, as he claims, take all reasonable steps, he would not have been subject to any local authority inspection. The 1980 Housing Act obliges councils to check for fire safety only in houses larger than 500 square metres in volume. The majority of multi-occupation homes are smaller than that.

Some councils check up voluntarily; others don't, and tenants can find it almost impossible to find out which category their council falls into. Yet in the past six years more than 700 people have died in bedsit fires in England and Wales.

Simultaneously, council-house building has dropped dramatically: in London it has fallen from 25,000 a year in the mid-seventies to just 5,000. Private-sector accommodation has become both scarce and highly priced, with the exception of an ever-increasing number of conversions to bed-and-breakfast or bedsit properties.

Householders' rights

Householders are obviously better off in every sense than the homeless living in bed-and-breakfast accommodation or bedsit-land. But what actual rights do they have?

For a start, there is no such right as the absolute ownership of the land on which the house stands, nor any real right to bolt the doors and shut out the world. There is an impressively comprehensive list of people who have a right to tramp through the living-room uninvited. The taxman can call at any reasonable time and demand access to your land and home to assess their worth. Customs officials have very wide powers to enter your home, day or night, provided they have obtained a magistrate's warrant.

Council officials can enter a council house on twenty-four hours' notice to make sure that any maintenance work is being properly carried out. Housing officials are also allowed to obtain warrants for entry if they believe housing regulations may have been breached. In addition, public health officials have a general right of entry (subject to twenty-four hours' notice) to investigate any breaches of public health regulations or bye-laws. Councils wishing to purchase compulsorily your home can walk in on the same terms. Any obstruction you might choose to put in their way can land you in court.

Farmers can be visited by agricultural officials with a general right to inspect wage sheets and employee records. Radio hams usually have to sign a compulsory agreement giving regulatory officials permission to enter their homes when they apply for a licence. Representatives from the gas and electricity boards can come in, either with your consent or with a magistrate's warrant. To obtain the warrant they need just twenty-four hours' notice of intention and a reasonable belief that there might be some sort of emergency on or around the premises.

The police have extremely wide powers under section 8 of the Police and Criminal Evidence Act to obtain a search warrant, provided they have reasonable grounds for believing that a serious offence has been committed, and that a search warrant would help the investigation. The Act defines 'serious' offences extremely widely – from treason to minor vandalism – and in practice allows the police themselves to decide whether an offence is serious or trivial. And there is no restriction on what they may remove from the house, whether or not it relates to the reason for the original search warrant having been granted.

National Insurance inspectors can walk into business premises at any reasonable time – even if the premises are in fact your home – to interview employers and employees and to inspect documents.

The list goes on and on: health officials, social workers, representatives of public utilities (who are also empowered to break the door down) – almost anyone in any official capacity can knock at the door and demand to come in. Of course, in the vast majority of cases there is little or no abuse of these powers. Officials of whatever variety are extremely unlikely to demand access to your family, workforce or filing cabinet in the dead of night without good reason. But the cherished notion of the home as a castle is no more than an illusion.

The system that allows these officials to call on you and come in is based on a notional bargain. Householders have many rights over their homes; in return they have many duties both to official bodies and the rest of the community – typically, their neighbours.

Although, as Sir Robert Megarry pointed out, there is no general right to privacy in this country, the law does have a stab at something similar. There are a host of common-law and statutory rights affecting the duties and responsibilities of neighbours. We shall look at the three main ones: trespass, light and nuisance.

Trespass

The phrase 'Trespassers will be prosecuted' has entered English usage and stayed there. It is, however, meaningless. Trespass is not a criminal offence and therefore cannot be prosecuted. It is, instead, a tort – a piece of wrongdoing actionable only in the civil courts. The police have no power to intervene or arrest the trespasser unless he has committed other offences.

The legal position was brought home spectacularly in 1982, when one Michael Fagan climbed into Buckingham Palace and ended up on the edge of the Queen's bed for a late-night exchange of pleasantries. Her Majesty had been in no danger, and Fagan had apparently no criminal intention towards any other member of the household, nor indeed towards the considerable fortune contained within the palace walls. The police proclaimed themselves powerless to act, and the Queen generously declined to sue Fagan for trespass. But if Her Majesty had had a lucky escape Leslie Attwell was considerably less fortunate.

Attwell is a Somerset farmer. In May 1986 he found 300 hippies, 100 old vehicles in varying states of dilapidation and a herd of goats encamped on his best thirteen-acre grass meadow in the hamlet of Lytes Cary. Neither a wealthy nor large-scale farmer, he stood to lose forty tonnes of hay which should have been winter feed for his stock. By the time the hippie convoy encamped on the thirteen-acre field, he had already lost other grass in other fields and was facing losses and legal bills of around £8,000. When the convoy rolled on to his meadow, he collapsed with a heart complaint.

To rid himself of the hippies, Attwell had to go to the High Court in London in the knowledge that its order to evict the convoy would not take effect for several days and that he had no likelihood of obtaining damages or costs from the 300 alternative-lifestyle enthusiasts who were ruining his livelihood.

Both he and the National Farmers Union subsequently campaigned for stronger powers to allow the police to arrest trespassers. And although a measure to strengthen marginally police powers was included in the 1986 Public Order Act, the government refused to create a law of criminal trespass. Until it does, trespassers will not be prosecuted.

Part of the problem is that any such law would restrict the rights, not just of itinerant hippies, but of other more law-abiding groups. The Ramblers' Association, for example, opposed any new law because it could worsen the existing problems ramblers already face with landowners blocking off public rights of way on their land.

The right to light

Esther Neville looked out of her Weymouth cottage window one morning in 1977 to find workmen building the foundations of a house fifteen feet away. Mrs Neville was not pleased – not only had she been told that no building would take place within sixty feet of her property, but as the house was built it rapidly cut off her view and light to her home.

Mrs Neville had a problem: there is no right in English law to a view. Householders cannot go to court if their neighbours put up buildings in front of their windows, provided that those buildings are on the neighbours' own land and do not interfere with or damage the householder's home or garden. (Of course, any significant building work requires planning consent, and neighbours have the right to object to any unwelcome development – although their objections are not binding on the local council planners.)

The closest the law gets to protecting our homes from being overshadowed by new buildings is the so-called 'right to light'. In legal theory a landowner owns not just the land itself but the soil beneath it and the air above it. Any unreasonable intrusion into this air-space can constitute a trespass – though, as we shall see, even that protection is severely limited.

But the ownership of the air-space does not necessarily amount to an automatic right to allow light to enter that air-space. The only way to acquire such a right is by written agreement with the neighbours or by what is known as 'prescription' – twenty years' continuous use of that unimpeded light.

That should mean that anyone living in a house more than twenty years old, or on a new estate built on the site of an existing house of that age, will automatically have a right to light (assuming of course that the light has been unimpeded throughout the twenty-year period). However, the small print of some title deeds specifically excludes the acquisition of such rights, and in any case it can only apply to buildings – so gardens or allotments remain unprotected.

But worse is still to come. Even when a right to light is established, there is no reliable definition of the amount of light guaranteed. Courts, as a rule, interpret the question on the basis not of how much light has been taken away, but on how much light remains. All of which makes legal action to resist an overshadowing wall or building a particularly hazardous prospect.

Nor is there any real certainty about how much air comes with the purchase of your land or home. In 1977, Lord Bernstein sued a firm of aerial photographers called Skyviews. The firm took photographs of all homes in a town or village from an aircraft and then offered the pictures for sale to the occupants of the houses photographed. Lord Bernstein was annoyed; he claimed that the company had invaded his privacy. But, not for the first time, the courts failed to uphold any right whatever to privacy.

Skyviews' plane had flown, said the court, at a reasonable height (from which, presumably, it had used a powerful lens). Lord Bernstein, like any other landowner, only had the right to such air-space as was necessary for the use or enjoyment of his land, and in this case there had been no infringement of that.

If the Bernstein decision seems a harmless confirmation of the rights of commercial air-photographers, it is as well to remember that its principles provide the legal legitimacy for surreptitious or illicit photographs of anyone in the country, by anyone, for whatever purpose. It is a judicial confirmation that the right to privacy simply does not exist.

Nuisance

The best protection afforded to privacy and the enjoyment of a quiet life is the legal right to live free from nuisance. It is a right we frequently invoke: surveys show that 80 per cent of people in Britain think their neighbours inconsiderate and one in four don't speak to each other.

In February 1987 Ronald and Patricia McSorley decided to invoke their right after two years of hell. The McSorleys live – or at least used to live – in Maidenhead Road, Windsor. In July 1985, their next-door neighbours moved.

Two men, Alan Krafft and Graham Geard, bought No. 125, Maidenhead Road with a loan obtained by deception from the Guardian Building Society. That summer the formerly neat, suburban semi was transformed by a gang of Hell's Angels who had moved in. The downstairs windows were barricaded and the front door replaced with an armour-plated version complete with the winged skull of the Angels' Windsor chapter.

After six weeks the McSorleys moved out, less intimidated by the Angels' taste in home decorations than by the axe-throwing contests, bird-shooting and extravagantly wild parties held in the garden.

They began renting another house at a cost of £525 per month, and, although their mortgage payments were frozen, the interest was still building up. By March 1987 they owed £5,000 more than the original £44,000 loan, and the home they had bought for £58,000 was virtually worthless. 'It has been valued at £90,000 – but no building society would give a mortgage on it,' said Mrs McSorley.

It was to take another two years before the McSorleys had the chance of returning to their home. In October 1987 the Windsor Angels placed 125 Maidenhead Road on the market, proudly advertising it as 'the second most famous residence in Windsor'. If the previous two years had been an expensive nightmare for the McSorleys, their unwelcome neighbours had at least found the experience profitable; the three-bedroomed 1930s semi-detached 'clubhouse' was priced at a breathtaking £114,950.

The 'right', then, to a quiet life and freedom from interference or invasion of privacy is at best uncertain territory – and more often unexplored and dangerously expensive of time, money and patience. But what of the other main cause of complaint for house-owners or tenants: repairs, renovations and improvements?

Building and the householder

House repairs and improvements provide a significant section of the building industry with employment and income. From double-glazing to home extensions, millions of pounds a year are spent on modifications to our homes. For the private customer (that is, not a tenant of a local authority or of a private landlord) with the right to choose what alterations to make to his house, the law provides certain safeguards: the work must be of reasonable quality and the materials used must be fit for the purpose. But there is a trap.

Many builders and home-improvement companies, embarrassed by a boom in cowboy firms during the mid-1970s began offering long-term guarantees on their work and materials. Unsurprisingly, thousands of people placed their trust in those guarantees – people like Chris Cunnell from Purley in Surrey. He purchased an eighteen-foot span of patio doors in 1978 from a firm then called Coldshield Windows Ltd.

> I chose Coldshield for the job because they were a national name, and because of the long-term guarantee they were offering.
> When the doors were put in in June 1979, they were left only partially complete. There were no draft excluders, so gales came howling round through the gaps; also, the door-locking mechanism didn't work.

Negotiations began with Coldshield about the defects. Repairs began which would last off and on until 1984.

> Early in 1984 one of the window units failed and the doors began steaming up (it wasn't the first time this had happened, either). So I tried to contact Coldshield, but I got no reply to my letters. I kept on writing – I even wrote to the parent company, but they ignored me as well.

That parent company bore the nationally advertised name of Moben plc. In fact, Moben – a household name in the fitted-kitchen industry – was just part of a wider group which owned Coldshield, Mulberry Home Extensions Ltd, and Wallguard Ltd – a damp-proofing company. By the time Chris Cunnell complained in 1984, however, the Moben group was in trouble. Derek Spring worked for the group and saw the situation deteriorate.

> In August 1984 we were getting complaints in about work done by Mulberry and Wallguard at the rate of about forty to fifty per month. The whole business was a mess, and the parent company decided on a rationalisation.
>
> We had been asking customers before then for deposits of around 10 per cent – indeed, less in some cases. But after August we were told to get a 50 per cent deposit up front: no work would be carried out unless half the bill had been paid in advance. I also began having difficulty getting jobs installed that I had collected the 50 per cent deposit on.

By August 1984, then, the Moben group was just about ready to demonstrate the two major flaws in the protection of houseowners from building-work problems. And by 26 November the process was complete.

The group went into receivership that day. It ceased trading – but the deposit cheques that salesmen like Derek Spring had been taking just days previously had all been paid in to the company and would never be returned. Nor would any work be done on projects either commissioned or half-finished.

Mrs Margaret Vives was one of the group's last victims. She, believing in the Moben name, had signed up with Mulberry Home Extensions Ltd. The initial deposit had been £400; but the start date for their extension seemed to be continually delayed. Then, on 22 November, the Mulberry salesman phoned.

> He said if we could pay off 50 per cent of the bill in advance they could start work the following week – which was fine because we wanted the extension to be ready for Christmas. In fact we were desperate to get it done. So we sent off a cheque for £2,700 on 24 November, which was a Thursday.

That was the last the Vives ever saw of their deposit. And as for the extension . . .

> We heard on the following Wednesday, the 28th, that the firm had gone into receivership on the Monday. We got on to our

bank straightaway, but by then it was too late – the cheque had been cashed. We wrote to the receiver – but he wrote back saying that after paying back various creditors like the bank the company would have no money left for people like us.

Mrs Vives and her husband were unsecured creditors and, as is all too often the case when a limited company collapses, unsecured creditors lose all their money. But problems stemming from the Moben collapse didn't end there. All those long-term guarantees were no more than empty promises, as Derek Spring explained.

There were possibly around 100,000 of those. They had been issued for various products marketed by the group – dehumidifiers, damp-proofing, double-glazing – and they had all been promoted on the Moben name. Now these guarantees – some of them for up to thirty years – were utterly worthless.

To add insult to injury the Moben name managed to survive; one of the last acts of the group, before it went into liquidation, was to change its name to CS Windows PLC. So when the company collapsed it did so under its new name. 'Moben', a valuable product name with a high public profile, was thus not tainted by failure and could be quickly adopted by a new company selling similar products – which is, in fact, precisely what happened. The Moben name is still in use today, even though the group which originally traded under that banner is in liquidation with a large number of unsecured creditors and unfulfilled product guarantees. (All of this is entirely legal – company law does not inhibit this 'protection' of a valuable trading name. Nor, we should stress, have we any information concerning products marketed under the Moben name since 1984, and we are not implying any criticism of the way the company currently runs its business.)

Product guarantees don't have to be worthless if the marketing company goes into liquidation; the Office of Fair Trading has campaigned long and hard for companies to insure their guarantees, and building trade organisations have offered such insurance policies for several years.

'That happens in far too few cases,' argued the OFT's director-general Sir Gordon Borrie just after the Moben collapse. 'In general law there is very little protection for the householder, so like all other unsecured creditors he or she goes to the back of the queue if the firm goes bust, having taken the money but not done the work.'

What was even more surprising was that in Wallguard's case separate guarantee insurance was available – but salesmen kept it very quiet. For the rest of the group, no such schemes had been set up.

Tenants' rights

The series of Rent Acts which govern the rights of tenants (and of landlords) are absurdly complicated. They are a uniquely twentieth-century innovation, brought in under political pressure from both sides of the political spectrum and thus ensuring a see-saw effect on tenancies contracted under the different Acts. (For example, tenants in occupation before August 1974 are protected by a different set of criteria from those in occupation after August, when the 1974 Rent Act took effect.)

All in all there are no less than fifty different statutes covering the subject. Add to this the fact that the protection principle behind the Rent Acts has been grafted on to a legal concept of land ownership that dates back to the Middle Ages, and the confusion becomes even deeper. In addition many judges have tempered the effects of some of the more radical Acts with traditional, unwritten Common Law rules. The result is a horrendously complicated mess.

It would take a book far longer than this one simply to deal with the intricacies of Rent Act legislation, so we won't attempt the task. Instead we will focus on the more common complaints and explain why the system has failed. And we will start with private accommodation.

Actually finding accommodation is the first step for the would-be tenant. In London this can be a particularly difficult task as there is always a large demand for relatively few suitable properties – which is where accommodation agencies come in.

There are dozens in the capital (and elsewhere) advertising their services, and even the smallest London agency can have up to 100,000 home-seekers on its books. The 1953 Accommodation Act makes it illegal for agencies to charge tenants before they sign an agreement for a home, but many agencies either don't know this or ignore the law. One day in October 1986 a campaigner picked out four agencies at random, all of whom charged 'administration' or 'registration' fees of between £5 and £40. Many would-be tenants are unaware that the practice is illegal – others are too desperate to complain. The alternative can be – quite literally – a night spent with the army of homeless people living out of cardboard boxes under London's archways.

But the problems don't end there. In September 1986 five students registered with the Busy Bees agency in Islington. They were given the address of a five-bedroomed flat in Archway Road, together with the name of the landlord. The students were desperate to find accommodation before the start of the autumn term and took the flat – despite some very obvious shortcomings. It had neither electricity nor hot water, though the landlord promised to put things to rights.

The students duly handed over one month's rent – £1,290 – and then paid Busy Bees their (perfectly legal) fee of £270. Two months later the ceiling fell in. The landlord had kept none of his promises.

To its credit, Busy Bees agreed to return its fee and to strike the landlord from its books. But the agency gave a revealing insight into the extraordinary lack of supervision of private accommodation. 'We'd need an army if we checked all our property,' was its manager's excuse to the students.

The students' accommodation was legally unfit for human habitation. There is a nine-point checklist which defines the legal standard of fitness, which covers the state of repair, stability, damp, natural lighting, ventilation, water supply, drainage, toilets and cooking facilities. The students' flat had no water, which took it outside the standard. But, in the crazy way of tenancy law, if it had running water it might have passed the test; a house may be infested with varying sorts of bugs and may have no electricity and yet be legally fit for human habitation.

The agency responsible for operating the checklist is the local authority environmental health department. But cuts in council staff have led to restrictions on the number of properties that can be monitored at any one time, which in turn leads to scandalous and inhuman conditions for tenants too poor or too desperate to find homes elsewhere.

From 1981 to 1984, an average of 400 people lived in squalid conditions at a large, privately run homeless people's hostel in the

London borough of Tower Hamlets. The hostel, Prince's Lodge, had just two unhygienic kitchens for the 400 tenants, who also shared filthy and inadequate washing facilities. The hostel was severely overcrowded, whole families of children sharing beds. Vermin roamed the corridors, where dustbins overflowed with refuse.

For four years the borough's environmental health team failed to inspect the hostel – despite a critical report on hostels in general by an independent charity which should, housing experts later claimed, have raised the team's awareness of the issue. In its defence Tower Hamlets gave just one reason for its failure: it did not have sufficient staff. As the housing crisis in London and in provincial cities grows, there will be many more Prince's Lodges.

If private landlords often appear to have improved little since the days of Rachman twenty years ago, the situation can be little better for thousands of council tenants.

In April 1986 a group of volunteer housing advice workers arrived in the remote Afan Valley, in the borough of Port Talbot, South Wales. For a week they travelled through isolated villages asking about people's housing problems.

What they found was a large number of council tenants who had been unable to persuade their landlord to carry out statutory repairs. One quarter of them had been waiting more than a year, and one man had waited fifteen years. Nor were their complaints minor grumbles: in 60 per cent of cases the complaints were of severely leaking drains or roofs, damp or condensation.

The advice workers approached the council on the tenants' behalf, but got little positive response. Only when they began preparing legal action did the council act, and even then it frequently waited until a matter of days before an individual case was due to go to court before sending out teams of repairmen. One solicitor acting for the tenants, Graham Jones, described court action as 'sadly, the only way to get things done in this area'.

Four months earlier, eighteen council tenants in Birmingham had been forced to take the city council to court to force it to carry out repairs. An eight-storey block of flats in Edgbaston had so much mould on internal walls that it posed a health threat, the court ruled. The tenants had told the city council that long before.

These two councils are far from being isolated examples. So why does it happen? Why are tenants' statutory rights not observed by local councils – who, after all, we might expect to behave rather better than the rogue landlords of the private sector?

Part of the answer is financial restraint: councils are prevented by rate-capping from raising more money from their electorate, and at the same time denied access to the City with all the money it could lend. This, coupled with an aging housing stock, leads to a crisis point.

There is another reason, however: an anomaly in the law. Local authorities are responsible for maintaining minimum standards in housing as part of their environmental health services. While this may work with regard to supervising the private sector, it can present a conflict of loyalties for health officers inspecting council-owned properties. The 1974 local government reorganisation ended the previously independent status of environmental health officers. Now they are effectively prevented from taking legal action against their own authorities.

Even when there is a willingness to act on housing-stock problems, it can sometimes fail to achieve results. Dozens of councils have, at varying times since the war, built homes out of pre-cast reinforced concrete (PRC). But the idea behind this – of cheap but sturdy homes – failed to take account of what would happen if poor-quality PRC was used. The councils – or rather their tenants – soon found out. The houses began to disintegrate. When tenants who had bought their homes tried to re-sell them, the scale of the problem emerged: twenty-four different types of PRC houses were identified as high-risk accommodation.

In 1984 Parliament passed the Housing Defects Act, which allowed for repair grants for the unlucky owners. A company, PRC Homes, was set up to administer the scheme through the National House Building Council, and for a while the tenants were encouraged. But the Act relied on the private design and construction industry to come up with workable repair schemes. At the same time it didn't guarantee them any work if they did devise such schemes. Research for a typical repair programme cost up to £20,000 for each of the twenty-four house types. Few companies took up the challenge, knowing that even if they did devise a successful scheme, and even if it was accepted, there was no certainty that they would be awarded the repairs contract itself.

Two years after the Act was passed only five schemes had been authorised. By October 1986, out of 22,000 faulty PRC homes, just thirty-nine had been repaired.

Before we leave the subject of housing rights we should acknowledge the existence of one system deliberately set up to handle and investigate complaints against local authorities – whether as landlords or in connection with any of their other services. Almost inevitably, however, it is a system with severe flaws.

Ombudsmen, more properly known as Commissioners for Local Administration (there is in fact more than one ombudsman keeping tabs on local councils, and Parliament has its own watchdog), have been involved in two of the cases we have cited in this chapter. In the case of Prince's Lodge one issued a damning report, saying that the council's 'failure to protect the interests of unfortunate homeless people' had been 'scarcely credible'. His conclusions were a savage indictment of Tower Hamlets Council.

Another Ombudsman's report, this time in 1977, had criticised Esther Neville's local council. Mrs Neville, who had discovered a building going up just fifteen feet from her window despite an agreement to the contrary, had complained to her local Council planning department. The planners promised to investigate. In the following months only one thing of significance occurred: the offending building was all but finished. At the last minute a council committee visited the site and ordered the building to stop. Mrs Neville was pleased.

She was less so when, at a subsequent meeting, they withdrew the order on the grounds that the building was too far advanced. She asked a local councillor to channel her complaint to the Ombudsman (a peculiarity of the system is that any complaint must be channelled in this way). He duly found the Council guilty of maladministration, and said that Mrs Neville had suffered an injustice. But that's as far as it went; he had no power to do any more than issue a second report on the Council's behaviour. According to Ombudsman Dennis Harrison, 'That is the end of it as far as the Commissioner is concerned.'

The Ombudsman, then, has little real power. And he handles a relatively low number of cases per year, despite having a reasonably large staff.

One victim of this system, Alan Severn, had complained after a pair of houses were built, quite improperly, right up against the footings of his semi-detached house in Yately, Surrey. The Council declined to act, because the buildings were too far advanced. The Ombudsman, however, did act: he roundly criticised the Council and asked it to keep in touch about what compensation it proposed to pay.

The Council proposed to pay Severn £600 for a drop in his house value of £2,300. Severn was not impressed. His verdict on the Ombudsman's power sums it up: 'The guy's heart is in the right place, but even with his aid and his findings I am still out of pocket. My house is no longer a semi, and his findings have not been acted upon. As far as I am concerned the Ombudsman is a toothless tiger.' His counterpart, the Parliamentary Ombudsman, spent 1988 trying to investigate maladministration by court officials. It proved beyond him.

We should note at this point a possible alternative remedy, and one which could carry a great deal more weight than the Ombudsman. It is possible in almost every case involving decisions of a public authority to go to court and seek 'judicial review'. Put simply, this is a device by which unfair, unlawful or irrational rulings can be overturned by a High Court judge.

In theory the process is very simple. The initial stages can be no more than a matter of filling in a form and submitting it to the court for a decision. Applying to the court costs only £10, though another £45 is added once the proceedings actually begin. The problems multiply ferociously from then on.

An applicant for judicial review would be hopelessly lost without legal advice. Judicial review has become the fastest-growing area of the law, and on its way it has collected its fair share of casualties. The services of a solicitor, and a barrister to go with him, are not cheap; and, as we have seen, the legal aid scheme does not always support those who most need assistance.

Fees aside, however, judicial review is a chancy business, resting less on well-defined laws (though they are always a factor) than on an individual judge's interpretation of natural justice. Even then the process may prove a waste of time. Judicial review as it is presently interpreted by the courts is 'concerned not with the decision, but with the decision-making process'. That was the view of Lord Fraser in a case known to lawyers as 'In re the Council of Civil Service Unions and others' but more commonly referred to as the GCHQ case of 1984. That case made it clear beyond doubt that the biggest court in the land – the House of Lords – believes that judicial review cannot decide whether any disputed decision by a public authority is actually fair, but merely whether that decision was reached after *a process* that was fair.

Judicial review has the potential to be a powerful and effective brake on public authorities – both local and national. To realise that potential legal aid in some form needs always to be available, and our judges must be prepared to examine the disputed decision itself, not just the way it was made.

THREE
A Free Country?

> 'It is by the goodness of God that we have in our country three unspeakably precious things: freedom of speech, freedom of conscience, and the prudence never to practise either.'
>
> Mark Twain, quoted in Daniel George and 'Sagittarius', *The Perpetual Pessimist*

Madeleine Haigh is forty-one. She is married, has two children and lives in Sutton Coldfield. She is a former English teacher and is not a criminal in any way, shape or form. Yet she spent several uncomfortable months knowing that she was under police surveillance. Her 'crime' was to express her opinions.

Political freedom

In 1981 Mrs Haigh wrote to her local weekly paper to protest about the cancellation of an anti-nuclear festival due to be held in Worcester. At the time she was not a member of CND or any other anti-nuclear or political group – she simply wished to register her protest.

Shortly afterwards Mrs Haigh was visited by two policemen who explained that they were investigating a case of mail-order fraud. Mrs Haigh became suspicious and telephoned her local police station to ask if they knew the officers. The police denied all knowledge of them, and of the alleged fraud investigation. Mrs Haigh became more suspicious still, and asked the police if the mysterious officers were from the Special Branch.

Once again the police issued a denial – a denial they stuck to for some eighteen months before admitting that, yes, it was the Special Branch that had knocked on her door.

The ensuing outcry led to the only enquiry into the Special Branch in its chequered 100-year history. Leon Brittan, then Home Secretary (and so ultimately responsible for the police force) gave evidence in its defence. On the question of Mrs Haigh's visitors, Brittan explained the reason for their curiosity. 'Mrs Haigh,' he said, 'had written to a newspaper in terms which were interpreted by the Special Branch officers concerned as indicating that she might be a person to support, or become involved in, public protests of a nature likely to become violent.'

Brittan did not say – and with good reason – that Mrs Haigh's letter actually indicated that she might support or become involved in some form of violent protest, simply that the Special Branch officers had interpreted it as such. He went on to tell the enquiry that he was 'broadly satisfied' with the work of the Special Branch, although mistakes did occasionally occur.

Mrs Haigh was rather less satisfied: 'It's hard to talk about the impact of surveillance on one's life without sounding hysterical and paranoid. I'm still frightened by what I'm doing. But the anger which has sustained me over these strange, recent years is stronger than any fear.' What Mrs Haigh was doing was not something illegal, and not something that should have made her frightened. She was – and is – ploughing through the lengthy procedure of making a complaint to the European Court of Human Rights.

In terms of the number of condemnations of Britain the Court has been forced to issue, this country has probably the worst record on human rights and civil liberties of any member nation. From telephone-tapping to torture the United Kingdom has been repeatedly found wanting when it comes to safeguarding its citizens against the State. This chapter is all about civil liberties and human rights. And because the test of any nation's stance on civil rights is how well it tolerates those whose opinions are unpopular, controversial or just plain awkward (though never criminal) many of the examples and case histories centre around fringe groups, campaigners and demonstrators. And whilst you may not agree with all their words, their right to say them is unquestionable.

Or is it? Back to Mrs Haigh, and let's look at the wording of the (European) law that she claims was broken in her case. She alleges that the United Kingdom government violated her right to 'hold opinions and to receive and impart information and ideas without interference by public authorities'. This right is not a creation of

English law, but of the European Convention on Human Rights (to which, as with the Euro-courts, we shall return). And as such it is not enforceable in any court in England.

So, is there any right in England to hold opinions such as those that caused Mrs Haigh so much trouble? And more important still, do we have any right to spell them out in print or anywhere else?

The answer is one you will read again and again in this book: not in so many words we don't. In theory, of course, we can think what we like. And so long as we don't break any one of a series of laws, we can tell the world about it.

What happens in practice, however, is rather different. There are a host of political and quasi-political organisations to which it is quite legal to belong, and yet joining them automatically qualifies you for surveillance by the police or security services. The surveillance can be obvious and clumsy, as Mrs Haigh discovered. Or it can be at the same time sophisticated and simple, highly technological and painstakingly manual – for example, culling information from press reports.

The anti-nuclear movement in general, and CND in particular, has aroused considerable interest amongst the security community. It is an interest that continues to bemuse many members of the movement, whose activities are specifically non-criminal and peaceful.

On 31 January 1985, Corrie McUaith dialled a telephone number in Cambridgeshire. It belonged to her friends, Tim and Bridie Wallis, a young Quaker couple active in the peace movement who happen to live almost next door to the Molesworth cruise missile site. Because of this their phone is often very important to peace protestors. It was to be very busy in the forthcoming Molesworth demonstration in February.

The phone rang once or twice and an answerphone picked up the call. 'This is Tim and Bridie Wallis's number,' it explained in an American accent (Tim Wallis is American). 'We are out at the moment. Please leave your name, address and phone number and we will ring you back.' Corrie called the Wallises twice during the next few days and got the machine both times, which would have been fine – except that the Wallises do not possess an answerphone. In fact they had noticed how whenever the phone rang it always seemed to stop before they could answer the call.

Nor was this an isolated problem on the Wallis's line. On 7

February Eric Rimmington phoned the couple. First he got the engaged tone – twice. Then, when he tried later, he didn't get the ringing tone at all. Instead he heard the background noise of a roomful of people. Ten minutes later it was the same story: though he managed to get through, the background noise lingered on, accompanied occasionally by two strange high-pitched squeaks. Yet another CND member was put through to the answering machine five or six times in March 1985.

Another year, another town. In the early summer of 1986 thousands of people were preparing for the 'Run the World' charity fund-raising event. On Sunday 25 May Sheffield Peace Action Network were planning a minor demonstration. One Network member, Richard Levitt, rang another, Trevor Edmands, to arrange a lift in his car. Trevor was out, but an answerphone message said: 'This is Trevor Edmands' address. Will you please leave your message after the pips.' Like the Wallises, Trevor Edmands does not possess an answerphone.

So where does this leave us? We all like to believe that in Britain we enjoy certain 'political' freedoms – freedom of thought, freedom of expression and freedom of assembly. Of course, all of these are subject to the general law of the land, but surely so long as we keep inside the bounds of the law we can think and say what we like, and do so in public with like-minded people if we choose?

This is where we came in. Madeleine Haigh, Tim and Bridie Wallis and Trevor Edmands were certainly free to think and say what they wanted – but not without interference by way of telephone-tapping and surveillance.

Freedom of thought

There is clearly a need for telephone-tapping in many serious criminal cases. The pop star Boy George, for example, had his phone tapped during 1986 by police investigating his involvement in a heroin ring. He was subsequently charged and fined for possession of the drug. But what of non-criminal cases – cases where the reason for surveillance or tapping is no more than a political dislike of another person's beliefs?

Cathy Massiter worked for MI5, Britain's domestic intelligence service, from November 1970 to December 1983. At first a secretary, she was quickly promoted to the rank of intelligence officer.

MI5 (like its foreign counterpart MI6) conducts its business largely in secret. Its annual budget is never debated by Parliament, no government willingly discusses its activities and its agents and officers have in theory no power to do anything to the rest of us in anyone's name.

The only indication we have of its aims and intentions comes from a 1952 directive from the then Home Secretary, Sir David Maxwell-Fyfe, to its director-general. 'The Security Service is part of the country. Its task is the Defence of the Realm as a whole. . . . You will take special care to see that the work of the Security Service is strictly limited to what is necessary for the purposes of this task.'

Thirty-two years later, on 10 December 1984, Maxwell-Fyfe's political descendant, Leon Brittan, gave the House of Commons his considered opinion, as Home Secretary, of the threat CND posed to 'the Defence of the Realm'.

> So far as the legitimacy of CND is concerned, I do not think it is for me to legitimise it or otherwise. There is no doubt that peaceful political campaigning to change the mind of the government and of the people generally about the validity of nuclear disarmament, whether unilateral or otherwise, is an entirely legitimate activity.

Brittan's reassurances came a little late in the day. Almost exactly a year before, Cathy Massiter had left MI5 in disgust at the way it had targeted CND and several of its officers for surveillance.

> I became concerned that the tasks which I, as an intelligence officer, was being called on to perform and the uses to which information which I gathered was being put were guided by considerations not solely related to the defence of the realm. . . . It seemed to me that the scale and nature of the investigation that we were undertaking into the peace movement – and into CND in particular – were determined more by the latter's political importance than by the real security significance of subversive elements in it.

The key word in Ms Massiter's statement is 'subversive' – and we'll come on to what a subversive is and who says so later on. But first let's examine the scale and nature of MI5's interest in CND –

an organisation which it had ceased to classify as subversive in the mid-1970s.

Cathy Massiter was told to apply for a warrant from the Home Secretary to tap the phone of CND's vice-president John Cox. She made the application to the Home Secretary in April 1983. Officially the reason for the bid was that Cox was a known member of the Communist Party and MI5 wanted to discover whether the party was secretly manipulating CND. Unofficially, Cox was a good excuse to obtain more material for files the service maintained on CND's chairwoman Joan Ruddock and its secretary Monsignor Bruce Kent.

Cox lived in Wales and would therefore need to keep in constant telephone touch with CND's national office. MI5 had a longstanding interest of its own in the habitually law-abiding Ruddock and Kent, but there were others pressing for information – notably a special department inside the Ministry of Defence set up in March 1983 to combat CND's growing public popularity. Cathy Massiter's view of the tap on Cox's phone could not be clearer:

> We had absolutely no evidence, as required by the guidelines, that he was concerned in any criminal activity or that he was engaged in any major subversive or espionage activity which was likely to injure the national interest. On the contrary, nothing from our [other] coverage of the Communist Party and its Peace Committee gave us grounds to suspect that they were manipulating CND.

Leon Brittan signed the warrant authorising the phone-tap in August 1983, and a huge, highly technological and extremely secret machine swung into action.

It is worth documenting the methods of surveillance in the UK, simply to demonstrate the awesome capabilities our masters possess to keep tabs on us.

Inside an externally innocuous building in Eccleston Street, close to London's Victoria station, is a nest of surveillance equipment. Known to the police as 'Tinkerbell', the centre is able to tap up to 1,000 phone lines at any one time. In another part of the building multi-channel tape-recorders and high-capacity storage discs record the conversations. Specialised word-filtering systems weed out irrelevant material, and advanced transcription systems provide a speedy print-out of the intercepted calls (in the event of a hitch in the proceedings there are a host of back-up listening stations and surveillance centres ready to take over).

The tapes and transcripts are taken just a mile across London to Curzon Street House, in the heart of Mayfair, where MI5 has its headquarters. John Cox's phone conversations took this route in August 1983.

John Cox was not the only person to attract attention. Cathy Massiter's evidence shows that MI5 also took an interest in Patricia Hewitt, now Neil Kinnock's press officer, and the Labour MP Harriet Harman; their files were opened in Curzon Street when both were officers of the National Council for Civil Liberties. The environmental organisation Friends of the Earth was also infiltrated by an MI5 agent. Union leaders were not exempt either; Margaret Witham of the Civil and Public Services Association became a target, as did both Mick McGahey and Arthur Scargill of the NUM (long before the bitter and violent coal strike of 1984-5).

What these disparate characters had in common was that the security services decided that they were 'subversives'. According to guidelines issued by the Home Office in 1984, subversive activities are 'those which threaten the safety or well-being of the State and which are intended to undermine or overthrow Parliamentary democracy by political, industrial or violent means'. According to Leon Brittan both elements of the test have to be satisfied if the label 'subversive' is to stick.

Neither Brittan nor the Home Office have managed to explain how, for example, Patricia Hewitt, Harriet Harman, Joan Ruddock, Bruce Kent and Friends of the Earth fulfil the qualifications, let alone the Tim and Bridie Wallises of this world. But then they don't really need to. John Alderson, formerly Chief Constable of Devon and Cornwall, is under no illusions that the present definition is hopelessly vague and that the police and the security services often simply ignore it anyway. He has estimated that up to 40 per cent of the information held by his own Special Branch was 'irrelevant tittle-tattle'.

Perhaps a more accurate description of what the people at the sharp end actually class as subversive comes from another former Chief Constable, Harold Salisbury. Salisbury moved to South Australia on leaving his job as head of Yorkshire's North and East

Riding Constabulary. He was appointed Police Commissioner and set about re-organising the state's Special Branch.

In 1978 the branch was disbanded, nearly all its files destroyed and Salisbury sent home after a judicial investigation had found its dossiers to be 'scandalously inaccurate, irrelevant to security purposes and outrageously unfair to hundreds, perhaps thousands, of loyal and worthy citizens.'

The records in question covered all the South Australian Labour Party politicians (local and national) and half the judges of the Supreme Court, together with prominent clergy, union leaders, environmentalists and homosexuals. The files included photographs of their subjects.

Salisbury, apparently unrepentant, subsequently appeared on British television explaining his definition of that important word 'subversive'. It covered, apart from obvious threats such as terrorists and avowed communists, anyone involved in the peace movement, anyone who appeared to be anti-establishment, to be or sympathise with homosexuals, to attack the virtues of family life – the criteria were very broad indeed. Nor did Salisbury think that what happened under his reign in South Australia would be very different from the state of affairs in Britain.

As for those people who might object to being on the security services list: 'If a chap doesn't like a file kept on him . . . that's the very chap a file should be kept on.' Which brings us to the conclusion that our masters have the motive, the manpower and the technology to cramp severely, if not entirely curtail, the first of our basic 'political rights' – freedom of thought.

We will return to the thorny problem of police powers in Chapter 6, but before we leave the shadowy world of telephone-tappers we should note the latest governmental compromise between the interests of the State and the rights of its citizens.

The Interception of Communications Act came into force in July 1985. The legislation was the government's response to a ruling in the European Court of Human Rights that Britain should have new legislation to protect people from unwarranted telephone-tapping. Rather than follow the spirit of the judgement – decidedly more liberal than the government would have wished – the Act simply laid down in statute form what was existing practice, and added provision for a complaints tribunal. Thus, only the Home Secretary can issue a warrant, and anyone who taps a phone without such a warrant faces two years in prison; the warrant lasts for six months before coming up for renewal; and it can cover either an individual or a set of premises.

The tribunal, with five legally qualified members, sits to hear complaints from members of the public. Its brief is to examine only whether a warrant has been issued and whether a warrant has been correctly made out. It has no power to take action if a warrant had not been issued, nor even to reveal whether a telephone tap has taken place at all. There is no right of appeal against its findings, nor any judical review of its decision. If anything, the law has made it easier for the tappers, and even more difficult for the public.

The government made clear its dislike of any investigation of its agencies' behaviour in a court case in July 1985 when CND attempted to have Brittan's authorisation of the John Cox phone-tap warrant declared improper. The government's lawyer told the judge, Mr Justice Taylor, that he should not attempt to decide whether the evidence provided by Cathy Massiter was accurate. 'The judicial investigation of facts of telephone intercepts is, in the policy of successive governments, damaging to national security.'

Freedom of expression

Much that applies to the restrictions on freedom of thought holds good (or bad) for freedom to express our thoughts. Indeed, much of the intelligence material to be found in the files of alleged subversives is gathered from public meetings and reported speeches as well as from tapped telephones.

Letters too appear to be susceptible, and once again CND provides a good example. Karen Lewton lives in Ovingham, Northumberland. She is a member of the CND Council. Between 17 September 1984 and 23 July 1985 she received twenty-three letters suffering from varying degrees of suspicious damage. The Home Secretary declined to confirm or deny that her mail had been intercepted; the Post Office suggested the problems were caused by a combination of machine damage and poor enveloping. Ms Lewton finds this hard to believe, which is not surprising given the several hundred letters that regularly arrive at CND headquarters in varying states of disrepair. And although Sir Ronald Dearing, then the Post Office's chairman, denied any liability for the damaged mail, CND did receive a 'goodwill payment' of £100 from the Post Office.

At this point you could be forgiven for believing that only those on the left of the political spectrum have anything to fear from our muddled, constitutionless laws on freedom, but this is not so. The right to free speech – if it exists at all – is the creation by default of a series of laws across the centuries. But the weight of law at the disposal of anyone who objects to someone else exercising his rights is quite staggering.

Many of the laws exist for the protection or prohibition of those three staples of British life: religion, politics and sex. Thus we have laws to prevent blasphemy and the incitement of racial hatred; we have the Obscene Publications and Customs and Excise Acts; we have the Official Secrets Act, the Incitement to Disaffection Act, the Vagrancy Act – not to mention a whole host of common-law offences, torts and misdemeanours from sedition to breach of the peace. But there are an equally binding set of what we choose to call conventions and traditions which inhibit or actually prevent free speech.

Judge James Pickles is not one of nature's revolutionaries. He is not, so far as is known, a CND supporter, nor yet a member of any subversive organisation. He is a judge and, as we have seen, judges by leaning and tradition tend to be neither angry nor young men. But Pickles risked losing his well-paid career as a circuit judge for exercising what he saw as his right to free speech.

On 22 March 1985, Judge Pickles aired his views on the inadequacies of our prison system in an article in the *Daily Telegraph* (which, like Pickles, is not noted for its subversive tendencies). At the time there was pressure on the judiciary from the government to shorten sentences as a result of prison overcrowding. It was a subject Pickles felt strongly about: in his view senior judges had long since given up opposing Home Office policies, and, worse, the public wasn't being protected as it should be.

Within hours, Sir Derek Oulton, KCB, permanent secretary to the Lord Chancellor (which is to say, a very high panjandrum indeed) wrote to Pickles saying that Lord Hailsham, the Lord Chancellor, considered the article evidence of 'judicial misbehaviour'. Under section 17 of the 1971 Courts Act, judicial misbehaviour provides grounds for dismissing a judge. Sir Derek went on to warn Pickles that he had a month to come up with a good defence. Either way, Lord Hailsham would 'proceed to consider your future on the circuit bench'.

Judge Pickles had long since ceased to consider his future on the bench as promising any form of promotion and so decided to join battle with Hailsham.

> I decided to stand up to the great and powerful Lord Chancellor and his powerful cohort. I wrote that I was appalled that Lord Hailsham should threaten to dismiss me. I would protect my position and reputation by any means available to me. If necessary I would make representations to both Houses of Parliament and the media.

Hailsham promptly issued a stern rebuke – and yet another threat.

> It has long been considered undesirable for a judge to contribute articles to the press, particularly on matters of current controversy. . . . Recent events, and in particular your article in the *Daily Telegraph*, show that you have not heeded the warnings which those senior to you have given. This must be the result of foolishness or a complete lack of sensitivity.

It either did not occur to the Lord Chancellor, or else he did not believe, that Pickles might actually be acting both within his rights and on principle. It was, Hailsham concluded, no part of Mr Justice Pickles' duty to express a desire to serve and protect the public outside the confines of his own court.

As for the question of rights, Pickles actually had a point – and on Hailsham's authority. Five years earlier, on 25 January 1980, Hailsham had written to all judges inviting them to approach his office for guidance should any member of the press or media be so bold as to invite them to speak publicly. But, he admitted, he 'had no power to give directions to my fellow judges'.

Instead, Lord Chancellors have traditionally relied on two weapons to silence the judiciary. The first, relatively subtle, weapon rests on the knowledge that the Lord Chancellor (who, it should be remembered, is often a party politician as well as head of the judiciary – the present incumbent, Lord McKay, is a rare exception) appoints and promotes judges by a secret and mysterious ritual, and to step out of line is to sacrifice promotion.

The second weapon is a convention known as the Kilmuir rules. These 'rules' are in fact simply a letter written in 1955 by the then

Lord Chancellor, Lord Kilmuir, to the BBC. The BBC had asked his permission for serving judges to give a series of radio lectures on the Third Programme about great judges of the past. Kilmuir refused, saying it was essential to insulate the judiciary against controversies of the day.

> So long [he wrote] as a judge keeps silent, his reputation for impartiality remains unassailable; but every utterance which he makes in public, except in the course of the actual performance of his judicial duties, must necessarily bring him within the focus of criticism.

Many judges now regard the Kilmuir rules as stuff and nonsense, and many ordinary mortals have become aware that it is often what the judges say in court that most frequently causes trouble. Nor should we forget, before we leave the subject of the judiciary, that these rules don't appear to bind all judges equally: top-ranking judges have at times made pronouncements in the press or on radio (the Scottish Law Lord, Lord McClusky, gave the 1986 BBC Reith Lectures, for example), and Lord Hailsham himself was no stranger to public utterances and controversy. But then, as we have remarked before, he was a politician as well.

So much for Mr Justice Pickles. But if that can happen to a judge, what hope is there for the rest of us? What, indeed, of the right to free speech? It's a question that might well have exercised members of the Royal Ulster Constabulary during 1986. (Like judges, the police are not renowned for the holding of subversive or revolutionary beliefs.)

As with all civil or public servants, police officers are forbidden to tell anyone anything, however trivial, without instructions from on high. But their various staff associations – the closest the police come to trade unions – are by tradition free to comment on problems facing their members, conditions of service and the like. This is a freedom exercised at well-attended annual conferences and through well-reported press statements. In the spring of 1986, however, with the prospect of a troublesome summer of rioting and sectarian strife ahead, the Northern Ireland Police Federation, which represents ordinary police officers, was formally instructed by the Chief Constable, Sir John Hermon, to refrain from any public comment.

As the Police Federation discovered, there is no law guaranteeing them their right to free speech. It was a discovery made around the same time by Tory MP John Carlisle. He is notable for, amongst other attributes, his firmly held belief that economic sanctions should not be imposed on South Africa. On 13 February 1986 he had been due to address a meeting of the Federation of Conservative Students at Bradford University. His chosen theme was to have been the right of sportsmen to play in South Africa.

Bradford has a large and, at times, vocal ethnic population. Carlisle found himself prevented from making his speech, and soundly roughed up into the bargain. Bradford University subsequently announced that it was modifying its 'open door' policy of allowing meetings on controversial subjects, while Carlisle began studying the law on the matter. What he found was that no specific right to free speech actually exists. Nor did the government have any desire to grant one, until it was ambushed in the House of Lords some time later and forced to concede a carefully qualified right to free speech on campus (although other gagging laws – breach of confidence, the Official Secrets Act and race relations legislation – would take precedence and wipe out any real freedom of speech). As a result the Education Bill of 1986 contains the only positive guaranteed right to freedom of speech anywhere in our laws.

Even inside Parliament itself MPs have found it hard to exercise any theoretical right to free speech. In addition to facing raucous chanting and jeering, they are frequently victims of the filibuster – a technique designed, as Labour MP Tam Dalyell found in the summer of 1986, to delay indefinitely speeches or bills such as his detailed criticism of the Prime Minister's recent behaviour.

Ten years earlier another politician was providing the testing ground for the very same principle. Richard Crossman, a former Labour Cabinet minister, died in April 1974. His executors set about arranging, as he had wished, the publication of his diaries. The diaries contained details of discussions and disagreements in Cabinet, which proved too much for the government to take.

All such diaries have, by tradition, to be submitted to the Cabinet Secretary of the day for political censorship. When Crossman's executors passed over the first volume of the memoirs, permission to publish was promptly refused on the grounds that secrecy in Cabinet was essential for good government. The *Sunday Times* subsequently, published excerpts from the diaries and was swiftly served with injunctions from the Attorney General to stop any further disclosures. One of the main planks of his argument was that of breach of confidence.

Although the *Sunday Times* had the injunction lifted on appeal, the Crossman case serves as a useful introduction to the frequent use of the confidentiality argument to gag free speech and the revelation of wrongs. Breach of confidence is a very powerful weapon in the armoury of big business or governments anxious to avoid public scrutiny of their dirty laundry. Governments are often particularly tempted to use it instead of the widely discredited Official Secrets Act. And they have done so with some success. Lord Reid, a Law Lord, explained in a 1968 case how the law can help.

> The business of government is difficult enough as it is, and no government could contemplate with equanimity the inner workings of the government machine being exposed to the gaze of those ready to criticise without adequate knowledge of the background and perhaps with some axe to grind.

This does not apply only to the business of government; the business of business – particularly, it seems, of bad business – must be protected by the law of confidence against the freedom of speech, even when that is in the public interest.

In 1980 the British Steel Corporation was losing large sums of the taxpayers' money, and documents circulating at a very high level within the Corporation revealed evidence of mismanagement. An employee passed them to Granada Television, which then used them in an interview with BSC's chairman. When the Corporation took Granada to court to make it disclose who had passed on such embarrassing information, the Court of Appeal decided to ignore the evidence that Granada had actually done a public service in revealing waste and sided with BSC.

It was the same story all over again in 1984, with the *Daily Express* in trouble for attempting to publish confidential documents belonging to a company called Lion Laboratories Ltd. Lion manufactured the new intoximeters intended largely to replace the breathalyser bag. The *Express* discovered (after an earlier 'Checkpoint' investigation) that the intoximeter was rather less than accurate. Two former Lion employees then offered the paper the company's own documents confirming its doubts about the machine's reliability.

On 8 March 1984, Lion issued writs for breach of confidence and quickly obtained an injunction to stop the *Express* publishing the allegedly confidential information. The ensuing court hearing quashed the injunction. The judge said that in certain circumstances public interest could be served by the disclosure of confidential information.

Even if we assume, however, that breach of confidence is no longer the reliable gag on free speech that it once was, there are plenty more laws for us to choke on. Chief amongst these is the law of contempt, which neatly silences anyone involved in a court proceeding. At its most basic, contempt law is there to ensure a fair trial by preventing prejudicial information being published. So, for example, it is an offence to write or say publicly that a man accused – but not yet convicted – of a crime has already been in prison.

Contempt can, however, be used as a far more sinister bar to free speech, and once again it is government and big business which provide the most telling examples.

The Distillers company began to make and market a sedative drug containing Thalidomide in 1958. It stopped in 1961 after 450 children were born with gross deformities; their mothers had taken the drug to ward off maternity sickness. Writs were issued against the company in 1968; some were settled out of court, others dragged on. In 1972 the *Sunday Times* published the first of a series of articles to draw attention to the children's plight. Immediately, Distillers complained to the Attorney General that the story was in contempt of court because some actions were still pending. The *Sunday Times* replied by justifying that first article and supplying a follow-up story which it intended to run.

There followed a lengthy chase through the courts to stop publication. The first court granted an injunction; a higher court lifted it; and finally the House of Lords forbade the paper to publish – despite the undoubted fact that the legal proceedings had been dormant for years and there appeared no prospect of any action coming to trial, and therefore no prosepct of any damages for the deformed children and their families.

Their lordships were more concerned with the evil, as they saw it, of 'trial by newspaper' than either the plight of the children or the right to free speech. Finally, in 1979, the European Court of

Human Rights ruled, as it has done so often, against the British government for violating the right to freedom of expression.

Even so, Lord Hailsham – then Lord Chancellor – refused to concede defeat: 'You,' he informed the *Sunday Times* when it claimed to have been vindicated by the Court, 'have got the European judgement wrong and I've got it right.' It was not, he insisted, a victory for press freedom in any way. And, in the topsy-turvy ways of the law, Hailsham's opinion was to be proved both right and wrong shortly afterwards.

Harriet Harman was in 1980 acting as legal officer of the National Council for Civil Liberties and as solicitor to a man called Michael Williams. He was suing the Home Office for damage after being detained in a special secret isolation cell in his prison. Ms Harman managed, after a good deal of argument, to obtain Home Office documents relating to the isolation cells, which she duly read to the court hearing Williams's case.

She later showed one of the documents she had read out to a reporter who had been in court. Immediately, she was prosecuted for contempt on the grounds that although the reporter had heard all that was in the documents (which were in any case then reproduced in the transcript of the hearing) it was improper actually to show them to him. The Home Office, which conducted this elaborate charade, spent taxpayers' money with abandon as the case dragged through court after court. Finally, it gave in at the doors of the European Court of Human Rights and agreed to pay the NCCL's costs.

The courts are certainly not fond of us airing our views about them – and never have been. On 15 March 1900 Mr Justice Darling, sitting at Birmingham Assizes, tried a man called Wells for publishing obscenities. Before the trial got under way the judge warned the press against publishing a full account of the case (newspapers are restrained from publishing obscene or indecent material even when it is a relevant part of a court case).

The following day, with the Wells trial over, the editor of the *Birmingham Daily Argus* published the following opinion of the judge:

> No newspaper can exist except upon its merits, a condition from which the Bench, happily for Mr Justice Darling, is exempt. There is not a journalist in Birmingham who has anything to

learn from the impudent little man in horsehair, a microcosm of conceit and empty-headedness, who admonished the Press yesterday. . . .

One is almost sorry that the Lord Chancellor had not another relative to provide for on the day that he selected a new judge from the larrikins of the law. One of Mr Justice Darling's biographers states that 'an eccentric relative left him much money'. That misguided testator spoiled a successful bus conductor. Mr Justice Darling would do well to master the duties of his own profession before undertaking the regulation of another.

For this the editor was fined the sum of £100, with £25 costs. To its shame, the law of contempt which prevents us from roundly criticising our judges has hardly changed since.

Freedom of speech is probably our single most important civil liberty. And yet, unlike other countries, our governments have not managed to give us an inalienable right to it. As a result, we in Britain are amongst the most heavily gagged poeple in what we choose to call the free world. And the irony is that we not only believe ourselves to have a right which doesn't exist, but we pity those in other countries whom we believe to be less free.

Freedom of assembly

The last, and most publicly visible, of our political 'rights' is freedom of assembly. It is more usually known as the right to meet and demonstrate in public against unpopular government policies or controversial events. And, as television news bulletins remind us almost nightly, demonstrating in public is one of our most frequently exercised rights. Once again our 'right' to meet and protest publicly is actually a myth. We have no such right.

As usual, we are only allowed to do what the law doesn't disallow, and the law disallows so much that were the police to enforce it in full it would be impossible to hold demonstrations and rallies as we know them.

As a result, the police find themselves using their discretion over the handling and even banning of public demonstrations. And the use of that discretion brings with it accusations from both sides of the political spectrum that police chiefs are meddling in politics. In fact, chief constables and officers alike find themselves trapped in the middle of an unworkable compromise, attacked both verbally and physically by one side (notably in long-running and bitter disputes such as the 1984-5 miners' strike) and with their backs to a crumbling and uneven wall of statutes – behind which shelter our politicians. In an attempt to codify the confused state of the law the government introduced the Public Order Act in the autumn of 1986. At the time of writing it was too early to see how the Act would work in practice, but in theory at least flaws began to be apparent before the ink had dried on the paper.

The new law gives the police more discretion rather than less, and in particular give chief constables the power to impose conditions on the size, location and duration of any open-air demonstration if they reasonably expect the demonstration to create public disorder, serious damage to property, the coercion of individuals, or serious disruption to the life of the community. And it's not just political demonstrations that are covered: religious meetings, pop festivals and football matches all come under the Act's umbrella.

The problem as ever, lies in the use of police discretion. The Act – whilst specifically avoiding the power to ban demonstrations – actually provides an effective backdoor method. All the police need to do is limit a demonstration to such an extent (for example, allowing five minutes instead of two hours, setting a location two miles away from the proper protest site, and severely limiting the numbers) that the protest becomes insignificant.

As yet we do not know how the police will act under this new law, but opponents of the law like Gerald Kaufman, Labour's former Home Affairs spokesman, have already voiced their fears. 'It will place the police in an intolerable position of taking political decisions on such occasions. It will erode their independence.'

Kaufman's concern was understandable. On the very day the Public Order Act, 1986, received the royal assent, the case of Hirst and Agu v. Chief Constable of West Yorkshire Police reached the Court of Appeal.

Hirst and Agu had been members of an animal rights group which, in January 1985, had demonstrated outside a Bradford fur shop. The shop in question was part of a spacious precinct and at the time was busy with shoppers. The demonstrators were variously holding banners or handing out leaflets to passers-by.

Both Hirst and Agu were charged with obstructing the highway with their demonstration. They denied the charge, claiming they were exercising their right to demonstrate. Both Bradford magistrates and the Crown court decided they had no such right, because standing on the highway holding banners and offering leaflets was not 'incidental to its lawful use'. In other words, no such right to demonstrate existed.

Fortunately for Hirst and Agu (and for any other would-be demonstrator) Lord Justice Glidewell and Mr Justice Otton, sitting in the Court of Appeal, decided otherwise. Mr Justice Otton said that the courts had 'long recognised the right to free speech to protest on matters of public concern and to demonstrate'.

Otton's view of the judiciary is altogether more rosy than that of many of its critics. Even so, and even if the courts do recognise a right to demonstrate, the Public Order Act largely takes it out of their hands. Part 2 of the Act effectively allows the police to ban such demonstrations in advance, so freedom of assembly will depend on the discretion of individual officers. Once again the police will be faced with a difficult decision which will inevitably be attacked by would-be demonstrators as political prejudice. The NCCL proposed a single solution: 'In our view, a statutory right of freedom of speech and assembly would clarify the limits of lawful activity and thereby lessen conflict.'

Before we leave the arena of political freedoms, a quick word on the curious case of the disappearing trade union. Employment law invests us all with a positive right (or at least a right by default) to belong to, and be active within, an independent trade union. Should an employer be unfair enough to discipline or dismiss us for enjoying this privilege we can immediately appeal to an industrial tribunal for re-instatement or compensation.

At least, nearly all of us can. During 1984 the government decided, unilaterally, that independent trade unions were not a good idea in the sensitive atmosphere of their civilian-operated spying centre, GCHQ. National security, it was said, was threatened by the existence of a union there which had once organised industrial action (although whether any damage was actually caused to national security is something of a moot point even amongst ministers). Perhaps unsurprisingly, the unions fought back and began a lengthy trek through the courts ending (in failure) at the European Court of Human Rights in Strasbourg.

The crucial point to emerge from both the British and European courts was that if a government decided that national security was at risk, it was quite entitled to strip its citizens of their rights to join a trade union. What's more, it is not up to the courts to question the nature of that threat: national security is a matter for the government, and only it can say what that means. Nor should we forget that trade unions, themselves sometimes act in a way calculated to deny members their rights, either through manipulation of their rule books or, in at least one case, by physical intimidation.

It is one of those typically British ironies that Mrs Thatcher's Conservative government has been responsible for bringing into force a comprehensive programme of trade-union reform aimed at strengthening the rights of the ordinary member, whilst at the same time stripping other employees of their right to belong to a union.

Personal freedom

Mervyn Griffith-Jones looked hard at the jury; the jury looked hard at Griffith-Jones. 'Is it,' he implored of them, 'a book you would wish to have lying around your own house? Is it a book that you would even wish your wife or your servants to read?'

The Old Bailey, more properly known as the Central Criminal Court, has seen many thousands of trials and heard a great deal of tosh. On the morning of 20 October 1960, Court Number 1 was awash with it.

The book which so alarmed Griffith-Jones – and potentially inflamed his entire household – was by then thirty-two years of age, and its author long dead. But the decision by Penguin Books to publish a paperback edition – cheaper and more readily accessible to wives and servants – of D. H. Lawrence's classic, *Lady Chatterley's Lover*, began a welter of prosecutions under our confused and confusing obscenity laws.

This section deals with what can be roughly lumped together as our personal, rather than political, freedoms. Chief among these (and in many ways the natural partner of freedom of expression) is the right to read what we like. And by now it should come as no surprise to find that no such right exists, except by default.

The right to read

The law covering what we read emerged historically from a desire to protect public morals and religion. Add to that our severe laws of defamation and the prospect of any 'right to read' narrows considerably. The most widely prosecuted area is that of obscenity and indecency (the old 'protection of our moral well-being' idea). And it was under just such a law, the then-new Obscene Publications Act of 1959, that Penguin Books found itself in the dock at Number 1 Court, the Old Bailey on that autumn morning in 1960.

Griffith-Jones, appearing for the prosecution, wanted the book declared obscene. He dutifully counted every four-letter word in the Penguin edition and listed them in order of numerical superiority. (Intriguingly, since D. H. Lawrence was not available to be censured for his writings, Griffith-Jones decided to try the fictional heroine of the title for the sin of enjoying sex. It was not a great success.)

Penguin's acquittal might have been expected to signal the end of obscenity prosecution, but not a bit of it. Over the next twenty years the Old Bailey and other palaces of justice saw yet more obscenity trials. Some had a limited success – in 1971 the men behind *Oz* magazine were sent to jail for publishing an obscene comic, only to be acquitted on appeal.

The problem with obscenity is that it is very difficult to define: the best official attempt came in 1868 in a case involving not pornography but religious bigotry. In it, and according to Sir Alexander Cockburn, then Lord Chief Justice, the acid test was whether the offending article tended to 'deprave and corrupt'. But a more honest judicial approach came in the midst of that boom-time for obscenity cases, the 1970s. 'Obscenity, members of the jury, is like an elephant. You cannot define it, but you know it when you see it.'

Another factor influenced the obscenity debate during those years – new technology, which made the production and distribution of genuinely pornographic material, as opposed to that which has some literary or artistic merit, a good deal cheaper. This, together with a corrupt system of bribes and blackmail between police and pornographers in London's Soho (traditionally the vice industry's capital), led to a classic confrontation of rights.

On the one hand, encouraged by official studies in Denmark and America showing pornography to be either harmless or even beneficial (Danish government statistics showed a dramatic drop in sex offences of up to 80 per cent after pornography was legalised), were those demanding their 'right to read' obscene books and magazines; on the other were those demanding their 'right' not to be confronted by gory or sexually explicit magazines whenever they walked into the local newsagents.

In a bid to sort out these conflicting claims the Williams Committee was convened by the Labour government in 1977. Its task was to examine the whole area of obscenity and make recommendations to solve the problem. The Williams Committee worked hard, viewed hours of the most noxious pornography, listened patiently to both sides and an assortment of academics, and finally produced in 1979 a draft bill to remove all traces of the worst pornography completely and to keep the rest out of sight of anyone who didn't go looking for it.

The Williams bill would have safeguarded the rights of those people who want to look at obscene material to do so, but at the same time would have kept it hidden behind closed doors. It was, arguably, the best of all possible worlds, though inevitably it didn't satisfy the extremes of either side. Sadly, the report has been gathering dust on a Home Office shelf ever since. By the time Williams reported the government had changed and the new Conservative administration was not interested in the report.

This leads us back to the chaotic state of the law – or, rather, laws. Each of the thirteen or so differing laws concerning pornography has a slightly different test of obscenity or indecency. The two main agencies which enforce this hotch-potch of statutes are the police and customs officers. Both agencies would like a simple unified law to tell them what they should seize and what they should leave on the shelf – an understandable desire, given the invariable public outcry whenever they either successfully prosecute obscenity or lose their case in the courts. Put simply, the present confusion has led to a series of embarrassing defeats by various courts. Thus in 1977 the citizens of Portsmouth were able (and sometimes willing) to purchase material depicting anything short of child sex, bestiality or torture, whilst their counterparts in Manchester found local police busily seizing the *Sun Book of Page 3 Girls*.

Her Majesty's Customs, too, has had its share of problems. In March 1986 a company called Conegate Ltd won a ruling at the European Court that a ban on lifelike, blow-up rubber sex dolls imported by the company into Britain from the EEC was unlawful and should cease. The case prompted one Law Lord at least to wonder (and surely with some justification) that if the dolls weren't obscene, what on earth was?

It was customs officers who were under fire again in another case that finished in 1986 – though this one was rather more important for the 'right to read' campaigners. On 20 August 1985 seven men and two women were committed for trial on charges of conspiracy to import indecent material.

All the accused were either directors or staff of a Bloomsbury bookshop called Gay's the Word. Evidence of their alleged crimes was seized in a raid on the shop in April 1984, and consisted of several copies of novels by Tennessee Williams, Gore Vidal, Christopher Isherwood and Jean Genet, in addition to serious medical and socio-medical works on homosexuality (all of which underlined the undoubted truth that this was a genuine bookshop and no sleazy pornographers' den). The trial was billed as the natural sequel to R. v. Penguin Books in the notorious Lady Chatterley case, and was intended to rule on our freedom or other wise to read 144 titles of literature concerning homosexual relationships. In the end the prosecution backed down and the case was dropped – which doesn't mean that it could never be brought again.

In an area of such sensitivity the resurrection of old laws or cases can never be ruled out – as Dennis Lemon discovered in 1978. Lemon was the editor of *Gay News*, a magazine which published a poem about a homosexual's conversion to Christianity and which metaphorically attributed homosexual acts to Jesus Christ.

There is at the time of writing, although moves have been made to scrap it, a crime of blasphemous libel. Before Lemon hit the headlines there had not been a prosecution since 1922, but that indefatigable guardian of public morals, Mrs Mary Whitehouse, brought the law back to life and won, as a result of a private prosecution, a conviction against Lemon which the House of Lords subsequently upheld. (Nor is it stricly necessary to involve a religious figurehead in gay sex to fall foul of the law, merely to make outrageous, indecent or scurrilous attacks on Christianity.) And though the crime of blasphemous libel may once again have fallen into disuse, the Lemon case reminds us that dormant laws can always be rudely awoken.

Sexual rights

The personal rights of homosexuals and other non-conventional couples are the least protected and the ones most frequently at risk. And while we may not share their sexual orientation – or indeed may even fear or resent their existence – few of us would deny their right to live quiet and unpersecuted lives. One test of our tolerance and freedom is the extent to which we allow minorities to find happiness in their own way despite our own personal dislike or revulsion.

Sadly, it is a test our laws all too often fail. The age of consent for heterosexual intercourse is sixteen, while for homosexual intercourse it is twenty-one – for no apparent reason. In April 1986 Mr Justice Glidewell warned gays that public kissing and cuddling could land them in the dock for insulting behaviour, and dismissed an appeal by two men against just such a conviction. Homosexuals are regularly routed out of the armed forces and discharged dishonourably, and the stiff warning the customs directorate was forced to issue to its own staff about discrimination against gay books during the 1986 trial was a salutary reminder that those who enforce the law may let prejudice affect their judgement.

Sadder still, perhaps, is the plight of Mark Rees. Rees was born with the physical attributes of a female, but the psychological make-up of a male. In later life he had hormone treatment and surgery to bring his body more in tune with his mind, and now considers himself male – as do his friends and acquaintances. The law and government of the United Kingdom, however, show no such understanding. He is unable under present law to have a birth certificate which shows he is a man – a denial which has on occasion caused him a good deal of embarrassment and distress. Nor may he marry – or at least he may not marry a woman.

Rees's predicament as a fully fledged transsexual is not one which many of us will experience, but it does highlight the tattered and inadequate state of our law in protecting the rights of minorities and the vulnerable.

The best example of the hypocritical and inconsistent way our laws decide who may do what with whom and where, is the rights of those women who choose to be prostitutes. It is not illegal for a woman to be a prostitute and given the incidence in the past twenty years of MPs and peers caught *in flagrante* with ladies of the night, we should not perhaps be surprised by this. It is, however, illegal for a woman publicly to solicit a man for sex – which effectively rules out one method of plying her trade.

And should she operate discreetly from her house, she may be convicted of a string of offences from keeping a disorderly house to allowing her premises to be used for prostitution. Anyone helping her, by allowing her to advertise her services, may face charges of living off her earnings – which just about covers every possible way of meeting clients.

Nor is this simply a problem affecting the many thousand full- and part-time prostitutes throughout the UK. The oldest profession will never disappear; prostitution is a capitalist dream – constant demand and constant supply. And the easiest, and most economic, method of business is street-walking (simply on the grounds that since the whole enterprise is doomed to prosecution, it is foolish to pay the overheads of renting rooms).

It was an economic equation discovered by the residents of Bedford Hill, Balham (amongst other places) in the early 1980s. Balham has traditionally been a working area for prostitutes since the introduction of a brothel to serve a local barracks in the eighteenth century. But times change, and people living in an otherwise unremarkable London suburb found themselves under constant siege from men looking for prostitutes. Ordinary women and young girls were regularly accosted by strangers asking for sex; doorsteps and garages were pressed into service as bedrooms. Understandably enough, the residents called for action.

It took several years in coming, but in 1985 the Sexual Offences Act limped on to the statute books to outlaw kerb-crawling by men looking for sex. Which should have helped the residents of Balham – and did after a fashion. Local police patrols, armed with a new law, protected the public's right to a quiet vice-free life and prosecutions of both men and women ensued. But there are two separate sections of Bedford Hill, though the outsider would be hard put to tell them apart; the bottom end is situated in one borough, served by one police force, the top end in and by another. The prostitutes simply shifted themselves, and the nuisance they caused, to the top of the hill, where the local police don't have the manpower to mount effective vice patrols.

All of this could have been avoided many years ago when the citizens of Southampton suggested state-run brothels as adopted by many other countries. Once again a potentially good idea was shouted down, and years' – perhaps decades' – more trouble for residents and prostitutes alike guaranteed.

If nothing else, this chapter should have shown how fragile – and sometimes illusory – our personal and political rights actually are.

How often have we said in response to some absurd or alarming infringement of human rights abroad that 'it could never happen here'? The sad truth is that if it hasn't already happened here, it can and quite possibly will do.

FOUR

The Source of all Discontents

'Far from being the basis of the
good society, the family, with its
narrow privacy and tawdry secrets,
is the source of all our discontents.'

Edmund Leach, BBC Reith Lecture,
1967

Bournemouth. November 1983. On top of a very small television in a tiny flat a small pasteboard invitation has pride of place. The invitation is to a child's birthday party. The child is Gemma. She is five years old. This is her very first party; it is also the first time she has been with her mother on her birthday. To get to her own daughter's party, Gemma's mother has been through hell.

This chapter deals with family rights as they affect both parents and children. It is in three parts: the first examines the 'care system' which supposedly underpins family life in times of crisis; the second deals with health care; and the third looks at education and the rights and responsibilities of parents, children and schools.

If Edmund Leach's bleak assertion is something of an overstatement, all three areas have proved contentious breeding grounds for litigation and legislation. The question remains, though: have we got it right yet?

In whose best interests?

Carole is proud of her small basement flat. It was all but derelict when she found it. Now the place shines and sparkles. It also has a homely feel for Carole – at least it does now Gemma has come home.

Carole (as in almost all cases in this section, the law prevents us from using surnames since they would identify children who have been in care) is one of a substantial number of parents who, through absolutely no fault of her own, lost her child into the care system. Getting Gemma back proved – as it often can – extraordinarily difficult.

Gemma was born in November 1978 when Carole was twenty. She had married just over a year earlier, but only weeks before she gave birth her husband left her for another woman. Carole was devastated. The couple had deliberately planned to have a baby; now she was on her own.

After Gemma was born Carole went home to her parents' house. But the house was overcrowded and rows developed. Carole grew daily more depressed and upset. The health visitor took her to see her local social services department. The social worker decided that Carole was suffering from post-natal depression and arranged for her to spend a couple of nights in Poole Hospital. She also – unfortunately in view of what would happen later – passed on her impressions of Carole to the hospital psychiatrist. For some reason the social services were subsequently at a loss to explain, Carole was labelled a 'silly, thoughtless, self-centred girl, showing no sense of being a caring and responsible mother'.

Quite how the social worker came to this conclusion is a mystery. The social services department now accepts that it was the complete reverse of the truth. Nonetheless, the stigma remained, and as a result the hospital psychiatrist diagnosed an underlying personality disorder. He too was later to admit that the diagnosis was utterly incorrect; Carole was perfectly healthy in mind and body, and a capable – if depressed – mother.

When she came out of hospital, Carole set about finding somewhere to live. She found a flat and moved in, but it was on a short-term lease only and she was soon moved out. She was at the time on her local council's priority housing list but, rather than sit out the long wait for a council property, Carole began looking for herself. With the help of the Samaritans she found a mother-and-baby hostel and moved in.

Meanwhile, the social services department had been making plans of its own. Unknown to Carole, Gemma was placed on the 'At Risk Register' because of the housing problem. When Carole moved back into her parents' home – the overcrowding having been eased and the rows all settled – the department moved in swiftly. It went to the magistrates' court and obtained a place of safety order.

Such orders are generally invoked when there is a danger of the child being physically or sexually abused. As the department was later to admit, there was never any question of either in Gemma's case. Carole remembers what happened next all too clearly.

> The social worker came round one day – it was 28 March 1979 – Gemma was less than six months old – and said she was going to take Gemma. I wouldn't let her. I put Gemma in the pram and pushed her up to my solicitor's office. She followed me and eventually took Gemma, and my solicitor told me there was nothing he could do because the social services had the power and were just enforcing their rights.

Carole was told that she could have her daughter back as soon as the housing problem was sorted out. Gemma was to be placed with short-term foster parents until Carole was ready for her. That reassurance was a lie.

The very day that Gemma was taken from Carole, the social services department held a case meeting. Carole knew nothing about it. Parents – and, as we shall see, children – involved in care cases have no right to attend case conferences that vitally affect their lives. At the meeting it was agreed to put Gemma out to long-term fostering. On 3 May 1978, Carole's daughter was given away to another couple for permanent foster care.

Throughout the first five weeks during which Gemma had been in care Carole had had complete freedom of access: she could see her daughter whenever she wanted – although conditions were far from ideal.

> I had to go along and sit in a bare room and Gemma was sort of put opposite me. By then they'd told her not to call me Mummy any more because this was very naughty . . . and it was very difficult for us both because we had to be supervised. It was awful just sitting there with my daughter opposite me who was obviously tearful and upset and completely confused.

After Gemma was taken to her long-term foster parents the social services department reduced the access to once a fortnight. Later they tried on two separate occasions to reduce it further still, and then to cut it out completely.

> They actually said in their letter that it was 'until the child's perception of parental and adult relationships is such that she can cope with them without precipitating the gross emotional distress exhibited at present' – which is quite a mouthful. What it actually meant was that I would never see Gemma again. I found out the social services had put her up for adoption. But they hadn't told me.

Carole fought this all the way. She knew, as the social services department knew, that Gemma only exhibited distress *after* Carole went away – not before or during her visits. The implications of that fact should have been obvious.

Carole took the department to court to challenge the care order it had by now taken out. The local magistrates refused her application on the advice of the social services department, but unusually asked her to re-apply six months later when she had sorted out her housing problem.

It was an unrealistic thing to say. Carole was discovering the care Catch 22. With Gemma with her she was a housing priority. Without Gemma she slipped to the bottom of a very long housing list – even though she was simultaneously told that she needed a proper home to get her daughter back. But Carole was determined. She didn't re-apply in six months' time; she spent almost a year looking for, finding and renovating a derelict basement flat. Then and only then did she go back to court.

In November 1982 Carole applied to the magistrates' court. It was to take until 2 February 1983 for the case to be heard. The hearing lasted four days, and at the end of it the bench discharged the care order and returned Gemma to her mother. Carole was overjoyed – briefly. 'Social services immediately came up to me and told me they were applying to make Gemma a ward of court. They said if I went anywhere near her I could be arrested.'

The department got its wardship order and Gemma stayed with the foster-parents. Carole once again prepared to go to court. The case finally came before Mr Justice Latey on 9 May 1983 – more than four years after Gemma had been taken away.

The case took seven days. Witnesses included the foster-parents, the head of the mother-and-baby hostel, social workers, psychiatrists – and Carole. In the end Mr Justice Latey's judgement savaged the social services department.

> The mother has throughout wanted her child back and has fought for it. Throughout several days of evidence not one of the witnesses for the social services department has said anything about the strain on . . . a mother who loves and wants her child. The strain of such a *modus vivendi* must go to the limits of human endurance . . . to have ignored this in their thinking is disquieting to say the least. . . .
> It is accepted now that there is nothing wrong whatsoever with the mother's mental or nervous health . . . nor is there a shred of evidence for the statement that she was a silly, thoughtless and self-centred girl, showing no sense of being a caring and responsible mother. No one suggests now that this was an accurate appraisal of her.

He went on to suggest that the actions of the social worker concerned may have been influenced by the fact that she had no children of her own. Worse, she was not fully supervised and did not take kindly to opposition.

> All the way through the evidence in this case I have been left with the uneasy impression that [she] was convinced that she was right in her judgement and decisions and resented any contrary view. Sometimes it seem that pique and *amour propre* have played a part.

The judge went on to note that the departmental team leader had not involved himself in the case, but simply accepted the social worker's opinions and explanations.

> In such cases it is really essential that there should be a further check, and this in my judgement is just such a case . . . some other social worker (preferably if I may say so one with children of his or her own) would have put a different complexion on the matter and would, I believe, have led to the postponement of a

decision to deprive this baby of her mother's care and to further efforts to keep them together and find a real home for them.

As to Carole's abilities as a mother, Mr Justice Latey was in no doubt:

> She has the deepest maternal feelings for Gemma. She has wanted her and fought for her from start to finish . . . simply because she loves Gemma. Far from being silly, or flighty, or irresponsible, she is a capable and resourceful young lady who has rebuilt her life, managed to find a home and, in her own time and spending her own money, she has gradually decorated and furnished it, converting it from a derelict building into a very nice home. And all this she has done for herself and Gemma in the hope that, against all obstacles, she would in the end have Gemma with her. She has already arranged for a playgroup, a school, and ballet and dancing lessons for Gemma. She is [a] splendid and admirable young woman. . . .

Four years after the social services department took her away, Judge Latey returned Gemma to her mother – and to her first proper birthday party.

> Everything's working out fine with me now [Carole said later]. And with Gemma. She's happy and settled. I think Gemma can adjust and I'm going to make sure that she will, because I don't want her to grow up a psychologically scarred person. But obviously it's had its effects on me, which are going to be long-term. I mean, there's no getting away from it: it's been five years out of my life – five very unsettled years and five very, very sad, tragic years.

But how could those five years have happened? How was it that a baby was taken from a mother who so obviously wanted, and was able, to look after it? Just whose best interests was the system protecting?

The care system

At any given time there are approximately 100,000 children in care in Great Britain – twice the number of adults in prison. They are taken into the care of local authorities in a variety of ways, through a bewildering array of courts, and can end up in a wide range of institutions with varying degrees of humanity and/or security.

The most obvious way into the care system is through the criminal courts. Juvenile offenders deemed to be out of parental control can be put into care by the juvenile bench. This category regularly makes up more than half of the number of those in care. We do not, however, propose to deal with this route in any great detail. The simple fact is that the juvenile justice system is a far more carefully regulated route (though still not perfect) than the alternative – 'voluntary care', a term which is sadly misleading. Compulsory care orders can also be sought by local authorities without evidence of crimes.

This is authorised under the 1969 Children and Young Persons Act. Under its provisions social services departments are under a duty to investigate if they believe that there are grounds in any case to bring care proceedings. If they find such grounds they may go to court and seek a care order. The juvenile court hearing this application must be satisfied that the young person concerned is in need of care and control which he is unlikely to receive unless it grants the order. Additionally, one of a series of specific conditions must be fulfilled:

1. His health or proper development is being impaired or neglected, or there is evidence of ill-treatment.
2. Evidence exists that a child of the same household has already satisfied these conditions or that someone who has been convicted of sexually or otherwise abusing children is or may become a member of the household.
3. The child is exposed to moral danger.
4. The child is beyond the control of his parent or guardian.
5. A school-age child is not receiving efficient full-time education sufficient to his age, ability and aptitude (only a local education authority may bring proceedings under this section).
6. The child is guilty of an offence other than homicide (he or she must be over ten years of age).

Care proceedings were described in one case as 'an objective examination of the position of the child ... not ... a contest between the local authority and the parent or, even more, the child and the parent'. (Lord Widgery in Humberside County Council *v.* DPR.)

Even so, many are contested. If a local authority is granted the order it then has the same powers and duties as a natural parent would have, and must exercise its powers to promote the welfare of the child. As we shall see, that legal duty is often upheld in a questionable manner.

These compulsory routes into care are thus 'policed' by juvenile courts. The criticisms of the care system revolve around three main aspects: the so-called 'voluntary' route, the behaviour of individual social workers and the provisions or infrastructure of care accommodation itself.

Voluntary care

The 'voluntary' route into care was created by the 1948 Children Act. Section 1 of the Act imposes on local authorities a duty to 'receive into care' any child in their area appearing to be under seventeen provided that one of three requirements is fulfilled:
1. It appears that he has neither parents nor guardian, or is lost or abandoned.
2. His parents/guardians are for the time being or permanently unable due to any illness or for any other reason to provide for his proper accommodation, maintenance or upbringing.
3. In either of the above cases, it appears necessary to the local authority to intervene in the interests of the child's welfare.

These are wide and powerful clauses allowing local councils to take children away from their parents – provided that the parents agree. In practice, however, research shows that many parents in this category feel that they have little option but to agree. Conditioning factors are typically illness, marital breakdown, poverty and homelessness. As in Carole's case, it is misleading to view as voluntary an agreement by a parent who has no home to go to for their child to go into care.

In theory again, the 1948 Act is not a long-term or compulsory measure. Section 1 in fact states: 'Nothing shall authorise a local authority to keep a child in their care if any parent or guardian desires to take over the care of the child.' In 1979, however, the House of Lords rather qualified this unequivocal undertaking by ruling that care does not cease automatically upon a parental request, and the child remains in the local authority's care until he is removed.

In practice, another Act has a bearing on this issue. The Child Care Act of 1980 endorsed the voluntary provisions of the 1948 Act, but added the right for local authorities to take out a 'parental rights resolution' – to all intents and purposes a sort of back-door care order.

The resolution, also known as a section 3 resolution, is theoretically passed by the selected members of a council social services committee. In practice this does little more than rubber stamp the recommendations made by the social workers. Before such a resolution is passed the young person's parents should be given written notice that it is being considered, and details of the reasons why. But parents have no enforceable right to go before the committee and explain their side of the story. Once the local authority has given the parents notice they have twenty-eight days in which to object to the passing of the resolution. If they do, the case goes before the juvenile court, where magistrates will make the final decision.

Therein lies another anomaly. Parents cannot appeal to a high court about a care order made by magistrates. The child or young person at stake has the right of appeal, but he will almost certainly have a different solicitor since his interests are not necessarily the same as his parents'. Quite why – in view of the emotional devastation wreaked by taking a child from its parents – there is no right of appeal is an unresolved mystery.

Once a child is in care there is a general right for the parents to have rights of access. Exceptionally, local authorities can refuse access; to do so they must serve the parents with formal notice of the decision. The parents then have a right of appeal to the magistrates' court. (In one of the very few pieces of progress in this field, legal aid was extended to cover families fighting care battles in 1984. Previously, the only child had been covered.) Once again, however, there is a loophole. Social services departments have a right to suspend access indefinitely. They do not have to give any indication of when it will be resumed; they simply have to avoid saying it has been terminated. From this no-man's-land position there is no right of appeal.

Very little official research is carried out into care-system statistics. The task of analysing exactly how the laws and regulations affect families is left to under-funded pressure groups. None the less, figures compiled by the Family Rights Group in November 1983 suggested that 8,000 children in care had been prevented from seeing their parents or other family members by social services staff.

The FRG study quoted the case of Ann Brown (not her real name) who had not been allowed to see her five-year-old son for three years. The social workers concerned insist that access has not been terminated but 'suspended under constant review'. No evidence had been put forward to suggest that access would harm the boy, and his foster-mother had even asked for access to be allowed. Because suspension does not qualify under the rules, Ann Brown had no right to challenge the decision.

The Group also claimed that bad social work practice had led to loss of contact between children in care and their relatives in another 30,000 cases – cases like that of Len and his fourteen-year-old daughter, Christine, who had been in care since the age of two. Len was not married to Christine's mother – though the social services department accepted that he was the girl's father and that there were no other relatives interested in her after her mother died. Yet they refused even to tell Christine that her father was alive and cared about her. Because access had not been suspended – it had never existed – Len had no right of appeal against the decision.

The rules governing access are, in the main, contained in a DHSS code of practice. And because codes of practice do not have the full force of law they are not challengeable in the courts.

These, then, are the rules by which social workers are empowered to intervene in family life, remove children from home and place them in care institutions, and thus ensure effective separation from their families. The powers are by any standards draconian. Sometimes they are abused. Unofficial figures suggest that up to 8,000 children a year are kept in care institutions needlessly, simply because an alternative resolution to their case has not been considered. Carole's experience showed how easily the word of one social worker can become law throughout an entire department and even influence experienced psychiatrists.

Yet we should not simply blame the social workers. Later in this chapter we will examine the very real pressures on them which can force dangerously wrong decisions. But first we need to examine how the law relating to children developed.

Children in law

English law has been particularly slow in recognising the existence of children – or at least their existence as anything other than a piece of personal or commercial property. The history of child-based legislation is a history of attempts to define the rights and responsibilities of their 'owners'. Rarely is there any mention of the child having specific rights.

At the beginning of the nineteenth century the concept of childhood was at best peripheral, at worst unknown to the law. The age of majority was twenty-one. Adulthood began at that age; below it was only infancy.

The State took similarly little interest in childhood: what parents did (or didn't) do to (or for) their offspring was deemed to be their own concern. It was in this laissez-faire climate that child labour, juvenile prostitution and murderous baby-farms flourished.

Significantly, when a legal doctrine known as *parens patriae* was created in the Dickensian murk of the Court of Chancery, legitimising the first State intervention between parents and children, it had less to do with social welfare than with property. The doctrine – the basis of all subsequent interventionist legislation – developed from the need to control the property interests of those legally disbarred by age from holding land. If the Court of Chancery became the first guardian of children's interests it was a highly selective one: only those fortunate enough to pass the property qualifications were within its jurisdiction.

Gradually, however, the Victorian years saw a shift towards more and more intervention. The judiciary became more willing to adapt *parens patriae* as a means of interposing the courts between parents (typically fathers) and their children. To do so they created the concept of 'the welfare of the child'. Welfare was interpreted generously to include moral and religious welfare as well as physical well-being.

The main concern of the courts in all this was the regulation of the adults' interest in the child, rather than the child's interest in itself or anything else. So the welfare principle was used to decrease the father's absolute rights to custody of his children, and expand the mother's rights. The welfare of the child was certainly not seen as a legal reason for intervening in cases of parental child abuse or neglect.

The first attempt at any such protection came with the Prevention of Cruelty to Children Act in 1879 – exactly seventy-five years *after* similar legislation to outlaw cruelty to animals. This Act, the enshrinement in statute law of prevailing judicial thinking and practice, managed to create 'childhood' as a recognisable legal entity worthy of consideration. But it did so at great cost: children became recognised as dependent on the law for protection and control. In other words they became objects for legal regulation rather than legal subjects with rights of their own. It is a legislative legacy still with us today.

At roughly the same time as child abuse came within the purview of the courts, a system for dealing with erring or delinquent juveniles was also developing. Until the middle of the nineteenth century children were subject to the same laws and routinely given the same punishment as adults. Technically, children under the age of fourteen were legally incapable of committing crimes, but from the age of seven this principle was 'rebuttable' – in other words easily ignored – by the simple facts of the alleged offence.

Thus, in 1833, a nine-year-old boy was sentenced to death for pushing a stick through a cracked window and pulling out tuppence-worth of printers' colourings. (The same principle applies today, though the age qualifications are different. A child aged under ten is legally deemed to be incapable of crime; between the ages of ten and fourteen he can be convicted if the court is convinced he knew what he was doing.)

It was in this mid-Victorian period that the idea of separating both delinquent and at-risk children from the rest of society – in effect the foundations of the care system – grew up. Although there was no specific juvenile court until 1908, reformatories were established for convicted juveniles; and by 1866 magistrates had established the power to send endangered children to 'industrial schools'. Endangered children included those who were vagrant or incorrigible, and those who were said by their parents to be associating with criminals or prostitutes – children, in short, who needed to be rescued, reformed and re-socialised. By 1894 more than 17,000 such children were held in industrial schools. By contrast, the reformatories had a population of just 4,800 delinquent young people. Both types of institution were charged with reproducing the conditions of working-class society (children from this background making up the major proportion of their population). So, as the industrial revolution took hold, children were trained for a future in a factory; education and literacy came a poor second.

In theory at least reformatories and industrial schools had differing approaches to their charges. The delinquent was deliberately separated from the neglected or abused child because he was assumed to have some responsibility for his present position. In 1896, however, an official committee of enquiry into the workings of reformatories and industrial schools effectively abolished the distinction. Children, it reported, were basically the same in either institution, and both shared identical disciplinary regimes. It was this principle which has dominated all subsequent child-care thinking; our attention has been diverted from what children do to what they are. In this way they become objects for our concern, never individuals who have taken a deliberate decision about their lives. From 1896 onwards children became legally bound up by a series of discretionary powers of intervention given to others. Because they were seen as being in need of care or control, little if any thought was given to safeguarding the rights of individual children. The 1969 Children and Young Persons Act set a modern stamp on this principle; juvenile courts hearing care cases provided an opportunity for social workers, backed by legal powers, to control the children who came before it.

The power of social workers

In the light of this history it is easier to understand – if not excuse – what happened to Paddy Brooks. At 12.45 p.m. on Thursday, 16 February 1984, Paddy Brooks was arrested. He was held and questioned by police in London for five hours. He was never shown a warrant for his arrest, was never cautioned or charged, and proceedings against him were never brought. Yet this was the culmination of more than eighteen months' harassment and disregard of the law by a social work department. Paddy Brooks's 'crime' was to love and want to care for his own daughter.

Claire Brooks was born in Scotland on 28 April 1982. At the time Paddy was working in Canada. He had been abroad for nine months and hadn't known his girlfriend was pregnant when he left. Claire's mother had decided during the pregnancy that she didn't want to look after the baby. And so, straight after the birth, she asked Highland Regional Council to take her daughter into care. The Council, using its powers under section 1 of the Social Work (Scotland) Act, 1968, obliged. Claire was taken into voluntary care, and almost immediately placed with foster-parents.

(In general, the law in Scotland is markedly different to its

English counterpart, but the care laws – at least as they affect this case – are almost identical. What happened in the Brooks case could happen in England as easily as it did in Scotland.)

In the summer of 1982, Paddy Brooks came home from Canada. He was stunned to learn that he had become a father – and upset that his only daughter was in care. 'I wanted to look after her. She was my first child, and yet she was being taken care of in someone else's house. I just knew that wasn't right.'

He began visiting Claire at the foster-parents' house in July. Almost immediately he told both the foster-parents and the social services department that he wished to have custody of his daughter. It was not a prospect that appealed to either party. The foster-parents had been given the impression by the social worker in charge of the case that they would be allowed to adopt Claire. In turn that social worker – an elderly, childless woman called Miss B. Barraclough – had fixed views regarding the impropriety of single men bringing up their own children.

By the end of October, Paddy Brooks had spent several months negotiating with Miss Barraclough's department for a formal access arrangement and for permission to have Claire home with him permanently. He provided character references, details of his background and a host of other documents the department asked him for. Claire's mother – who fully agreed with his request for custody – had re-registered Claire's birth with Paddy Brooks's name entered in the box marked 'father'. But that proved insufficient to satisfy Miss Barraclough.

On 14 November Brooks formally applied for the discharge of his daughter into his care from that of Highland Regional Council. It took Miss Barraclough until 11 January the following year to respond: 'I have to inform you that the Regional Council does not accept that you are a parent in terms of the Social Work (Scotland) Act, 1968, and Claire will not, therefore, be discharged into your care.'

The Act in question does not recognise – and nor does any English law – the rights of the father of an illegitimate child. So although Brooks was Claire's father in real life, the law maintained a fiction that he was not. None the less, he could be Claire's legal guardian if her mother agreed. She did, and on 17 February signed a document giving him full parental rights and responsibilities, appointing him Claire's legal guardian, and giving him an entirely free hand in her future. The document was swiftly lodged with the Council, and once again Paddy Brooks asked for his daughter to be handed over.

On 3 March 1983, the Council's legal department wrote back. Claire would not be released, even though it was accepted that Brooks was entitled to give notice of the ending of the voluntary care arrangement.

> The council have a duty in terms of Section 15(2) of the Social Work (Scotland) Act, 1968, to keep a child in their care so long as the welfare of the child appears to them to require it and the child has not attained the age of eighteen. It is under this section that the council are objecting to releasing the child. . . .

All of this was true – as far as it went. The Council knew (or at least it certainly should have known) that if a child's legal parent or guardian wanted to remove her from voluntary care, the only way the social services department could stop him was to take out a parental rights resolution. At no stage did Highland Regional Council ever take out such a resolution.

Instead, the Council encouraged Paddy Brooks to have the case heard in court. In the meantime Claire was growing up – she was by now almost a year old and had lived with her foster-parents all her life. They, in turn, were becoming irritated both by the access which Brooks had arranged via the Council and by the very real possibility that they would lose the child they had been led to believe would stay with them for ever. Friction began to develop and the couple – perhaps understandably – put pressure on the Council to reduce access or reschedule it at inconvenient times for Brooks. The Council, in the shape of Miss Barraclough, agreed. To her the issue was simple: it was not natural for a single man, twenty-seven years old, to want to look after his own child – particularly a little girl. She dismissed his plans to give up work to care for Claire as irrelevant.

Brooks duly started legal proceedings – proceedings which were held up by considerable delays in granting him legal aid. In the summer of 1983 the case was put on ice and negotiations were reopened with the Council on the basis of a suggestion he put forward.

Paddy Brooks's sister, Patricia, was a trained nursery nurse and nanny. She wholeheartedly approved of her brother's attempts to win custody of Claire. 'I'd seen him with other children, relatives and friends. He was simply marvellous with them. In fact he would make a better mother than I ever could. Yet the Council wouldn't allow him to look after Claire because he was a man.'

At the time Patricia Brooks lived and worked in Australia, but she agreed to come home to Scotland to help look after Claire if the Council felt that that would make a difference. In May 1983 she had a formal interview with Miss Barraclough. As she had understood it, if the social worker approved of her and her qualifications the Council would drop its opposition to Paddy Brooks's custody appeal. For its part Highland Regional Council denies that there was ever any such arrangement. Either way, its social services department refused to be swayed. Once again the legal action was resumed.

By December 1983 the case was still unheard. Brooks gave the Council the statutory twenty-eight days' formal notice of his intention to reclaim Claire. Still the Council did nothing. On 20 December the case finally came before Inverness sheriffs' court – the approximate equivalent of a stipendiary magistrates' court in England. The sheriff reviewed the evidence, heard witnesses from both sides (as well as from the foster-parents in the middle) – and then decided that he had no power to handle the case. It would have to go to a court of higher jurisdiction.

The transcript of his ruling makes interesting reading. With regard to Paddy Brooks's ability to look after Claire, the sheriff noted:

> In principle there is nothing to show that he could not physically care for Claire adequately. His accommodation is also adequate. There is evidence that his ability to meet her physical needs is adequate.
>
> Her mental and emotional well-being is another matter entirely. It is very unusual in my experience – a view echoed by Miss Barraclough – for a single man of twenty-seven years of age to be seen to be so determined to have custody of his eighteen-month-old female illegitimate child, but that does not in itself in any way indicate his unsuitability to have her. I discount the evidence that other single men have coped successfully with raising small female children as each case has to be looked at on its individual merits.
>
> Nothing in [Mr Brooks's] demeanour in the witness box

indicated one way or the other whether he was suitable to ensure normal, healthy, mental, emotional and physical development in an eighteen-month-old female child.

Miss Barraclough, as the sheriff recorded, had indeed made her opinions quite clear. Brooks's lawyer asked her in the course of the hearing why she thought a single, twenty-seven-year-old man was not a suitable person to look after his own daughter. Her answer was revealing. In Miss Barraclough's opinion single young men should be in the pub 'talking about beer and football' with their friends, not staying home and looking after children. As a display of old-fashioned prejudice it was without equal. It was also the basis for refusing to release Claire from 'voluntary' care.

By the end of December Brooks had come to a decision. Claire was eighteen months old – fast approaching an age where any court would think twice about separating her from the household she had grown up in. Equally, he had fulfilled his legal responsibilites by giving, as her lawful guardian, twenty-eight days' notice of his intention to remove her from care. And the Council had not taken out parental rights. On the last Saturday of the month Paddy Brooks took his daughter out during a regular access visit. Instead of returning her two hours later, he drove across the border out of Scotland towards his parents' house near London.

He subsequently telephoned the foster-parents' house to reassure them that Claire was safe. He then telephoned us.

In the meantime Highland Regional Council's social services department had made a formal complaint to the Northern Constabulary that a young child had been unlawfully abducted by its natural father. The council failed to tell the police that Brooks had given them the required twenty-eight days' notice (and therefore had not in fact committed any offence). The police also failed to understand that they had no cross-border powers to arrest Paddy Brooks as the council had demanded. ('I have to tell you,' one senior officer later confided, 'the social workers seemed more interested in getting Brooks arrested than in the welfare of the wee girl.')

At the time Brooks was living in a pleasant flat in south-east London. We put him in touch with the Family Rights Group, which in turn advised him to commission an independent social worker to report on his relationship with Claire and his ability to look after her. Before the visit was arranged, Brooks was arrested.

On the morning of 16 February he had been to a branch of the Bank of Scotland in Threadneedle Street, in the heart of the City of London. He wanted to transfer funds from his account in Scotland to London. The bank asked him to return an hour later to allow time for the necessary arrangements to be made on the phone. At 12.30 p.m. he returned and was again asked to wait – this time just for a few minutes. At 12.45 p.m. he received his money and walked out of the bank. As he crossed the road he noticed a man following him. He began to hurry away; two streets further on two police officers grabbed hold of him.

> I was taken to the police station and held from 1 p.m. to 6 p.m. When I asked to see the warrant I was told it was in Scotland. I wasn't asked to give a statement – they only wanted my London address so they could go and get Claire. But they didn't seem worried that she would be upset that I hadn't come back from the bank.

By 6 p.m. it had become clear that a mistake had been made. Brooks's solicitor, alerted by friends, had contacted the Inverness Procurator Fiscal (who had agreed to the arrest); the solicitor pointed out that Brooks had given twenty-eight days' notice and had therefore not committed any offence. In London Paddy Brooks was released and allowed to go home to his daughter.

And what, all this time, of Claire herself? Had she suffered through being removed from her foster-home to live with her father? On 7 March 1984 the report from the independent social worker was presented to the sheriff's court at Tain, near Inverness. Brooks had by this stage moved out of London to his parents' home in Reading. He still didn't dare risk moving back to the Highlands. The social worker wrote of Claire:

> She was [at the time of his visit] very neatly and cleanly dressed, appeared well-nourished, and presented herself as a very happy and inquisitive little girl throughout the observation.
> She paid a great deal of attention to her father, whom she referred to as 'Daddy', and to a lesser extent she involved her grandparents in her play activities, referring to them as 'Grandma' and 'Grandad'. Mr Brooks responded well to his daughter's attention, playing with her, getting her to identify

objects, making her laugh and generally handling and relating to her in a confident and competent manner.

I observed no sign of stress in Claire at all. The names of her foster-parents' other children were mentioned at my request, and although she appeared to recognise them and repeated them later, this did not observably upset her in any way. . . .

Asked about his future commitment to looking after Claire, I was impressed by Mr Brooks's well-balanced outlook. He told me he would envisage remaining unemployed so as to devote full-time care to Claire initially whilst she needs it most, but eventually, when she becomes old enough for nursery and then school, he would hope to be re-employed and feels confident he could obtain work through his contacts in the [Highland] area.

From the evidence of my observations, Claire is happy and well cared for with her father at present and he seems firmly committed to her long-term care with both an appreciation of her needs and an expressed willingness to co-operate with agencies such as social services for help and advice as necessary. . . .

As to the eighteen months of heartache and rejection as a suitable father by Highland Regional Council:

It appears that as a single male he was not taken seriously enough by social services despite his persistence, regular contact with his daughter and the numerous precedents of successful child-rearing by men. . . . Asked why he wants his daughter full time, Mr Brooks told me he loves her, he is part of the family, and as he is able to care for her and fulfil her needs it is in Claire's best interests to be with him.

Shortly after that the Council dropped its opposition to Paddy Brooks looking after his daughter. Six months later he moved back to the Highlands, where he is now married. Claire is, by all accounts, a cheerful and friendly little girl. Paddy Brooks is just grateful the case is finally over.

In October 1986 the British government lost the first round of a potentially lengthy battle at the European Court of Human Rights. The petitioner, a single father identified only as John, was challenging the same legal principle which had prevented Paddy Brooks from being accepted as a father with rights to care for his child. The government told the court that the differing status of unmarried fathers and mothers from that of married couples was 'objectively and reasonably justifiable'.

The Brooks case – like that of Carole and Gemma before it – shows how social workers can exceed their authority and make appalling decisions on the basis of irrational prejudice. Decisions which can shatter all those affected by them.

Further evidence – if more were needed – came in July 1987 in a secret enquiry report into the behaviour of Birmingham social services department. The report disclosed that an Asian woman, identified only as Mrs P., was subjected to a prolonged campaign to separate her from her baby. On one occasion, on 18 November 1979, a social worker and a policeman literally snatched the six-day-old baby girl from her mother's breast.

The family spoke no English and the social worker hadn't bothered to bring an interpreter. The independent enquiry report added: 'Mrs P. became hysterical and Mr P. felt numbed and paralysed – and broke down in tears. They had not been prepared for the removal of their new-born baby. . . . Who is responsible for this dreadful failure to speak to a mother whose baby is being removed without warning?'

The report showed that social workers had been right to be concerned about the family. Two years previously Mr P. had admitted in court to shaking his son. The boy was found to be brain-damaged and Mr P. was convicted of injuring him. But the department had failed to notice doubts subsequently thrown on the conviction. Mr P.'s first language is Gujerati, in which the word for shaking is the same as the word for rocking. More importantly still, new medical evidence indicated that the boy had been born with brain damage.

None the less, a case conference called during Mrs P.'s pregnancy – a conference to which no one who had had any dealings with the family was invited – decided to separate her from the forthcoming baby.

Four months after the November raid, magistrates dismissed the social services department's case and returned the baby to her parents. Despite this, she was again taken into care three years later when a cut was found on her arm. Social workers refused to accept Mrs P.'s explanation that the child had been hurt while out playing.

(Mr P. was, incidentally, in Scotland at the time of the incident.) Once again, magistrates returned her to her mother.

In November 1984 Birmingham social services made a third attempt to remove the child. Mrs P. had taken her to hospital with a cut above one eye. A social worker asked the little girl how it had happened, and chose to disbelieve the child's answer that she had fallen against a coffee table at home. Yet subsequent forensic tests on the table confirmed the story. Once again, magistrates re-united her with her parents, but this time it took nine months for the case to come to court. In the course of the last two attempts to take the child into care social workers completely failed to speak with her teachers. Had they done so the school report would have painted a picture of a happy, well-cared-for little girl.

The problems of social workers

At this point it is only fair to record the particular stresses involved in social work. Underfunding is endemic in a profession forever walking an impossible tightrope between over-intervention and complacency of the sort that led to the deaths of Lucy Gates, Maria Colwell, Jasmine Beckford – and a depressingly long list of other cases of fatal child abuse.

In addition, research completed in 1986 indicates that social workers can expect to be physically attacked once a year. Mandy Smith was a 24-year-old generic (non-specialist) field social worker when she was attacked by a client. She is now nervous in her job and afraid of more violence. She was given no time off after the attack and no counselling to help her over what was by any standards a vicious and potentially lethal assault. 'I went into the house of a woman I'd known for a few months. For what I saw as no reason at all she just set upon me – swinging me round the room by my hair, thumping me in the head, then pinning me down on a chair and saying I wasn't going to leave the house alive.'

Mandy Smith was lucky – the woman's son came in and saved her life. Others are less fortunate; cases of murder or manslaughter are disturbingly more common than they used to be, but still rarely make an impact on the government or public.

'People assume that the police are in a risk-taking business, but they don't make the same assumption for social workers,' a spokesman for the British Association of Social Workers warned. At the time BASW had at least three cases of social workers killed while on call on its books. 'If a policeman is killed on duty the sympathy extends from 10 Downing Street downwards. If a social worker is killed we get no such supportive noises, yet there is a tremendous fuss when something goes wrong.'

The strain of constant potential violence (in late 1983 a survey by Cambridge University Institute of Criminology showed that one in three social workers in England and Wales had been attacked during the previous five years), and a widespread belief that their profession is ill-regarded and only worthy of attention when a child is battered to death, has led to a steady loss of confidence among many social services staff. In October 1986 the local government union NALGO produced a survey which claimed that many social workers were 'burnt out' by their early forties.

The problem has an additional knock-on effect. Many social workers now privately admit to advising trainees and colleagues not to become emotionally involved in any way with their clients. The results of such a policy when dealing with young and vulnerable children in care can be devastating.

Children in care

So far we have dealt with the system in relation to parental rights. But how does it deal with its consumers – the 100,000 children who depend on local authorities for their mental and physical development? According to Ron Lacey of the mental health organisation MIND, 'For many youngsters, and particularly adolescent youngsters, it's no bloody good at all.'

MIND became involved in examining the care system after persistent claims of human rights abuses involving mental health techniques being forced on children in care. We shall examine these shortly. But MIND also had a general criticism of the system.

> The evidence presented suggests that the child care system is built on confusion which has accumulated and been reinforced by layers of legislation, conflicts of practice and goals, and a steadfast refusal to face facts.
> Notions of care, treatment and protection have tended to suffocate the principles of natural justice. Perceptions of how the system works and what it is for, vary alarmingly among those

who can assign people into it and those who provide it, and these seem to bear very little relation to how the consumers, children and their families, experience the end product; indeed it is the consumers who, on this evidence, seem to be most realistic. Objectively, the consumers of the care system are likely to be the poor and disadvantaged. Admission into the care system may be a recipe for personal destruction. Some survive, but others embark upon a career of institutional living, perpetual supervision, dependency and delinquency. [*In Whose Best Interests?*, MIND, 1980.]

In other words, the thinking behind 'care' has progressed very little since 1896 and the industrial school and reformatory system.

In theory, of course, the care system embodies that welfare principle laid down by mid-Victorian judges and specifically spelt out in the 1980 Child Care Act:

In reaching any decision relating to a child in their care, a local authority shall give first consideration to the need to safeguard and promote the welfare of the child throughout his childhood; and shall so far as practicable ascertain the wishes of and feelings of the child regarding the decision and give due consideration to them having regard to his age and understanding.

How well does the reality live up to that principle? In February 1983 the House of Commons Social Services Committee held hearings into the state of the care system. Denise Simpson gave evidence. Her statement is a lengthy one, but we reproduce it in full because it is all too typical of complaints from consumers of the care system.

Some people believe that the Local Authority always act in a 'child's best interests'. Well, unfortunately, this didn't happen to me.

At the age of thirteen I was given a full care order by the local juvenile court for minor offences I had committed when I was twelve. (Up until this time I had been in voluntary care of the National Childrens' Home from the age of three months.)

A case conference was held to decide where I should go. Later I learned that they had seriously considered putting me in Moss

Side or some other adult mental hospital. However, at ten minutes' notice I was taken from the Home to an all-girls Assessment Centre (formerly a remand home – which still ran along the same lines). I was here for seven weeks, during which time I absconded seven times as it was the 'in' thing to do. On returning from my last two absconsions (I was never out for more than a few hours) I acted out, i.e. threw objects across a room. Because of this the police were asked to handcuff me while a doctor was brought in and forcibly gave me an injection of Valium. When asked if I had calmed down I replied 'no', so the doctor got out another needle and gave me a dose of Largactil.

On my last return from absconding I was taken to semi-secure. (A room with a bed in it and windows that don't open.) I was kept here for over a week and special agency nurses were assigned to look after me. The only thing that kept me occupied during this time was watching the nurses crochet and learning to do it myself.

At the end of the week I had had enough so I tried to break out. However, this proved unsuccessful and the police were brought in immediately. There then followed a scuffle because I refused to be stripped by the staff and the police. More police were brought in and I was handcuffed before being thrown on the bed and given over 200 milligrams of Largactil.

The next day I was moved to a secure unit in Southampton; altogether there were six nurses looking after me each day. I had no contact with any other children despite the local doctor telling the superintendent that he was 'concerned at the way I was being isolated from children of my own age, and strongly recommended that this should not continue'.

Each day throughout my three-month stay I was given 125 mg of Largactil (orally). If I refused to take these tablets, then the doctor would be called to give me an injection.

After this three months I was moved to an open assessment centre. This didn't work out for various reasons, so I was moved back to the secure unit, where I stayed for a further eight months. I was treated the same way as I had been before (drugs etc.). I was allowed out six times in the last two months of my stay, and the only reason I left this place was because I ran off.

After a week of being 'on the run' I was picked up in London and taken to a girls' secure unit in Middlesex. Here I was seen by a psychologist; and the following quotes are from the psychological report he wrote on me.

Absconding and subsequent violent behaviour which Denise exhibited in Redhatch and Fairfield Lodge are essentially normal, since they are patterns of behaviour which people normally develop in situations where they are confined against their will, unless controls are very tight or a programme is created to avoid conflict situations.

She does not appear to be particularly delinquent or to have done very much by the standards of present-day delinquency, and nor does she appear to be particularly violent, unless placed in conflict situations where the naturally expected reaction is one of violence or, less frequently, apathy.

I twice tried to abscond from here; the second attempt was unsuccessful and I was thrown into my room, where I proceeded to smash it up out of sheer frustration. I was taken into the lounge where several nurses, staff and police were standing; they threw me on the sofa while I was given another injection.

It would be just as reasonable to conclude that since Denise has spent all her life virtually in care, that Denise's present predicament is the result of the failure of the caring and educational services as to labelling her as having a personality disorder, which is simply shorthand for being unable to define what the problem is.

I never knew where I was going to be moved to next or when I would be allowed to settle down. I had already been moved fourteen times since being in care. I was fed up with all the labels being stuck on me like having a 'personality disorder' or being 'disturbed'. I was eventually told that I would be moving to a Youth Treatment Centre in Birmingham (a long-term secure unit for 'seriously disturbed' young people). On the date I was supposed to move I was told that I would now be going to a Youth Treatment Centre in Essex on another date.

Since the day I first had my care order, I was given no education whatsoever, despite having asked for it at every available opportunity, as well as pointing out that it was illegal not to receive education.

I was also disappointed at the lack of contact I had with my family and close friends as they were only allowed to visit once. All my mail was opened and read at each secure establishment I have been in.

I remained in the Youth Treatment Centre for three years. The first six months of my stay was spent in a totally secure house, where I was allowed out (with staff) about six times. Each night we were locked in our 'rooms', which contained an unmoveable wooden bed, a small cabinet, pretty curtains hiding a 'plastic' bullet-proof, flame-proof, shatter-proof 'window' with metal bars behind it.

I was then moved to a less secure house (supposedly) where I could go out more frequently. The education here was minimal, mainly catering for the 'slow' ones.

Fortunately, I didn't have to take drugs here (although by this time I wanted them as I had become addicted). I only had injections here when the staff could not control me, or if they thought I was going to be violent.

My last injection resulted in me being rushed to hospital (after I had fainted) and having a stomach pump.

Absconding was looked on as a serious 'crime' and each time I returned (sometimes of my own accord) I was locked up in a cell or my room.

I haven't really elaborated on what happened to me in these secure units because it would take a whole book to do so. I have just given general information to give a brief idea.

What happened to me in these institutions has happened to a lot of other young people who go through the 'care' system often through no fault of their own, but because there is no one to turn to, to complain to, then this sort of treatment is allowed to continue under the pretence of 'acting in the child's best interests'. (Hansard, 9 February, 1983.)

Denise Simpson gave evidence on behalf of NAYPIC – the National Association of Young People in Care. By the time we interviewed her she had fulfilled the MIND prediction of a continuing institutional life for many care cases; she was serving a short sentence in a low-security womens' prison.

Denise was not unique. NAYPIC and the Children's Legal Centre have consistently drawn attention to gross violations of the human rights of children in care. Both have called for a Children's Charter to safeguard fundamental rights: the right to freedom of association, the right to adequate accommodation and food, the right to some form of privacy and the end of letter-opening by home staff, the right to refuse medication, the right to have a say in future placements. None of these rights exist in law.

In theory, of course, a child – in care or anywhere else – has the same common-law rights as an adult. It follows, then, that the child has a right to sue in, for example, cases of alleged assault. But how does a child in care go about doing so?

The testimony of Denise Simpson (among others) led to a tightening up in the use of secure accommodation to house children in care. On 25 May 1983, new DHSS regulations banned local authorities from locking up children in secure units for more than seventy-two hours unless a juvenile court had sanctioned this. The government also drew up a list of 552 accredited 'lock-ups' – units which range from forty-bed buildings to single cells. The regulations also banned the practice of locking children in care in their rooms, or locking internal doors so that they were confined to specific areas of an institution, unless sanctioned by a court order. Lock-ups also needed to have functioning alarms to comply with the DHSS rules. All these were restrictions put on local authorities, and therefore rights given to children in care.

There is, however, no system of enforcing them. Both NAYPIC and the Children's Legal Centre have long campaigned for an independent complaints system to be set up. It still doesn't exist. And although there is an assumed right to legal advice for children in care, some secure units can in practice exclude almost anyone they choose from their premises.

Furthermore, it may not be in the best interests of staff to support the children against the local authority. In April 1986 David Sherwell, a social worker in charge of a Salford assessment centre – Park House – was dismissed by the Council for gross misconduct. In fact he had refused to admit a child to the unit because it had no functioning alarms. He was abiding by the DHSS regulations; the Council was not. He was acting in the childrens' interests; Salford City Council was not. David Sherwell was sacked. 'I had been complaining about the alarms for years and finally decided I couldn't go on risking these children's lives. There had been an incident some time back of a child using a light bulb to cut himself. . . . I had to take a stand.'

Salford City Council's response when the case came to light was that it, not the DHSS, was running Park House.

The institutions which brought the issue of children's rights in care into the clearest focus, in 1984, were a private hospital called Spyway and its sister unit at the charitable St Andrews Hospital in Northampton. The regime adopted by a joint team of consultants to both units represented a microcosm of all that is wrong with the care system – at least as far as its consumers are concerned.

In fairness to both 'institutions' it should be recorded at the outset that neither was a shady backstreet operation. Both units promoted themselves with glossy advertising brochures, and both were served by an exceedingly well-qualified team of medical consultants led by an eminent mental health specialist, Dr Gavin Tennent. Equally, and perhaps more disturbingly in the light of what follows, there is no doubt that Dr Tennent and his team sincerely believed that that programme they had developed was in the best interests of those in their care.

However, we must also note that after the allegations made by former inmates received widespread publicity, St Andrews modified the treatment programme, and Dr Tennent left that hospital to concentrate on the Spyway unit. (There is, we must stress, no implication of anything untoward in his resignation.)

What, then, was the programme which caused so much controversy? Both St Andrews – a well-established psychiatric hospital – and Spyway were, in 1984, at the forefront of promoting a private-enterprise solution to the problem of troublesome teenagers in care. For a weekly fee of up to £900 Spyway, and three secure units at St Andrews, accepted 'disturbed' youngsters who were deemed to be beyond the control of local authority care staff. (The units also took private patients.)

There were two elements to the treatment programme devised by Gavin Tennent. The first was a rigorous 'behaviour modification' programme; the second was a largely experimental drug therapy scheme.

Behaviour modification as a concept began in the United States. Crudely speaking, it involves the offering of rewards and incentives for good behaviour. By the time it reached St Andrews and Spyway, behaviour modification was a well-established practice in both mental illness and difficult care cases.

During the early 1980s a committee of the Mental Health Commission – the government-appointed body which regulates psychiatric practice – was considering the pros and cons of behaviour modification. It was eventually to lay down guidelines on the use of the concept and on what should and should not constitute its 'rewards'.

By any standards both units went further than any other programme in this country. Linda spent several months on a behaviour modification ward at St Andrews. 'It was run by a token system, where you had to earn tokens for food, tokens to go out – you had to have paroles to go out, one hour every afternoon, and that's if you were more or less a saint, a saint for the whole day.'

This was the reward system. New inmates started on level one and earned tokens through 'good' behaviour for basics like food, association with other people and exercise in the grounds. If enough tokens weren't earned by the end of the day an inmate would not be given a meal. Instead, he or she was given Complan. Inmates could lose up to five meals a week in this way. Similarly, the right to 'ground parole' – free exercise periods in the hospital grounds – had to be earned, as did association with friends and visits from relatives.

In the opinion of some of Dr Tennent's colleagues in the medical establishment this regime was far from ideal. Dr Derek Russell-Davies, Emeritus Professor of Psychology at Bristol University, was one of the doubters.

> The idea of behaviour modification is that behaviour is modified by being rewarded. So if a kid does something that you approve of you give him a privilege, that's his reward. If he doesn't do it you deprive him of the privilege. The difficulty is when you deprive him of something that he should normally expect to have. There's a very difficult line between having something as a privilege and not having something that you ought to have.

Critics of Dr Tennent's programme argued that every child, whether in care or not, has an inalienable right to proper food, free association and contact with friends or relatives. As Rachel Hodgkin of the Children's Legal Centre pointed out, all these are guaranteed by the European Charter of Human Rights.

> We were very concerned about what happened at St Andrews and Spyway. They operated a system of rewards and punishments, which they call medical treatment, and we believe there should be definite legal controls on what punishments can be used on anybody. We know there are certain inalienable human

rights: the right to liberty, so long as it can be shown that the individual is not a danger to himself or others; the right to unrestricted meals; the right of access to friends and relatives and the right to communicate privately by letter or telephone. We also think, and this is endorsed by law, that they have a right to explicit, informed and continuing consent to their medical treatment.

Dr Tennent's use of extremely powerful psychotropic and other drugs was the second major cause for complaint – and with it went the issue of consent. For those young people placed in St Andrews and Spyway by their local authority consent might as well not have existed. It is true that there were consent forms, but these were signed by the social worker rather than the inmate. It was the social worker who consented to whatever drug treatment Dr Tennent's team chose to employ.

Yet the law is quite clear: children under sixteen have a right to consent to or refuse treatment. (What makes this all the more worrying is that the DHSS keeps no statistics on the use of drugs on children in care. In contrast, the Home Office keeps annual figures on the types of drugs that have been used on different types of prisoner, the time and the place.)

Inmates arriving at one of the behaviour-modification wards would often be given an EEG scan of the brain. At the time, Dr Tennent believed that a sort of epileptic explosion in part of the brain was responsible for the bad behaviour of teenagers who came to his units. Accordingly, he treated this 'episodic discontrol syndrome' with a long-established drug called Tegretol, generally used on *grand mal* epileptic seizures. Many youngsters were forced to take this drug. If they didn't they lost tokens and risked either missing meals or being downgraded to a lower level, with a consequent loss of ground parole.

Additionally, ex-inmates repeatedly alleged that they were given heavy doses of tranquillising drugs like Serenace, Lithium or Largactil – sometimes forcibly. Dr Tennent has subsequently denied over-using the drugs, but admitted that they were occasionally forcibly administered to 'damp down the fire' in 'very disturbed young people'.

In theory the forcible injection of drugs in this way could be grounds to sue for assault. Both units operated as closed environments, however; visits from relatives and social workers were often discouraged, and even the inmates' lawyers occasionally found it hard to obtain access to their clients. Mike Lewenden, a Northampton solicitor, had five clients on closed behaviour-modification wards at St Andrews in the summer of 1984. During one week, when the youngsters faced court review hearings to decide on their future, Lewenden found that they were denied access to legal advice.

> The people there get parole on a points system, and of course if they fail to achieve the right number of points by the relevant time they don't go out on parole – even if it's to see their lawyer. The whole system, it seems to me, is very much like the way a monkey is trained – you know, it rings the bell and gets the grape.

It's worth remembering at this point that many of the young people in St Andrews and Spyway had never been convicted of an offence and had never been given the opportunity to discuss their future at a case conference. They were simply regarded as troublemakers – typically for absconding – by their local authority, and placed in Dr Tennent's units. The youngsters themselves had a rather more direct phrase: 'We've been dumped in a loony bin.'

It was this way of treating children in care that most worried Ron Lacey of MIND.

> We'd been getting complaints about these places since 1976 – we've even had a petition which ten of the residents sent to us. When we got it I rang the medical superintendent and he invited me up to have a look at what was going on.
>
> When I got there I didn't see anything that could be described as brutality. However, what I did see was a group of young people, most of whom were in local authority care, not on mental health orders, and yet who were in a mental hospital. Of course they had histories – many of them – of getting into trouble with the law, and they were complaining to me about the use of drugs, the lack of consent, and the behaviour-modification programme. But most of all they were complaining about being locked up in a loony bin.
>
> So I looked into what sort of youngster ended up in there. About 60 per cent of them had been put into care at the age of

nine; from that point on they had a series of placements, one
after the other, and then by the time they became adolescent –
surprise, surprise – they became delinquent. But if you move
anyone around from pillar to post like that I don't think it's
surprising that they grow up with a few problems. That's the real
problem, and the programmes at St Andrews and Spyway –
unintentionally of course – just obscured it.

The real villains of the piece are the local authorities who are
providing a care system which for many youngsters is no bloody
good at all.

Youngsters like Linda, who was sent to St Andrews, agree
wholeheartedly.

I was six when I was taken into care for protection from my
parents. I went through about twenty-nine children's homes;
even though I'd never committed a crime in my life I was put
into remand homes and other lock-ups.

All right, I was disturbed – of course I was disturbed *then*.
Eventually, when I was fifteen, I took an overdose with a bottle
of drink. When I woke up I was in a psychiatric hospital – a
locked ward. I went from there to another psychiatric hospital.
Then I was taken – they said I was out of control – to St
Andrews.

Linda is extremely bitter about her life in care, and about Dr
Tennent's treatment programmes. But she has another, more visible, legacy from 'care': her arms are a fretwork of slashes and scars.
In the locked secure unit she fell into the (all-too-frequent) 'cutting
syndrome' – slashing her arms with sharp objects or broken glass.
At St Andrews and Spyway such behaviour was punished by loss of
'privileges'.

In the end my anger turned towards myself because I couldn't
express my anger back at them for fear of losing tokens. Everything I'd ever done I was being punished for. In the end I
believed I was bad, I was so sure that I was bad, so I just carried
on destroying myself, cutting all the way up my arms.

Interestingly, in America, where this type of behaviour-modification programme started, safeguards were introduced a decade ago to place far more responsibility on the institution to safeguard its inmates' well-being. In almost any state in America if a child in care cuts his wrists it is legally deemed an act of negligence on the part of the institution. In England, at Spyway and St Andrews, it was grounds for further punishment.

Elizabeth Arnold checked herself into St Andrews, suffering from chronic depression. She was not in care but endured the same regime and became friends with many youngsters who were.

Dr Tennent did not work on a regular behaviour-modification programme. It is supposed to work on a system of rewards, but the way it worked there was just to put the fear of God into you. You had no right to eat, for example, no right to wear clothes – it was really a system of punishment. Eventually people who were on those sort of wards broke down and gave in.

Allegedly they were then behaving socially, but I've seen people coming out of those wards who are seething heaps of rage and yet will tell you, 'I've learnt to control that behaviour now, there's nothing wrong with me.' Which is rubbish – the original problem, whatever it was, is still there.

To social workers like John Smith, who had responsibility for youngsters in both Spyway and St Andrews, the regimes were an abhorrent abuse of children in care. 'I know the kids can be difficult and downright bastards – I've been a policeman in my time so I know what it can be like. But there is no way, no possible way in child care, that it is right to attempt to break children down like that. Even if it succeeds it's too great a cost.'

Dr Tennent claimed some success for his programme. A research study he had commissioned showed some improvement in the majority of a sample group studied. But his units fulfilled a more symbolic role than just 'correcting' by methods more akin to a *Clockwork Orange* society a few of the thousands of children in state care. They symbolised a care system still based on the Victorian principle of intervening in children's lives without allowing them any say in what is to happen to them.

The sad irony of this system of second-class juvenile citizens is that even the social workers who maintain and run it admit that it is often unnecessary. In September 1986 the incoming president of the Association of Directors of Social Services, Mr Brian Kay, warned that children were being taken into care unnecessarily or kept there longer than was needed because social workers lived in fear of another Jasmine Beckford or Maria Colwell case. The circle has been completed. Social workers in fear of being publicly pilloried take too many children into care; parents facing unjustified care proceedings live in fear of never seeing their child again; and children in care all too often live in fear of institutional abuse and misery. It really is no way to bring up a generation.

Health rights

If, then, doctors have a *de facto* 'right' to force medical treatment on at least some of their patients, do the patients have any reciprocal rights? Is there any enforceable right to medical care?

The concept of a right to medical treatment came with the National Health Service Act of 1946. Prior to that health care was dependent on money or charity. The NHS Act, driven through Parliament in the face of fierce opposition from the medical profession, was intended to place the entire nation on the same medical footing. Regional boards were set up to administer the various voluntary hospitals that served the poor; medical treatment, drugs, glasses and false teeth were all to be provided free of charge.

Since 1946 the NHS has expanded to become one of the country's biggest employers and has pioneered surgical and medical techniques that have become the envy of the world – from ante-natal check-ups to heart transplants. But subsequent legislation has done little to create an inalienable right to immediate health care, building on the well-intentioned but non-specific aims of the 1946 Act. At the same time the health service has come under ever-increasing pressure, as our population grows and lives longer.

The closest our law comes to granting a specific right to medical treatment is the 1977 National Health Service Act, but even that Act does so only by implication. It imposes a duty on the Secretary of State for the DHSS to provide hospital services 'to such an extent as he considers necessary to meet all reasonable requirements'. Clearly this is not the same as granting an inalienable right, and depends on the discretion of a government minister.

The first major challenge to the exercise of that discretion came in November 1987. Significantly, it quickly failed.

Tuesday, 24 November 1987 was an important day in the short life of David Barber. David had been born five weeks earlier with a coin-sized hole in his heart. By 24 November a vital life-preserving operation had been postponed no fewer than five times. On each occasion his parents had been prepared to see their son undergo major surgery; on each occasion a shortage of specialist nursing staff forced postponement. On 24 November the Barbers went to the High Court seeking a ruling that would require surgeons at Birmingham Children's Hospital to operate immediately. The court ruled against them. It would, the judge decided, be 'inappropriate' for the law to intervene on their behalf.

The Barber case spelt out clearly the fact that there is no enforceable right to treatment. It also highlighted the plight of thousands of children and adults forced to wait years for vital surgery. At the Birmingham Children's Hospital alone, thirty-five children had their heart operations cancelled at short notice in the months of September and October 1987. Nor is Birmingham an isolated example. Area health authorities all over the country reported similar statistics in the wake of the David Barber case. In October 1986 two London paediatricians had organised a petition by doctors and surgeons, warning that they were unable to do their jobs properly because of a shortage of specialist nurses. The petition was delivered to the DHSS. It went unheeded, but within a year David Barber proved the point.

Within days of the Barber judgement the National Audit Commission produced a damning report on hospital delays. It showed that in a sample of just five regional health districts more than 11,000 badly needed operations were not carried out because of the lack of trained nursing staff. Simultaneously, government ministers claimed that the staff shortage was not caused by a lack of funding. That claim was manifestly untrue. Money is the key to the shortage of specialist nurses – a shortage which caused the postponement of David Barber's surgery and the death of at least one baby in the same health district. Eventually, David Barber did have his operation, but died within days.

The average NHS nurse can expect to earn up to £10,650 a year after six full years of training – less than many dustmen. If a nurse decided to undergo specialist training for theatre or intensive-care qualifications, she (or he) receives no extra payment even after qualification. Yet the pressures are immense. Margaret Farley is twenty-seven. She is one of only twenty-four intensive-care unit nurses at Birmingham Children's Hospital. The unit needs another twelve nurses to operate at full strength. 'We have to work our days off to ensure the operating theatres can run. I took an ICU course and got an extra qualification in treating pre-term babies, but I get no more money for my extra skills.'

Margaret Farley has been a nurse for nine years. She earns £10,000 a year. In London a newly appointed bus driver earns the same amount.

> There is a very high turnover in ICU staff. It's a rewarding but stressful aspect of nursing. Extremely ill children can be very unstable. They can be so unstable that you hardly dare turn them over to change a nappy. If it has come to the end and we can do no more it is a terrible moment when we have to decide to disconnect the drains and drips and ventilator – that part never gets any easier. Then we dress the baby up in a posh frock or a Babygro and give it to the parents so that they can be alone.

Small wonder, then, that many nurses simply decide not to put themselves through this kind of stress for so little reward. Small wonder that more than 1,000 nurses annually leave the NHS for much larger salaries in private hospitals. Small wonder that David Barber's parents went to court.

November 1987 was a key month in the short history of health care rights. By the time David Barber's case came before the High Court, more than forty years after the NHS was born, evidence was mounting that health care in Britain was beginning to resemble the pre-1946 days of money-oriented treatment. In November 200 hospital consultants in the West Midlands signed a letter addressed to the chairman of their regional health authority. In it they warned that hospitals in the area would not be able to cope with the needs of patients in the coming winter. The consultants put it bluntly: there was simply not enough cash to keep the system running, and that would lead to ethical problems over who to treat and who to ignore.

Two of them painted a picture of typical hospital chaos:

Routine surgical admissions – described as routine even though they are for operations that are required urgently – are frequently cancelled at the last minute due to the fact that beds have been taken by emergency admissions.

We had a patient with cancer of the stomach whose admission was cancelled. That is somebody in an ideal world you would see one morning, bring in and operate on the next day. The only way to get this gentleman admitted was through casualty as an emergency. Then we said, 'This man must come in, he must have a bed', and he was therefore moved from the routine admissions to an emergency admission.

The reason for all this was quite simple: the hospital – and many others like it in inner-city areas – didn't have enough beds or enough staff to keep up with the demand. And this is a demand not for state-of-the-art micro-surgical techniques but for the basic, bread-and-butter medical care we have come to take for granted.

One of the doctors went on to describe being forced to leave patients – including the very old – waiting on trolleys in the casualty department corridors for up to twelve hours while a vacant bed was found or created.

I have had eighty- and eighty-five-year-old patients with broncho-pneumonia, with heart attacks and with strokes, sitting on trolleys in casualty all day. They are waiting for beds. That leaves me phoning around; it also leaves me responsible for them but not able to treat them. There are treatments that cannot be given in the casualty department.

Even when a bed is found, it may be in the wrong type of ward where staff are not trained or even supplied with the basic equipment necessary to treat that type of patient. And it comes down to one thing: money. For however much this or previous administrations spend on the NHS has simply not been enough to provide a nationwide and efficient health care system for all.

The cash crisis, coupled with an ever-aging population calling ever more frequently on the NHS, has caused an additional problem. Junior hospital doctors – typically just out of medical school and in their first job – are often required to work 100-hour weeks. The implications of this are obvious: their ability to concentrate and to diagnose correctly tail off dramatically towards the end of their shifts. Mistakes occur – mistakes which can be literally a matter of life or death.

We should not, in all fairness, blame these overworked doctors. Yet that is precisely what the law requires of us, because in order to receive compensation for a doctor's mistake the patient has to prove negligence. And establishing that can be a monumental task.

For a start, the definition of negligence is very precise. Negligence is defined as 'the omission to do something which a reasonable man, guided upon those considerations which ordinarily regulate the conduct of human affairs, would do; or doing something which a prudent and reasonable man would not do'. (A definition spelled out in the case of Blyth *v*. Birmingham Waterworks Co. in 1856.) A simple and honest mistake by a doctor – even if it costs the patient his life – is not evidence of negligence.

Furthermore, doctors in Britain belong to one of two professional insurance companies – the Medical Defence Union and the Medical Protection Society. According to the pressure group Action for the Victims of Medical Accidents (AVMA), the organisations habitually impede compensation settlements. 'In almost every case liability is not admitted by the doctor, and their societies act just like insurance companies disputing every claim,' says Derek Kartun, spokesman for AVMA. 'Although we are dealing with decent people, the system makes them behave callously and without regard for the victim.'

On 14 May 1981, David Woodhouse, a twenty-seven-year-old married man with four young children, went into hospital for an operation to remove his appendix. He was routinely anaesthetised and the surgery performed, but he never woke up. David Woodhouse became a man in a coma, lying inert in a ward in Hereford Hospital.

The district administrator took immediate action; he recorded all the events surrounding the case and notified the area health authority. He also advised all the doctors involved to contact the Medical Defence Union. The area health authority checked the anaesthetic equipment and found it in normal working order (though, of course, it could have suffered a temporary fault during the operation). It then attempted to set up first a members' investigation and then a full independent enquiry under a legally qualified chairman. It was at this stage that the MDU entered the fray, instructing its members not to take part in any enquiry into the Woodhouse case. There has never been a public enquiry into what happened on 14 May 1981; no one who is admitted to Hereford Hospital can know just what caused David Woodhouse to go into coma – and therefore whether they risk the same fate.

AVMA receives an average of 1,000 requests for help every year; it does so despite shunning publicity for fear of an avalanche. It is clear from the cases it does handle that there is a sizable pool of patients who suffer at the hands of the medical profession, and that the compensation system either requires them to wait for years before receiving compensation or, worse still, denies them any hope of such a settlement.

In December 1985 the case of Linda Thomas made the point perfectly. She was awarded £679,264 after a routine operation to remove her tonsils went wrong and she suffered a brain haemorrhage and a heart attack. But the operation took place in 1975. Linda had been made to wait ten years for compensation from her anaesthetist and South Glamorgan Health Authority. It is cases like hers that make AVMA frequently attempt to dissuade victims from taking out a negligence claim; the distress and sheer length of time involved can cause ill health in itself.

Even then – and ironically – the timescale has another damaging effect on the compensation system. If the fight has been a long one the ultimate bill is likely to be higher. That in turn puts up insurance premiums and makes doctors extremely reluctant to take on difficult cases or carry out unnecessary tests in simple ones for fear of ruinous litigation.

In 1977 the highest sum awarded in a medical negligence claim was £132,970. By 1985 the record sum awarded had spiralled to £679,264. In August 1986 the MDU increased its subscription fee by more than two-thirds.

There is a simple way round all this: no-fault compensation. Such a scheme was introduced in New Zealand in 1982. Under it there is generally no need to go to court for compensation or to prove negligence. Payments are made from a special fund set up by the government, and are closely related to the future needs of the victim. Payments are generally much lower than the highest awards in the UK, but are supplemented by an index-linked income for life of up to £250 a week.

Additionally, if the award made by the State-run Accident Compensation Corporation is disputed and cannot be resolved by a review body or an independent tribunal, the victim or his relatives can take the case to court. In essence the New Zealand ideal has been to take compensation claims away from lawyers and the adversarial atmosphere of the court-room. 'The aim,' says Derek Gibson-Smith of the ACC, 'is to cut out legal fees, and we are not out to see how little we can get away with.'

Although the doctor concerned is protected from civil law suits under the scheme, he can be disciplined or even struck off. Victims and families have the right to ask the New Zealand Medical Association to investigate the case.

What chance is there of a similar system being introduced here? Promisingly, the MDU backs it, but the government, in the form of the Lord Chancellor's Department, has no plans to institute a no-fault compensation scheme. Instead the LCD ordered a review aimed at streamlining the present system and cutting costs by removing the right to a full court hearing in minor cases. This is probably the worst of all the worlds. If we must have an adversarial system to determine compensation, it makes little sense and bad justice to cut off access to that very process.

Education and the family

It would be wrong to leave this chapter without considering the rights of parents (and children) in education. After all, school is the most important formative influence on children outside the family and can have a marked effect on future employment prospects.

The main piece of legislation in this field was the 1944 Education Act. It imposes a duty on parents to ensure that a child receives 'efficient full-time education suitable to his age, ability and aptitude'. At the same time it required local education authorities to provide suitable schools. By and large the Act has survived the test of time well – although it never actually defined what a suitable education was. Nor did it spell out what a suitable school should be – which is where the problems begin.

In many LEA areas school buildings predate the 1944 Act by at least a century. Many are unsafe, shored up with makeshift girders and posts, yet our children continue to be led into them for compulsory education. Many teachers, like Caroline Rees, live with the fear of a major accident in their classroom. Ms Rees teaches twenty-six children aged five and six in a classroom divided by a row of scaffolding poles. The poles are there to stop the roof above falling in.

The rest of the school, Lincoln Green Primary in Leeds, is no better; by March 1987 headmaster Stewart Forster had been forced to abandon upstairs classrooms because the floors were unsafe. Elsewhere dry rot, wet rot and leaks plagued the building, gutters had collapsed and the playground surface was so bad that the children were banned from using it.

The problems at Lincoln Green are not new – a replacement school has been promised for the past fifteen years. But government cutbacks in local authority spending have meant that school-building and repair plans have to be shelved.

For parents and teachers alike there is no way to force a change through the courts; there is no education statute which defines any obligation as to the standard of school accommodation. This is why Chapel-en-le-Frith infant school in Derbyshire has been stoically awaiting disaster.

The school has 239 pupils, all aged between five and seven. It is split into two sites 300 yards apart. On one is the main building, erected in 1837. Across the road are a series of temporary classrooms put up forty years ago. Behind them a railway goods line runs within fifteen feet of the huts; every time a loaded 2,000-ton train passes by the school literally shakes to its foundations.

Generations of parents and teachers have been fighting for a new school for thirty years. In November 1986 Education Minister Kenneth Baker said: 'I can make no promises for this school or any other.'

Successive case laws have made it clear that should an accident happen and children be injured while at school the local authority can be sued for negligence. But English law does not allow such action to be taken before an accident actually happens – which is why the parents of Chapel-en-le-Frith have been waiting . . .

In July 1987 the Assistant Masters' and Mistresses' Association called for a legally-enforceable standard of school buildings to ensure a safe environment. At the Association's conference one teacher, Victor Luscombe, spelled out the problem:

> Successive governments have reduced educational expenditure. As the cuts began to bite, local education authorities were left with the unenviable choice of reducing the quality of teaching or

reducing the standards of non-statutory provision. The result was predictable.

Yet at the time the Association was meeting education had suddenly become a top priority for the newly elected Conservative government. Kenneth Baker promised a bill to radically improve (amongst other things) parents' right to choose their child's school.

In fact the 1981 Education Act already provided some measure of parental choice, but allowed education authorities a loophole. Under section 6 of the Act, LEAs can refuse to accept a parent's choice if it would prejudice the provision of efficient education or the efficient use of resources.

The loophole is wide enough for any LEA to duck out from an inconvenient choice. Additionally, many authorities began imposing so-called 'artificial limits' on the numbers of pupils to be allowed into any one school. The issue came to a head in the summer of 1987, when more than twenty parents in Dewsbury, West Yorkshire, demanded the right to send their children to a particular local school. Calderdale Council rejected the demand and insisted that the children be sent to another school in its catchment area. The case was clouded by racist overtones – the school rejected by the Dewsbury parents had an overwhelming majority of Asian pupils – but highlighted the weakness of the 1981 Act.

Under the Act there is provision for an appeals procedure to force LEAs to reconsider unpopular decisions. Calderdale Council refused to change its mind, so the Dewsbury parents exercised their final statutory right of appeal to the Education Secretary – the same Kenneth Baker who was simultaneously promising to introduce a new law guaranteeing parental choice of schools.

As part of their appeal the Dewsbury parents produced evidence that Calderdale was maintaining an artificially low intake level at the school they wished their children to attend. The Education Secretary declined to entertain their appeal.

The Dewsbury rebels sent their children to a makeshift school held in a local pub – and did so quite legally until Calderdale gave in. The 1944 Act allows parents to arrange private tuition for their children in any suitable place. It also allows parents to educate their own children, provided that the local authority is satisfied with the standard of tuition.

John and Lynette Cameron satisfied their LEA that they were

more than well qualified to teach their three teenage daughters at home. The Camerons, from Earley in Berkshire, are both trained teachers. But in 1986 they launched a case on the long road to the European Court of Human Rights because, they claimed, their right to home teaching was being undermined by the DHSS.

Under normal circumstances two of the couple's three daughters – one aged fifteen, the other seventeen – would attract for their parents child benefit of £7 a week each, but a clause in the Child Benefit Act has robbed the Camerons of the benefit. Under its provisions the DHSS does not recognise the home as an educational establishment. And to qualify for benefit, the Camerons' daughters are required to attend a recognised educational establishment.

'The money aspect isn't the important thing,' Lynette Cameron said. 'It's the principle involved. But to a lot of other parents the loss of child benefit is a very important consideration.'

Perhaps *the* most important consideration, though, is actually getting the right schooling for your child. By and large, although faced with dwindling budgets and a diminishing supply of textbooks, most schools manage to fulfil the spirit (if not always the letter) of the 1944 Act. Children with special educational needs can, however, be caught in departmental crossfire as rival government agencies fight not to pay the bill.

The 1981 Education Act changed the previous policy of segregating children with special needs. Under its provisions LEAs – wherever reasonably possible – were required to keep such children in ordinary schools rather than send them to specialist schools. That at least was the theory. In May 1986 the Centre for Studies on Integration in Education (CSIE) – part of the Spastics Society – found that many parents and children were getting a very poor deal.

In the CSIE study half of the sixty-five English and Welsh LEAs were found to have failed to explain to parents (as required by the Act) how they went about assessing a child's needs, and that the parents could object to their assessment. Most failed to give any more than piecemeal information.

Lack of information is not the only problem facing parents of 'special needs' children. John and Teresa Wallace took Oxfordshire Education Authority to court in November 1986. Their nine-year-old son Allan, who suffers from a chomosome disorder, had been refused vital speech therapy by the authority a year previously – despite an admission that he had special educational needs and a recognition that the 1981 Act required LEAs to cater for such needs in ordinary schools. The bid failed. Lord Justice May told the couple (in an unenforceable *obiter dicta*) that the provision of Allan's speech therapy 'should be a matter for the health authority'.

Such decisions do not bode well for the future of integrated schooling. Yet at the same time parents like Lucy Goodison, whose daughter Corey is brain-damaged, face the prospect of their LEAs closing down special schools. Ms Goodison, once a supporter of integration, is now campaigning to keep Samuel Rhodes School in London, where her daughter has made rapid progress, open. If the Oxfordshire decision were repeated nationwide, children like Corey Goodison could be caught in the crossfire.

Crumbling schools, home education bills, special needs, parental choice: the unifying factors are well-intentioned but vague legislation – and a cash crisis.

As long as education cut-backs continue, the statutory rights of parents, children and teachers will continue to be eroded or simply unenforceable. Of course cut-backs are not new in themselves, but the scale of them – and of the problem areas needing money – is. And it is pointless, as we have observed elsewhere, to create rights unless the infrastructure to enforce them is maintained.

Perhaps the most telling – and saddest – picture of the decline in education is none of these obvious examples. It is, instead, the relatively new creation of sponsored teaching materials. In a survey in September 1986 the National Consumer Council found that one-third of their random sample of such textbooks were inaccurate and half were overtly biased in favour of the sponsor.

The assessors found one booklet for schools from the Kelloggs company in which the brand name appeared ninety-six times in just eighteen pages. In another, produced for children by Lever Brothers, a guide was entitled 'How to tell the difference between a good quality dishwashing liquid (like Sunlight Lemon Liquid) and a cheaper dishwashing liquid'. Levers produce Sunlight.

If educational standards can be privatised to that extent, what price our rights?

FIVE

Masters and Servants

'"When *I* use a word," Humpty
Dumpty said in a rather scornful tone,
"it means just what I choose it to mean –
neither less nor more."'

Lewis Carroll,
Through the Looking Glass

The building which houses the Supreme Court of New South Wales is a modern, unfussy block; it has none of the Victorian subfusc of the original parts of Britain's Old Bailey, nor the gothic extravagance of the Courts of Justice in the Strand.

By November 1987, the British government had chosen to spend an estimated £2 million and fourteen months preparing itself for a lengthy courtroom battle. It should perhaps have known better. If the Sydney court building is clean-cut and uncomplicated, the Australian view of law and government can be similarly straightforward.

The issue ostensibly at the heart of the case was a serious breach of confidence and official secrets by a former government employee who wanted to publish a book of his memoirs. In reality, the ex-employee was a former member of MI5, the British domestic security service, and his memoirs contained dramatic allegations that MI5 had illegally bugged and burgled its way across London. At one stage it had even plotted the downfall of the then Labour Prime Minister, Harold Wilson. For good measure Wright also included allegations that the former head of the Security Service had been a Russian spy.

Wright's claims were, by almost any Western nation's standards, serious and legitimate matters of public concern. Many of them had previously been aired in public by journalists and authors. Yet in September 1985, the British government decided to embark on what became a protracted legal battle to suppress the book, *Spycatcher*. Its conduct of the case has been the clearest exposition of the way we are governed in Britain. By the time the government's three QCs, teams of solicitors, press officers and the then Cabinet Secretary, Sir Robert Armstrong, arrived at the New South Wales court block the case had descended to the levels of Lewis Carroll's absurd fantasies. Inside that court building every word of Peter Wright's MI5 allegations was officially agreed to be true and accurate, but outside the court the allegations remained untrue, inaccurate and unprintable – according to the very same government officials. Truth, to the British government, meant different things within the space of a few feet. Humpty Dumpty would have been impressed.

The theory of government

This chapter is concerned with the governance of Britain – who is master and who is servant? And what rights do both have when the other breaks the rules? Who actually creates a law, and under what pressures or circumstances? And in whose best interest are they planned? Do they always apply equally to both governments and the governed, to master and to servant?

As we have seen, this country has no written constitution; instead we have a series of conventions which, in theory at least, regulate the way government operates. The structure starts, at the top, with the Queen, in whose name government is carried out. Underneath her are the three principal arms of government: the Executive, the Legislature, and the Judiciary. The constitutional convention is that the Executive – comprising all government ministers, officials and departments, including the most senior body, the Cabinet – is the servant of the Legislature – the Houses of Parliament – and is charged with putting into effect the laws those Houses pass. In turn the Judiciary attends to their enforcement.

In theory, all three arms are separate and independent – though the ultimate master of all is the Legislature. The practice is, of course, rather different.

The reality of government is that the monarch, in whose name all is done, has no power whatsoever. And rather than being the simple servant of the wishes and intentions of both Houses of Parliament, the Executive is actually their master – and a strict, uncompromising master at that.

All this may sound dry and rather irrelevant. What, after all, does it matter who is the ultimate boss, provided the work gets done? The answer lies in the nature of that work. Although every government clings stubbornly to the fiction that it simply implements the will of the majority of the population, each has its own dogma, creeds and beliefs that it wishes to enact regardless of pubic opinion. Nor is all its work simply directed towards that goal: the function of government in Britain is as often as not to serve itself and prevent the public from finding out.

To that end all governments employ strong-arm forces both within and without the palace of Westminster. Inside, the task is to keep MPs in line and behind the government; outside, the task is to keep politically sensitive operations secret.

Secrecy is endemic in Britain; it exists throughout Parliament and in local councils up and down the land (we shall examine the way local authorities often ride roughshod over their electorate later on in this chapter). The reason it exists is quite simply that information is power – without it there is no effective challenge to laws, edicts, actions or decisions taken by those in charge. Secrecy is the British Disease.

Governments and Parliament

Britain is nominally a democratic country, ruled by the trinity of Executive, Legislature and Judiciary. In fact, of course, it operates as a refined form of Cabinet dictatorship, subject to loose democratic control in Parliament; this makes the flow of information to MPs crucial to the democratic system, and by extension crucial to all of us.

Governments communicate information in a wide variety of ways: through Green (discussion) Papers, White (proposal) Papers, statements in the Commons or in public, or through the workings of a mysterious body called the Lobby – of which more shortly. In addition, MPs traditionally have the right to acquire information independently from ministers – usually through special select committees set up to enquire into or monitor specific issues, or through the device of Parliamentary Questions.

Parliamentary Questions can be either written or oral. In either case the aim is to make the minister answering questions about his department's activities provide complete and accurate information. But if you pick up any copy of Hansard (the verbatim daily account of proceedings in Parliament) you will see that the reality is starkly different: ministers have mastered the arts of evasion and half-truth. Thus, when Leon Brittan was Home Secretary, he was asked for details of firearms registered in each police area of the country. Hansard records his answer: 'Such information is not recorded centrally for England and Wales and could not be obtained without disproportionate cost.'

Similarly, when Dr Rhodes Boyson, then an education minister, was questioned about the *per capita* cost of tools and materials for woodwork, metalwork and pottery in schools, he explained, that: 'The information is not available as the returns . . . do not differentiate between materials and equipment used for different subjects.'

At first sight neither of these two examples appears materially to affect our lives. Yet the question of resources in education is crucial to our children's schooling – schooling for which taxpayers (and, on their behalf, MPs) are responsible. And, with the number of violent crimes involving firearms rising year by year, it is surely not unreasonable for Parliament to want to know just how many guns are licensed, where and by whom. Yet the government chooses not to say, claiming that the figures are unavailable at a proportionate cost – whatever that means. In fact the cost of providing information is often cited as a reason for not answering MPs' questions.

On other occasions ministers simply 'tough it out'. On 15 November 1983 the following question was asked of the DHSS: 'How many National Health Service beds have been taken out of use since 9 June as a result of restrictions on expenditure?' The answer was brief and unenlightening: 'The information requested is not available.' Why not? Such statistics and analysis are kept routinely by district health authorities. Even if ministers and officials were not actually monitoring just how many beds were de-commissioned due to spending cuts (and it's hard to think they do not), a few phone calls or letters would have produced the necessary figures.

As a refinement to the 'unavailability' response, some ministers and their departments have perfected the technique of answering a question by simply re-phrasing it. So, on 30 November 1983, the following exchange took place:

Question: 'How often does the Radiochemical Inspectorate inspect sites licensed for the disposal of radioactive wastes?'
Answer: 'The number of visits is determined by the radiological significance of the disposal.'

By this circular path the minister avoided parting with any information whatsoever. (It is sheer coincidence that all the ministers quoted here are Conservatives; both main parties have an equally dismal record on the provision of information to Parliament.)

Evasion is not the only shot in a government's locker. There is a list of subjects about which MPs cannot even ask questions (a list which was, almost inevitably, itself secret until disclosed by the *Sunday Times* in 1971). Some of these no-go subjects are ludicrous. MPs may not, for example, request information about the day-to-day business of either the White Fish Authority or the British Sugar Council; equally taboo are questions about the wages paid to agricultural workers.

Some closed subjects have more serious implications, however. Neither the activities of MI5 nor its sister unit MI6, are ever the subject of ministerial answers. Similarly out of bounds is the subject of the British Nuclear Police, a shadowy body accountable to the Home Secretary; yet he may not be questioned by MPs on the issue.

Every year the Civil Aviation Authority records details of near-misses, when one aircraft flies uncomfortably close to another, but the figure is not available to Parliament. Every year the Home Secretary authorises a number of telephone taps by the police and security services, but no MP may question him on the propriety of his decision in any individual case (assuming that an MP can ever find out whether a telephone intercept was in fact authorised and carried out) – even when the case is long over and closed.

The operational behaviour of the police may also prove a taboo subject. In the autumn of 1986 the Scottish Liberal MP Archie Kirkwood began asking questions of the Scottish Crown Office about the seemingly bizarre death of a Glasgow solicitor and anti-nuclear campaigner called Willie McRae. McRae had been found in his car on a remote Highland moor with a bullet in his head, and suicide was assumed. Yet his papers were discovered outside the car, and the gun which killed him was some twenty yards away on the other side of the car – circumstances which made suicide look distinctly unlikely. But no Fatal Accident Enquiry (the Scottish equivalent of an inquest) was ever held.

Instead, a simple announcement was made that there were no suspicious circumstances surrounding the death. Kirkwood began by asking to see a copy of both the pathologist's post-mortem report and the official police enquiry. He was told that both were confidential – even though there was no further action planned on the death.

Puzzled, he submitted a further thirty-six questions about the incident. To lodge questions MPs must go through a department called the Table Office. To his amazement Kirkwood found that the Table Office refused to accept thirty-two of the questions on the grounds that they dealt with information contained in the police and post-mortem reports – which the Crown Office had already refused to release. Amongst other subjects on which he had sought information were details of the road and weather conditions on the night McRae died – that information had apparently become a State secret.

And yet, according to the Prime Minister, it is part of a minister's job to produce information for MPs. In 1984, Mrs Thatcher, rejecting calls for a Freedom of Information Act, said:

> Under our constitution ministers are accountable to Parliament for the work of their departments, and that includes the provision of information. A statutory right of public access would remove this enormously important area of decision-making from ministers and Parliament and transfer ultimate decisions to the courts.
>
> Above all, ministers' accountability to Parliament would be reduced and Parliament itself diminished. In our view the right place for ministers to answer for their decisions in the essentially 'political' area of information is Parliament.

Mrs Thatcher's argument is essentially humbug. The sovereignty or supremacy of Parliament is one of those trite fictions which few MPs believe, but even fewer will attack. The reality of parliamentary life is that the government only answers those questions it welcomes or those which it cannot avoid, and successive governments have allowed 'traditions' to develop by which sensitive areas of parliamentary life go unchallenged. Before committing herself so boldly to the cause of ministerial responsibility for information-giving, Mrs

Thatcher might have been well-advised to consult Hansard for 21 November 1979.

At the time, the scandal of Sir Anthony Blunt's unmasking as a Russian spy was dominating Parliament. The Prime Minister was asked how many people had been questioned after the defection of Blunt's colleagues Burgess and Maclean in 1951, and how many civil servants had been sacked. Her reply hardly conforms to the rosy image of ministerial responsibility she outlined in 1984. 'Not all those questioned were themselves under suspicion, and *it would not be in the public interest to give numbers.* A number of people left the public service or were transferred [our emphasis added].'

The Prime Minister – the only government minister with responsibility for spies and full access to information about them – was then asked if she would answer questions on the security and intelligence services. To no one's great surprise she refused. In fact Mrs Thatcher has provided a short list of barred topics about which she refuses to answer questions. It includes 'security matters; telephone interception; Cabinet committees and detailed arrangements for the conduct of government business' – in short all the major responsibilities of the Prime Minister plus a few of those rightly belonging to her most senior Cabinet ministers.

The other main method by which MPs can obtain information from government departments is the select committee system. There are, confusingly, two varieties of committee in Parliament: the standing committees, which examine draft bills, and the select committees. The latter cover the work of all ministries and departments, monitoring policy and performance. Prior to 1979 the select committee system was disorganised and scanty. After that date a committee was set up for every government department, thus creating, in theory at least, a workable system of accountability. Inevitably, however, there are problems.

The committees, made up of members of all major parties, operate on an inquisitorial (rather than party politically adversarial) system – which should provide a reasoned and detailed method of dissecting an issue. But too many MPs – particularly those who are, or have been, in government – tend to view this as an unwelcome distraction from the main business of politics – the voluble abuse of your colleagues and rivals. Michael Foot, for example, the former Labour Party leader, habitually referred to the pre-1979 committees as 'sewing parties'.

More importantly, perhaps, the committees suffer from a lack of research commitment and back-up. Unlike the powerful Congressional committees in the United States, Westminster's select committees are not serviced by teams of dynamic young lawyers who can make their names in ferreting out inaccuracies, inconsistencies and plain lies by government departments. Instead, they are often former Foreign Office staff, frequently close to retirement, who are unlikely to go out of their way to upset the departmental apple-cart.

Worse still, the committees' powers to summon ministers and officials to give evidence is a good deal less impressive than might at first appear. There are many examples in the history of select committees of departments refusing to allow their ministers or senior civil servants to testify.

In February 1976 Harold Wilson, then Prime Minister, refused to allow Harold Lever to appear before a committee looking into the government's rescue of the Chrysler car company. Lever, who held no portfolio within the government, had been sent by Wilson to see the Shah of Iran and attempt to persuade him to switch a contract from Chrysler to another British-based firm. Wilson didn't want the committee to question Lever about details of the trip – nor about previously leaked splits in the Cabinet over the Chrysler issue.

Then, after the select committee system got fully into its stride in 1979, the Attorney General at the time, Sir Michael Havers, barred the Director of Public Prosecutions from appearing before the Home Affairs Committee which was investigating deaths of people in police custody. The Attorney General is both politician and independent law officer; the DPP is simply a law officer and senior civil servant. Amongst other tasks, his job is to decide, on the basis of evidence supplied by the police, whether any individual case stands a more than 50/50 chance of successful prosecution. There can be no legitimate reason for protecting him from the select committee system.

Of course, legitimacy is a commodity often in short supply. On 6 July 1984 it was noticeable by its absence.

Michael Legge was, at that time, head of the Ministry of Defence's general (non-Nato) policy division. On that day in July he sent an internal memo to his Armed Forces Minister, John Stanley. Its subject was a request by the Foreign Affairs Committee for a series of MOD papers. The papers themselves related to the sinking two years previously of the elderly Argentinian cruiser,

General Belgrano, during the Falklands conflict. From the date on which the *Belgrano* was sunk, 2 May 1982, there had been a sordid and entirely unnecessary deception of Parliament by the government over the circumstances of the action.

After the hostilities were over the Foreign Affairs Committee had begun an enquiry into the future of the Falkland Islands. This led them to consideration of the various peace plans which had been put forward and, since it had been alleged that the *Belgrano* had been sunk to avoid just such a plan, into an investigation of the government's actions and subsequent conduct. On 28 June the Committee formally asked for a list of 'all changes in the Rules of Engagement [ROE] issued to HM Forces in the South Atlantic between 2 April and 15 June 1982'. It fell to Michael Legge to draft a reply.

By the summer of 1984, the cover-up had not only been instigated and perpetuated, it had also been abandoned once (briefly and only within the MOD) before being re-adopted. With this in mind Legge recommended refusing the Committee's request. He put forward several reasons: the rules were classified; they would need paraphrasing to be intelligible, which would be too time-consuming; and finally: 'In addition a full list of changes would provide more information than Ministers have been prepared to reveal so far about the *Belgrano* affair. . . . I therefore recommend that we should avoid these difficulties by providing the committee with a more general narrative . . .'

Legge's first two reasons were nonsense – and he must have known it. For one thing, they were self-contradictory – by paraphrasing them the ROE would no longer be classified. Equally, whilst it was true that providing the information would be time-consuming, that is not accepted as a proper reason for refusing to do so. The real reason was the third: ministers had kept Parliament in the dark, deceiving MPs about the *Belgrano* affair for two years, and could not now change course. Clive Ponting, the MOD civil servant who was ultimately to lose his job over the *Belgrano* cover-up, was stunned.

> This advice was fully in line with the directions given by Michael Heseltine [then Secretary of State for Defence] and John Stanley in April and May about the way information should be released

to Parliament. But this was going a stage further than the refusal
to provide information to a persistent backbench MP.

Ministers were now involved in blocking an enquiry by a
Select Committee which had the right to enquire and get truthful
answers. Ministers were also going to provide a misleading
memorandum that would at best be 'consistent with previous
statements' and which had the clear purpose of blocking any
further enquiries. [Clive Ponting, *The Right to Know*, Sphere,
1985.]

Ponting knew that what Heseltine, Stanley, Legge and the rest of
the MOD were planning was quite simply a complete breach of the
good faith that is supposed to govern all departments' relationships
with their monitoring select committees. At first he could not
believe that they would carry on the cover-up. But on 13 July 1984,
Stanley signed and sent an anodyne note along the lines suggested
by Legge's memo to the Committee. Ponting turned the issue over
in his mind for two days. Then, on 16 July, he mailed a copy of the
memo to the Labour MP Tam Dalyell – the backbencher who had
pursued the government rigorously for the past two years over the
Belgrano affair – together with a draft letter to him that had been
suppressed because it gave too much away.

Dalyell, an ascetic, uncompromising Scot, suddenly found that
he had irrefutable evidence that Parliament and the Foreign Affairs
Committee had been deceived. After much consideration he decided
to place Ponting's papers before the Committee members so that
they could see for themselves how the MOD was misleading them.
The Committee then decided to ask Heseltine to give evidence and
explain just what was going on. Incredibly, members also agreed to
hand back the Ponting papers to the MOD. 'Within ten days they
were back inside the Ministry of Defence. . . .This was an extraordinary decision by a Select Committee of the House of Commons
which had been misled by the Government. Where was Parliament's
old ability and duty to stand up to the Executive and assert its
rights?' (Clive Ponting, ibid.)

Where indeed? Ponting, a high-flying civil servant who had
believed in the creed of duty to Parliament, not merely loyalty to his
current political masters, was subsequently charged with breaking
section 2 of the Official Secrets Act, which is hauled out depressingly
regularly to silence anyone who dares to warn us what a government

is up to. He was acquitted, though he lost his job and career. None of those involved in the far more serious business of deceiving Parliament – Michael Heseltine, John Stanley and Michael Legge – faced as much as a slap on the wrist for their conduct.

Two very important doctrines run in tandem with the historic theory of the separation of powers: Cabinet responsibility and ministerial responsibility. The former, reflecting the dominance of the Cabinet of any government over the rest of Parliament, is designed to ensure that whatever arguments go on behind closed doors on any given policy, all Cabinet ministers adopt the same stance in public. What of course this means is that Ministers who disagree with a particular policy are effectively silenced if Cabinet thinking goes against them.

This doctrine of 'don't tell the others' even extends to disclosing the existence of Cabinet committees and what they may or may not have discussed. It was as a result of this that Judith Hart, Minister for Overseas Development in the last Labour government found herself in an invidious and embarrassing position. Hart was being pressured to set up a group of civil servants from a number of Whitehall developments to coordinate and improve foreign aid. In fact just such a body already existed – but because it was a Cabinet committee, and because all such bodies are officially secret, neither she nor her colleagues felt able to tell a Commons committee dealing with the issue about the group.

Apart from the fact that, for no good reason, Parliament – in the shape of the Commons committee – was being kept in the dark, this absurd situation grew more farcical still. James Callaghan, the Prime Minister, sent round a note to all his Cabinet colleagues swearing them to secrecy over the aid group's existence. He then promptly let it be known that the decision to deceive the Commons had been a collective Cabinet agreement.

Callaghan was quite probably unduly naïve in believing he could get away with this breathtaking piece of double-speak. Within months of his instructions being sent to the Cabinet in February 1978 they had been leaked to the press. Headed 'The Prime Minister – Personal Minute', it gives a revealing picture of how honest and open governments are (or in reality are not) in their relationship with Parliament. Callaghan wrote:

> Consistently with the practice of all former Prime Ministers I
> have always refused to publish details of Cabinet Committees or

to answer questions in the House about them. Hitherto this has
led to some allegations in the press about Whitehall obscurantism
but little interest or pressure in Parliament itself. There is
however now some evidence that Select Committees would like
to interest themselves in the Committee system, and may be
seeking to erode the present convention. I have therefore been
considering the case for taking the initiative and disclosing
details of the Committee structure.

However much consideration Callaghan gave to taking such a bold step, he predictably decided on standing still.

I do not believe that we could in any event disclose the
existence of the GEN groups. [GEN groups are the *ad hoc*
Cabinet committees set up by each administration during its
term of office; GEN is short for 'general'.] This is partly because
of their ephemeral nature and partly because disclosure would
often reveal either that very sensitive subjects were under consideration or that we had something in train about which we were
not ready to make an announcement.

Disclosure of the main standing Committees would thus give a
partial picture only. Moreover, having gone as far as this I do not
believe that it would be possible for me to hold the line and
refuse to answer any further questions about the composition and
activities of the Committees. At the minimum we would have to
reveal the names of the Chairmen. This would make it harder for
me to make changes; and it would have implications for the
responsibilities of Departmental Ministers since Select Committees would try to summon the Chairmen of Cabinet Committees
to give evidence in addition to the responsible Minister. . . .I
have therefore decided that we should not change our stance on
this matter.

What all this gibberish actually meant was quite simple: if
Callaghan agreed to tell Parliament what his Cabinet committees
were, there would be an immediate demand to know what they did.
All of which would make it very difficult for him to continue to
keep Parliament in the dark. In short, it would be very inconvenient
to have MPs getting in the way of running the country.

The situation is so absurd that should you try to explain it to the average American or Western European voter he would stare at you in disbelief. Americans, for example, have the protection of a piece of legislation called the Sunshine Act, which in essence requires almost all governmental business to be done (and be seen to be done) in public. Ironically, Parliament here has endorsed this principle – but only where it doesn't apply to itself. Local councils in England and Wales are forced by law to allow the public into all their full committee meetings, and there is pressure for this to be extended to their sub-committees. Yet at Westminster the very existence of some committees must remain a closely guarded secret.

It was against this ludicrous backdrop that the twin doctrines of Cabinet and ministerial responsibility were to be played out in the Westland affair. Westland was an ailing British helicopter manufacturer which had close contacts with, and was a major contractor to, the Ministry of Defence. By 1985 it was in deep financial trouble and on the lookout for a rescue bid.

Two were forthcoming. The first, favoured by the company, the Prime Minister and Leon Brittan, then Trade and Industry Secretary, came from the American Sikorsky helicopter company; the second, announced some time later, was from a European consortium of companies with defence and aerospace interests. It was backed, very publicly, by the Secretary of State for Defence, Michael Heseltine. The Cabinet argued long and hard over the issue. Finally it decided on a public stance of non-intervention, leaving Westland to make up its own mind. But behind the scenes it was made known that the Prime Minister favoured the Sikorsky bid and was irritated by Heseltine's support for the Europeans.

And there the matter should have ended. According to the constitutional doctrine of Cabinet responsibility, Heseltine should have accepted the majority view of his colleagues and kept quiet. He didn't. He launched a high-profile crusade to promote the consortium's offer, sincerely believing that it was the better option for Westland and for Britain's defence interests. Suddenly Cabinet responsibility was dumped and Brittan and Heseltine began a public squabble.

In all probability neither the squabble nor the abandonment of Cabinet responsibility matter overmuch – at least not until the doctrine is next wheeled out to justify some absurd piece of secrecy. But what followed was far worse.

In December 1985 Heseltine wrote to Westland shareholders

warning them that, in his view, accepting the American bid could lead EEC countries and companies to steer clear of contracting work to the British helicopter firm in future. The letter was the clearest indication to date that Heseltine had no intention of abiding by the Cabinet decision. Perhaps understandably, Margaret Thatcher was furious. She told Brittan to refer the letter to the government's law officers. On 6 January 1986, the then Solicitor General, Sir Patrick Mayhew, wrote to Heseltine pointing out 'material inaccuracies' in his letter to Westland.

Hours later the letter had been officially leaked to the Press Association for distribution to all national newspapers and broadcasting organisations – despite the clear and unequivocal rule that advice from law officers is never made public.

What had happened was that Brittan's department had issued it almost as soon as it received a copy. But the civil servants did so in the belief that they had the authorisation of either the Prime Minister herself, or her officials at Number 10. In fact, the head of information at the Department of Trade, Colette Bowe, had apparently been most reluctant to leak the letter, and only did so on explicit instructions from the Prime Minister's Press Secretary, Bernard Ingham.

The law officers were outraged by the leak. On 10 January the Attorney General, Sir Michael Havers, had a tense meeting with Cabinet Secretary Sir Robert Armstrong. He threatened to resign unless those responsible for the leak were brought to book. Initially Armstrong prevaricated, but Havers cut him short. 'I have spoken to the Director of Public Prosecutions and I will have the police in here if you don't immediately hold an enquiry.'

On 13 January the Prime Minister agreed to an enquiry to seek out those who authorised the leak. Mrs Thatcher maintained that she had no foreknowledge of the leak, though her officials had authorised or agreed to it. Finally, and exhibiting the only piece of honourable conduct in the whole sorry saga, Brittan accepted ministerial responsibility for his actions and those of his officials, and resigned. (Heseltine had also resigned, refusing to be silenced by the principle of Cabinet responsibility over Westland.)

Once again that might have been the end of the affair. But no one quite believed that the Prime Minister knew nothing of the leak until after it happened – and certainly found it hard to swallow her claims that she didn't know the identity of those responsible until after Sir Robert Armstrong's enforced enquiry. And so the Select Committee on Defence began its own investigations – and the constitutional problems grew deeper.

The Committee, dominated by Conservative MPs, began work in a properly inquisitorial mood. But it needed to hear evidence – frank and honest evidence – from those involved. In particular it needed to question Bernard Ingham, Leon Brittan, Brittan's principal private secretary John Mogg, Colette Bowe and Nigel Wicks, the Prime Minister's private secretary.

Mrs Thatcher had earlier named all five officials as involved in the leaking in a Commons statement after Armstrong's enquiry. But she refused to allow them to appear before the Defence Select Committee to explain or justify their behaviour. The Prime Minister took the traditional line that officials are accountable to ministers, and ministers alone are accountable to Parliament. (Although this is the traditional constitutional position, numerous select committees had previously interrogated named officials about individual items of policy on which they had advised ministers.) The government, then, refused to allow the civil servants to appear. The Committee could have insisted. But the chairman, Sir Humphrey Atkins – a former Cabinet colleague of the Prime Minister – chose not to. Instead, the Committee planned to rely on the close questioning of Leon Brittan. Specifically, the Committee wanted to know when the need to leak the letter was first discussed with Number 10; who in the Prime Minister's office authorised the leak of selected passages from the Mayhew letter; and why, if Mrs Thatcher was to be believed, Brittan had said nothing to her about his role in the affair until the Armstrong enquiry revealed it.

Leon Brittan chose simply to refuse pointblank to answer those – and dozens of similar – questions. He got away with this because he had, by the time the Committee got into its enquiries, resigned from office. To date there are no official answers to those questions. Brittan's career may be (temporarily) over, but the Prime Minister, Ingham, Wicks, Mogg and Ms Bowe emerged unscathed. Mogg has even been promoted.

So why does Westland matter? Wasn't it, after all, a small storm in an already-cracked teacup?

The importance of the Westland affair is that it showed clearly for the first (though, as we shall see, not the last) time how government ministers cheat and dissemble, ignore in private the conventions of government they propound in public, and seek to prevent those with information from passing it on to those with a duty to investigate.

Almost a year after Westland erupted the government, in the shape of Sir Robert Armstrong, wrote to all permanent secretaries in Whitehall departments instructing them to stop their staff spilling the beans to select committees. He quoted the government's reply to the Defence Committee's report on Westland, which concluded that civil servants giving evidence to such committees 'should not answer questions which are, or appear to be, directed to the conduct of themselves or of other named individual civil servants'.

In the face of a storm of protest from MPs the government retreated and promised to withdraw the instruction – at least until after the Commons had had the chance to debate the issue.

If, then, governments can (and do) regularly pull the wool over Parliament's eyes, what chance is there of the general public ever finding out the truth?

Governments and the people

Up until now we have concentrated on the dodges and deceits that governments use to keep Parliament in the dark. Given that there is no written constitution, merely tradition and precedent, to guide their hands, it might appear that this is an easier task than withholding information from their electorate. Not so.

There is a substantial body of statute, common and case law designed to keep secret both trivial and important official information. In this section we shall examine the way governments manipulate the public through an information machine that is itself secret – and what it does to 'whistleblowers', idealists and journalists who dare to tell the truth out loud.

There is, in Britain, one inflexible rule of government: everything done by it, for it, or on its behalf is officially secret unless someone officially says it isn't. There is no obligation in this country for Whitehall to inform anyone of its activities. To reinforce this notion – unique in a Western democracy – a series of cynical conventions and obstructions have been developed to impede the free flow of information to those who ultimately foot the bill – the electorate.

We have already seen some of these techniques – notably the 'breach of confidence' laws – in action. In addition to wide statutory powers, governments occasionally resort to crude political thuggery to stifle informed debate: they either confiscate the information or simply forbid its publication.

In 1981 the National Advisory Committee on Nutrition Education (NACNE) – its members are all government appointees – drew up a damning report on the food we consume. Its conclusion was that our diet is the biggest single cause of the diseases from which we, as a nation, suffer and ultimately die. The NACNE team, headed by Professor Phillip James, identified fat, sugar and salt as the main culprits, and suggested a high-fibre alternative diet which would, if adopted, have adversely affected the home market for sweets, processed and convenience foods.

For two years the report was kept secret. And when it did emerge, it was not officially sanctioned. On 3 July 1983, the *Sunday Times* revealed its contents after receiving a leaked copy. The findings were immediately attacked by the food industry – in the shape of the British Nutrition Foundation, which it funds – and by the DHSS. The BNF's director, Dr Trevor Shrimpton, told the *Sunday Times* that the report would not be published. The DHSS said that it had no intention of publishing either – though Professor James was free to do so. The DHSS spokesman didn't elaborate on how James was expected to fund publication.

In the end the NACNE report was published in September 1983 by the Health Education Council – ironically a Quango funded by the DHSS. Within a year of publication, the Health Education Council flatly contradicted the report's conclusions: 'What we eat,' a subsequent HEC pamphlet advised, 'is not necessarily the most important key to good health.'

Both the NACNE report and a subsequent book, *The Food Scandal*, indicted the food industry and the way it lobbies governments. The authors of the book, Geoffrey Cannon and Caroline Walker, alleged that the Department of Health had been subjected to secret pressure by lobbyists on behalf of the food industry. Some of these had influenced officials in the Department of Trade and the Ministry of Agriculture, Fisheries and Food, who had in turn influenced the Treasury, which had then put pressure on the Health Department.

All this had been done in secret, behind securely closed doors. Cannon and Walker described the NACNE affair as 'our own Watergate', and concluded: 'Britain is a centralised society in which a remarkable proportion of decisions are taken behind closed doors.' (Cannon and Walker, *The Food Scandal*, Century, 1984.)

The lobbying by the food industry against the NACNE report is not unusual. Although political lobbying in Britain is a very recent development, its influence is beginning to spread. And, this being Britain, it spreads insidiously and in secret.

There are approximately thirty-five firms specialising in lobbying MPs and government. Many are one-man, shoestring operations (like private detectives, there are no regulations governing who can lobby whom in this country) and probably no more than six companies carry any real clout. Those that do, invariably boast ex-employees of politicians from almost all parties. So, for example, in the best known firm – Gifford, Jeger, Weeks – Andrew Gifford used to run David Steel's private office; Jenny Jeger is the daughter of the Labour politician Lena (now Baroness) Jeger, and also worked for Jim Callaghan when he was at Number 10; and Wilf Weeks used to be with Ted Heath, the former Conservative Prime Minister.

GJW models itself very closely on the American corporate lobbyists – it takes on single issues, specialises in opening selected doors and whispering in the ears of the important. GJW worked for Westland during its fight to see off Michael Heseltine and his European consortium (though it was not involved, of course, in the political shenanigans surrounding the affair), and persuaded a previous Minister for Trade, Lord Cockfield, to refer an unwelcome American bid for the auctioneer's Sotheby's to the Monopolies and Mergers Commission. The Office of Fair Trading, which deals with takeovers as a matter of routine, had recommended against referring the bid.

At times, professional lobbyists can work in the public interest. For example, in 1986, Ian Greer Associates (whose fifteen-man staff is largely composed of high-ranking ex-civil servants) simply drew the constitutional and legal implications of the government's plans to privatise the Devonport naval dockyard to Lord Denning's attention. Denning looked into the matter, was appalled by what he found and promptly forced through a series of amendments to the enabling bill in the Lords. The name of Ian Greer Associates, and the influence the firm had exerted on behalf of its client (the City of Portsmouth, where the dockyard is sited) were never mentioned. Lobbyists in this country like to work in secret.

'We believe,' said another lobbyist, Peter Luff, 'that the story should come from the horse's mouth, not the trainer's.' Luff works for Good Relations Public Affairs Ltd. Set up five years ago as an offshoot to a PR firm, it had an annual turnover by 1986 of more than £750,000. Luff formerly worked as a political adviser to Edward Heath and the Conservative Cabinet minister Peter Walker. His colleagues Peter Shipley and Paul Tyler have similarly good contacts: Shipley was a member of the Number 10 Policy Unit, and Tyler is an ex-Liberal MP and Liberal Party chairman. Impressive men with impressive friends, though those whom they lobby are occasionally far from impressed.

In 1986 Good Relations started a campaign on behalf of International Paint. The company marketed an anti-fouling paint for yachts which, its critics claimed, was not only poisoning the sea but killing off oysters as well. The Ministry of Agriculture, Fisheries and Food had persuaded the Department of the Environment to ban the product – much to the delight of those who made a living from harvesting oysters.

Good Relations waded into the scientific evidence for contamination and claimed that it was 'not overwhelming' – though it had been good enough for MAFF and the DOE. The lobbyists then persuaded 1000 yachtsmen to write to the DOE, mobilised the yachting press and obtained the support of the Royal Yachting Association. The result: the ban was lifted and International Paint given time to come up with an alternative.

William Waldegrave, Secretary of State for the Environment, denounced it as 'the worst case of single-issue lobbying I have ever come across'. Peter Luff said: 'When he said that I knew we were getting somewhere.'

Not all lobbying is carried out by specialised firms of consultants. The pro-pesticides lobby, for example, is one of the strongest in the country. It operates in a far more subtle manner. There are in Britain two bodies which are supposed to regulate the use and assess the safety of pesticides. The government's own body is the Pesticides Safety Precautions Scheme (PSPS). Any chemical passed by the PSPS is allowed to advertise the fact on its tins. But no firm *has* to submit its products to the scheme, which is entirely voluntary and works on a 'gentlemen's agreement' between MAFF and the agrochemical industry. The evidence needed by the PSPS to assess the safety of a product is often provided by the manufacturing company. Details of independent tests carried out by the PSPS, the results these produce and the follow-up studies (if any) are never published. The PSPS works in complete and utter secrecy.

The PSPS does, however, pass on its findings to the second watchdog body, the Advisory Committee on Pesticides (ACP). This Committee is a Quango, staffed by scientists. How they are chosen, and on whose recommendation, is kept secret. So too are their deliberations on the safety of any product to come before them: they simply approve or reject a given chemical.

Because of this secrecy the agricultural workers' union describes the ACP as a 'toothless watchdog'. Peter Walker, while Minister in charge of MAFF, described the ACP as being made up of top-ranking independent scientists, but at the time none of the Committee had worked with pesticides in the field – only in laboratories – and one of its members had been heavily funded by Shell. Shell is a major force in the agro-chemical industry and was, at that date, involved in a major controversy over its extensive use of the pesticide 245T.

Although PSPS – and therefore ACP – evaluations are secret, evidence can be obtained of the effectiveness of these watchdogs. In the autumn of 1983 it emerged that fourteen separate pesticides had been cleared for use in America on the basis of deliberately falsified evidence. The same preparations had also been passed as safe by PSPS and ACP. Conservation groups immediately asked the two bodies whether the same fraudulent data had been involved in the PSPS tests. They also wanted to know whether the pesticides concerned were going to be banned.

The PSPS announced that the chemicals would not be banned in the UK, because it had cleared them. But it refused to say on what data it had based the decision. Nor would it say whether independent tests had been carried out. Finally it refused even to say which fourteen pesticides were involved. All the information was secret.

Checking through the US Freedom of Information Act provided us with the American brand-names of the pesticides – but not the British ones. The Act did, however, throw a little more light on the potentially dangerous way in which the pesticide lobby and its watchdogs work in Britain. Researchers found, by using the Act, that another weedkiller, Dichlobel, had been passed as safe in America without a single test being carried out to check whether it caused cancer, birth defects or infertility, or damaged the nervous system (all potential side-effects of agro-chemicals). They asked

PSPS if such tests had been carried out here, but the information was not released.

So much for lobbyists. What of the Lobby?

Governments and the media

The Lobby's role is to receive official press releases, and to act as the main channel for passing information from the government to the public. It comprises a privileged group of journalists who are officially given access to briefings and 'leakings' by politicians every day of the week.

In 1971 the government-appointed Franks Committee on the Official Secrets Act took evidence from Jim Callaghan, later to become Prime Minister. The Committee pressed Callaghan about the willingness of some ministers to give out unattributable information which, under the Official Secrets Act, it would be otherwise illegal for the journalist to obtain. Callaghan explained the situation in a memorable phrase: 'You know the difference between leaking and briefing: leaking is what you do, and briefing is what I do.' There is one other difference Callaghan might have mentioned: leakers are prosecuted, briefers are not.

Briefing – the provision of unattributable information to journalists by ministers and their offices, takes place on both a formal and an informal basis. In both cases the Lobby is the vehicle.

Once a week about a hundred accredited political journalists – the Lobby – trip up a flight of stairs in a corner of the Palace of Westminster to ask polite questions of the Prime Minister's press secretary and, later, the Leader of the House. They are also given a briefing on the views of the politician in question (e.g.: 'The Prime Minister thinks that . . .'). They go through the same ritual with the leader of the Opposition, with Cabinet ministers and with the political representatives of the main parties in the Lords. At these demure and cosy gatherings one rule is sacrosanct: no mention may be made in any story of the source of the information.

A similar easy anonymity descends on the corridors of Westminster with regard to the other method of channelling information through the Lobby: individual briefings, inevitably over drinks or dinner.

The results can be seen almost every day in our national newspapers and in the broadcast media, stories which ostensibly originate in 'Westminister circles', or 'senior government sources'. In general, these phrases are simply a code meaning either the Prime Minister, via his or her press spokesman, or an individual Cabinet minister.

Is there, then, any harm in this system? Isn't it simply another manifestation of the particularly juvenile quality of British political life? Sadly, no. The Lobby allows itself to be used to fly governmental kites, convey misinformation, and disinformation, or generally shift the blame for something unpleasant on to someone else.

For example, on 3 April 1969 Harold Wilson, then Prime Minister, instructed his Press Secretary to tell the Lobby that Jim Callaghan had been soundly reprimanded in Cabinet that day by the Prime Minister. The Lobby duly ran the story. It subsequently turned out that there had been no such reprimand.

In his memoirs Wilson recalled a similar incident. Where the Lobby was used to plant a story without the Prime Minister taking responsibility. He was having trouble at the time with the left-wing MP Tony Benn, then in Cabinet and upsetting the City.

> During the Jamaican conference . . . the High Commissioner gave a reception for the British press corps in the garden of his residence. At the appropriate point I asked Harry Boyne, political correspondent of the *Daily Telegraph*, a paragon of discretion, to disengage himself for a little while and go to a room the High Commissioner had reserved.
>
> I was waiting there and I stressed that while he could use the story – that Tony Benn was going to be moved sideways to another department – it should not be datelined 'Jamaica' . . . the Telegraph accordingly ran a story 'from our political staff' that Tony was to be moved to pastures new. [Harold Wilson, *Final Term*, Weidenfeld and Nicolson, 1979.]

The Lobby still allows itself to be used in this way today. Early in 1987, Bernard Ingham, the Prime Minister's Press Secretary, gave the usual weekly background briefing to lobby journalists. On this occasion he chose to communicate Mrs Thatcher's belief that the leader of the Labour Party, Neil Kinnock, had lost credibility as a potential leader of the country.

In normal circumstances, and outside the Lobby, such information would have been unlikely to grace the pages of even the most pro-government newspaper: it simply wasn't news, given the habitual hostility between Thatcher and Kinnock. But because the source of the story could be – had to be – wrapped up in a cloak of euphemisms, it appeared more credible as a news item. After all, 'Senior Tory officials convinced Kinnock has lost credibility' has a more solid ring to it than the opinions of a Press Secretary.

The story duly led the front pages of many newspapers. The fact that, at the time, there was no shred of fact to back up the view simply didn't matter – the Lobby rarely questions those who feed it titbits.

There are times, however, when its masters exceed even the Lobby's relaxed attitude to accuracy and fair-dealing. On 9 May 1986, the Commons Committee on Privileges removed its accreditation from a lobby journalist called Richard Evans. Evans, a reporter for *The Times*, had been leaked a draft report from the Environment Committee on radioactive waste. The leak had been in the best traditions of journalism, and seemed entirely within the habitual behaviour of the Lobby system, in that it was clandestine and entirely unattributable. *The Times* promptly published excerpts from it.

The Environment Committee was not pleased. The *Times* report was completely accurate, and no one had been defamed or treated unfairly, but it was an *unauthorised* report. The Committee set about finding the culprit. None of its members was prepared to own up to having leaked the report, and Evans took the view that it was not for him to disclose a good source. In the end he paid the price for doing his job. The Privileges Committee banned him for six months and removed his *Times* Lobby pass. The MP who leaked the story was never found, nor punished.

There is a parallel to this sorry saga which exhibits the same double standards. MPs from all parties have interests outside the House; some are retained by particular firms or organisations as 'advisers' – in reality little more than part-time lobbyists. Parliament recognises the inherent dangers of this practice and a register of Members' interests exists so that the suspicious, the vigilant and the cynical can check an MP's support for a particular cause against any private interest he might have in the matter.

The problem has been that the register is voluntary. Some members – prominently the former Ulster Unionist MP Enoch Powell – openly refuse to have anything to do with it. Others are simply careless about the precise details. Against this background, and with an ever-increasing number of share and City scandals, pressure has increased for the register to be made mandatory. Almost inevitably the Commons voted against the move – but at the same time, 1985, decided to impose a similar mandatory register of the interests of journalists covering parliamentary affairs.

Official secrets

The 'blackballing' of Richard Evans, is, however, a minor landmark in the history of governments' efforts to keep their electorate in the dark. By far the most powerful weapons are the twin threats of ESTACODE and the Official Secrets Act.

ESTACODE – the staff discipline rules of the Civil Service – specifically forbids officials in government departments from talking to journalists (with the exception of the hundreds of press officers who are employed to do just that). The rules go much further in restricting the flow of official information than the truly draconian Official Secrets Act. They also manage conveniently to confuse the code with the law – as the following excerpt from the 1971 Franks Committee report makes clear.

> *Question:* 'Most of these declarations require the signatory to state that he is aware of various things, one of which usually is that he must not disclose information which he has acquired in the course of his duty without previous consent in writing from the Department. Would you agree with me that while to have consent in writing may be a prudent precaution it is actually imposing a requirement which is not imposed by the Act?'
> *Sir Phillip Allen* (Permanent Under Secretary of State, Home Office): 'Entirely.'
>
> *Question:* 'And similarly, most of these declarations require that the person concerned shall submit two copies of the proposed publication, which again it appears to me goes further than the Act?'
> *Sir Phillip:* 'Yes.'
>
> *Question:* 'Do you agree that it is a fair comment to make that these declarations are imposing or putting further obstacles in the way of publication, which go beyond the Act?'
> *Sir Phillip:* 'Yes, I do.'

Question: 'And in fact that most of these declarations, given that they ask the signatory to say he is aware of various obligations, mis-state the effect of the Act and exaggerate its importance?'
Sir Phillip: 'Yes.'

What then of the Official Secrets Act, this 75-year-old piece of panic legislation? To understand its workings we need to remember the circumstances of its passage through Parliament one hot Friday afternoon.

The summer of 1911 had been sultry. It had also proved a trying month for a government beset by a major railway strike, public frenzy over spying and the rapidly escalating arms race with imperial Germany. By Friday 18 August the country was caught in a bout of anti-German jingoism, and the second spy trial within a year was in full swing in London. The army had been mobilised and issued with live ammunition.

It was this atmosphere that allowed the Official Secrets Act – almost certainly one of the worst-drafted pieces of legislation ever to reach the statute-book – to be whipped through the House in an unprecedented rush. The second and third readings of the bill took less than thirty minutes.

Major General J. E. B. Seeley was Under Secretary of State for War, and it was he who pushed the bill through.

I got up and proposed the Bill be read a second time [he wrote later], explaining, in two sentences only, that it was considered desirable in the public interest that the measure should be passed. Hardly a word was said and the Bill was read a second time; the Speaker left the Chair. I then moved the Bill in Committee. This was the first critical moment; two men got up to speak, but both were forcibly pulled down by their neighbours after they had uttered a few sentences, and the committee stage was passed.

The Speaker walked back to his chair and said: 'The question is, that I report this Bill without amendment to the House.' Again, two or three people stood up; again they were pulled down by their neighbours, and the report stage was through.

The Speaker turned to me and said: 'The third reading, what day?' 'Now, sir,' I replied. My heart beat fast as the Speaker said: 'The question is that this Bill be read a third time.'

> It was open to any one of the members of the House of
> Commons to get up and say that no bill had ever yet been passed
> through all its stages in one day without a word of explanation
> from the minister in charge. But to the eternal honour of those
> members, to whom I now offer, on behalf of that and all
> succeeding governments, my most grateful thanks, not one man
> seriously opposed, and in a little more time than it has taken to
> write these words, that formidable piece of legislation was
> passed. [Quoted in David Williams, *Not in the Public Interest*,
> Hutchinson, 1963.]

The Major General probably understated the gratitude of successive administrations for such a convenient barrier to the passage of information. Although additions were made in 1920 and 1939, and there have been sporadic attempts at reform, the Act has remained substantially the same for seventy-five years.

Section 1 deals with spying and is relatively straightforward. It prohibits the handing over of military information which could help an enemy. There is without doubt a need for this type of legislation; every country has laws against spying, and few people would argue against them.

It is section 2 of the Act which has aroused the most hostility, caused the most controversy — and launched the majority of prosecutions. Very little of its 350-word sentence has anything to do with the proper defence of the realm. Yet, according to the Franks report, there are 2,000 differently worded charges which can be brought under it.

At times the prosecutions can be ludicrous. In 1984, the Attorney General sanctioned the prosecution of an accountant inside the Home Office's prison department. His alleged offence had been to reveal details of the toy typewriters made by inmates of certain prisons. He was eventually acquitted.

In April the same year a reporter from the monthly newspaper *Voice* sat, stunned, as an official of the Department of the Environment quoted every word of section 2 at him over the telephone. He had rung the Department about a rescue dig it had begun near the Iron Age village of Chrysauster, in Cornwall. A local farmer, in order to get a reclamation subsidy, had reclaimed land nearby in which there were known to be other Iron Age remains. The subsequent DOE rescue dig unearthed human remains and grave-goods. The *Voice* reporter had rung to ask for details of the exact find; after listening with increasing disbelief as the official quoted section 2, he asked why the information should be kept so secret. He was told it was 'a confidential and sensitive issue'.

Two and half years later Kevin Buckley had an altogether more sinister experience. Buckley, thirty-two, is an inventor. In October 1986 he made an application to patent his latest brainchild, a non-nuclear method of generating electricity via an injection-nitration engine. Within hours of receiving his application the security branch of the Patent Office, acting on behalf of the Ministry of Defence, was on the phone to his Cheshire home, threatening him with the full rigours of a section 2 trial and two years in prison unless he kept very quiet indeed.

Buckley had fallen foul of a little-known section of the 1977 Patents Act which gives the Ministry of Defence the right to 'call in' inventions in the interests of national security. 'At first they spoke to my father, who was quite frightened about talk of official secrets and asked me when I came in from work what I had been up to. The official spoke to me the next morning but refused to discuss the matter with me on the telephone.'

Eventually the MOD decided that Kevin Buckley's engine was of no military significance and not likely to endanger national security. It is now going through its patent stage unhindered. But what of the Ministry? An official there explained that since everyone involved in calling in useful inventions is subject to the Official Secrets Act, the MOD couldn't discuss its use of the Act in the Buckley or any other case.

If all these examples appear absurd, typically bumblingly British or even mildly amusing, there have been more serious cases.

In the autumn of 1983 Sarah Tisdall, a 23-year-old clerk in the Foreign Office, picked up two papers dealing with Cruise missiles. Both were marked 'Secret'. Whitehall documents are graded in four categories, apart from those it regards as innocuous or 'unclassified' – in which case the only barrier to disclosure is the ESTACODE: 'Restricted', 'Confidential', 'Secret' and 'Top Secret'. (In reality these can be translated into: 'bland', 'mildly sensitive', 'rather secret', and 'genuinely secret'.)

The type of material which falls into each individual category is as follows:

a. Top Secret. (This can only be authorised at Assistant Secretary

level or higher.) Plans for the military use of space; policies which, if publicised, 'would prevent our achieving highly important national ends'; a variety of defence and security documents, as for example the plan to impose direct rule on Northern Ireland in 1972.
b. Secret. 'Highly embarrassing disagreements with a friendly government'; legislative priorities agreed by the Cabinet; details of any planned changes in tax or of current pay negotiations 'which might damage confidence'; forecasts of future economic performance, such as inflation; emergency plans to deal with strikes in essential industries; the full list of government bunkers; vital military information such as photographs of important or strategic sites.
c. Confidential. All exchanges with foreign governments together with Foreign Office minutes relating to other countries; anything to do with wage bargaining or unemployment figures and policy; future fuel policy discussions; industrial subsidies; the balance of payments and long-term development papers; all local government, regional planning and land development documents; all information about weapons design and developments; all 'routine political reports'.
d. Restricted. All draft bills; all Cabinet committee memos; all instruction manuals and routine office circulars (even down to the price of canteen meals); all telephone directories.

The Franks Report, trying to bring back some sanity to the issue of official secrecy, implied that the latter two categories could safely be scrapped. To date nothing has been done.

The documents, then, which Sarah Tisdall picked up were stamped 'Secret'. One dealt with security and safety measures to be put into operation when the Cruise missiles arrived; the other centred on how to handle the political implications of the arrival. This document, a memo from Michael Heseltine, then in charge at the MOD, was addressed to the Prime Minister. It was primarily concerned with the party political policy, and how best to neutralise the effect of a CND anti-Cruise demonstration. In short it was a treatise on how, in the best traditions of government, to manipulate public opinion. It had no business bearing a security classification.

Tisdall felt strongly that it was wrong for this manipulation to take place behind a veil of official secrecy. She sent both documents to the *Guardian* newspaper, though the security plans themselves were, in the event, already fairly well known outside Whitehall.

Tisdall was not an anti-nuclear campaigner: she did not agree with either CND or the Greenham Common women protesting about Cruise missiles. 'In the present circumstances we have to have nuclear weapons,' she later explained. 'But as to the way they were to be brought into the country, I felt this was indecent, sort of doing it by the back door, and I couldn't stomach it. I felt the public had a right to know what was being done to them.'

The *Guardian* duly published a story based on the Heseltine memo. It failed, however, to destroy the documents – and neatly landed Sarah Tisdall in the dock at the Old Bailey, on a section 2 charge. She was convicted and sentenced to six months in prison. It was by any standards an excessive sentence. Mr Justice Cantley told her when he sent her down:

> If secret documents are leaked for publication, that must weaken the confidence of the country's allies in the trustworthiness of the Department of Defence. It is very important that people in a position of trust should not flout their obligations in the expression of their own views.

He didn't mention a public's right to know. Nor did he draw attention to an opinion poll at the time the documents were mailed which showed a majority of the population against the deployment of Cruise. Sarah Tisdall went to prison 'pour encourager les autres'.

Even that cynical objective appears to have failed, however. Within a year Clive Ponting would send MOD documents to Tam Dalyell, MP, and later take centre stage at the Old Bailey. In neither his nor the Tisdall case was national security really at stake. Yet both were charged under the Official Secrets Act. In Ponting's case, the trial judge, Mr Justice McCowan, actually accepted this principle. 'It is not necessary,' he told the jury in his summing up, 'that the disclosures should have breached national security.' No other judge, in no other case, had pinpointed so well the 'Through the Looking Glass' qualities of section 2 official secrets trials.

The Thatcher government has instituted more prosecutions under the Act than any previous administration: its tally includes nine civil servants in as many years. But in the seventy-five-year history of the Act not one minister has been prosecuted – not even the notorious

Jimmy Thomas, Colonial Secretary in the 1930s, who twice revealed Budget secrets to his cronies, enabling them to make a fortune on the insurance and stock markets. It is a shameful record. The Act should be repealed and replaced with a genuine anti-spying statute; instead, a new and harsher measure is being planned. Section 2 must be scrapped altogether.

Even without the Official Secrets Act, however, the government has the power to prosecute – even persecute – those who 'blow the whistle'. In the autumn of 1987 the government of the United Kingdom lost its appeal against a ruling in a New South Wales Court allowing the ex-MI5 spycatcher Peter Wright to publish his memoirs. Wright's allegations of plots within the security service to topple the democratically elected government are so serious that the trial judge, Mr Justice Powell, felt that there was a general public right to know.

This principle may apply in Australia, but in England the Law Lords eventually ruled against future publication of such 'insider' allegations. In October 1988, at a cost of £4 million, the government got the verdict it wanted: MI5's tradition of secrecy was more important than the sanctity of a democratically elected government?

(What made the government's case all the more ludicrous, and forced the Cabinet Secretary Sir Robert Armstrong into being 'economical with the truth' – his phrase – was that the allegations had already been aired by other authors, with the help of other ex-MI5 men. Still, the government stuck to its guns, that the very fact that an ex-MI5 agent was making them *directly* caused quantifiable and irreparable damage to the security services.)

The Wright case is a prime example of government secrecy, dishonesty and irresponsibility gone mad: it demonstrated a Humpty Dumpty-like disregard on the part of the government for the real meaning of its words and actions. But what has all this to do with the ordinary man in the street? However reprehensible, do matters of secrecy and national security policy actually affect our daily lives?

Probably not in many cases. But national government sets a pattern which local government is only too happy to follow. Local council decisions affect us all: we all pay rates, send children to school, use buses, sports centres or other public buildings. And in many cases we have rights – statutory rights – to know about them. All too often, however, those rights go unenforced and neglected in favour of a blanket of secrecy.

Secrecy in local government

Early in 1984 the Community Rights Project set out to discover how easy it is for us to get the information we are entitled to. Staff were handed a list of the documents supposed by law to be available to any member of the public – and told quite simply to go and ask local councils if they could see them. The results of the exercise were 'disgraceful – even alarming'. Why?

The project targeted sixty-one boroughs. All thirty-three London boroughs were included, together with those in the Greater Manchester area, West Yorkshire, the West Midlands, Tyne and Wear, and Avon. They started with the most fundamental of the public documents – the local byelaws. Researchers all over the country simply asked to see a copy. What they were told makes dismal reading.

Salford Council: 'We wouldn't give out that kind of information.'

Kensington and Chelsea: 'Apply in writing, giving the reason to the Chief Executive.'

Calderdale: the bye-laws were 'not available'.

Trafford: 'They're not available – why do you want to see them?'

The Local Government Act, 1972 (section 236[8]), says byelaws 'shall at all reasonable times be open to public inspection'. All the councils that refused were breaking the law, in the name of secrecy.

It was the same story all over the country: wherever the researchers went there was something they couldn't see. In Bolton, the council refused access to its register of air pollution (inspection guaranteed under the Control of Pollution Act, 1984). 'We're supposed to have a register, but we don't need one; and even if we did have one you couldn't see it as it is confidential information and comes under the Secrecy Act [sic].' Quite simply, that isn't true. Bolton's housing officials were 'too busy' to provide housing information which must legally be available to the public. The council added: 'Write to the Director. You're not entitled to the information anyway.'

So much for simple enquiries. But what about council meetings? All full council meetings and all council committee meetings (though not sub-committee meetings) must be open to the public. But inevitably there's a let-out clause. The public can be excluded from any part of the meeting 'whenever publicity would be prejudicial to the public interest by reason of the confidential nature of the business to be transacted or for other special reasons'. (In theory the Local Government (Access to Information) Act, 1985, will tighten that definition and make it harder to hold secret meetings: as yet, however, it is too soon to assess its success or failure.)

The residents of Cambridge found out about confidential council business the hard way. They were worried about a proposed building development in an area known as 'The Kite'. The council and a firm called Grosvenor Estates wanted to redevelop the site, which would have involved wholesale demolition. The residents tried to attend council meetings to keep tabs on the progress of the scheme. For eighteen months they were frustrated: the first item on each agenda was a resolution to exclude press and public. Even when an agreement was signed for the development it was kept secret, and the leader of the opposition group of councillors was only able to see a copy after he had promised not to discuss it with anyone – not even his own constituents.

'The Kite' may have been a special case, but as an example of council secrecy it is by no means unique. We have already seen how information on education is kept secret from the very people who need it most – parents.

Public enquiries

Before we leave the arena of official information and the general public we should sound a note of caution about public enquiries.

Taxpayers spend hundreds of thousands of pounds on public enquiries into major areas of concern: nuclear power stations, reprocessing plants, motorways and the like. The system is often held to be proof of a living spirit of democracy. After all, although the government chooses the chairman for the enquiry he is, in practice, his own man. But there are flaws. Typically, the proposer of the scheme in dispute – generally a government department or large company – is backed by teams of lawyers, accountants and secretaries. Equally typically, the objectors, unless funded by some benevolent organisation, go into the fight alone and unaided. This can cause serious financial hardship, and even the best prepared objectors cannot match the expensive professionalism of the large corporation or Whitehall department.

It was a problem recognised in September 1986 by the Commons Environment Committee. In a wide-ranging paper it proposed paying compensation to objectors who, after all, helped determine national policy. 'We are suggesting that the government ought to carry out an analysis of what it would cost the state to do this, against what it costs when people object to proposals in their area,' Committee chairman Sir Hugh Rossi explained. As yet there has been no official response – but the omens are not promising. On 19 September, just two days after Sir Hugh's Committee reported, Home Secretary Douglas Hurd took a swipe at pressure groups – the very people Rossi wanted to fund publicly.

In a speech to the Royal Institute of Public Administration, Hurd said that ministers and MPs needed to shake themselves free from the 'strangling serpents' embrace' of pressure groups. If the Home Secretary didn't mention public enquiries by name, the suspicion lingers on that objectors will get no help with their costs.

The Environment Committee report was not, however, wholly to the advantage of objectors. Rossi's team suggested a modification of the system to cut costs and delays. Instead of objectors being able – as at present – to argue against, say, a nuclear reactor being built near their village because nuclear power is inherently dangerous, the government of the day would be able to establish a principle beforehand that nuclear power is acceptable, and this would then become unquestionable. Only the finer points – precisely whose village should be affected – would be open to debate.

There are those, of course, who argue that such an abridgement of the system would make little difference. These critics point to the long-running Sizewell B enquiry which reported early in 1987. The enquiry endorsed a proposal to build another nuclear power generator on the existing Sizewell site – despite objections which lasted for more than a year.

The enquiry actually finished taking evidence some time before it reported. In the interim period the nuclear reactor at Chernobyl in the Soviet Union exploded, leading to the world's worst nuclear contamination disaster and an estimate that thousands of people across Europe would die of nuclear-related cancers.

Despite the fact that this happened a few months before the report was finished, there was no mention of Chernobyl in the body of the enquiry report. The chairman, Sir Frank Layfield, had felt that it was outside his brief to include – and not worth recalling the enquiry to take evidence of – any possible effect, similarity or lessons to be learnt from the explosion. Critics of the public enquiry system say there is no clearer example of what is wrong with objectors' rights.

Data protection and you

Jan Martin doesn't look like a Baader-Meinhoff terrorist. She doesn't think, talk or act like one either. It comes as no surprise to those who know her that she isn't, and never has been, a member of any terrorist organisation whatever.

In fact Ms Martin, an independent film producer, never gave the subject of terrorism any undue thought until 1978, when she started work on an advertising film for the major British company Taylor Woodrow. On the day she was due to start filming the company refused to allow her on to their premises – they had been told by Special Branch police officers that Ms Martin was a suspected member of the Baader-Meinhoff gang.

She denied the accusation, of course, but found it hard to convince her employers. She was finally told either to disprove the story or to look for work elsewhere.

Jan Martin was about to discover that inaccurate, absurd and damaging information is regularly kept on file about millions of us every year – and that the same information is fed secretly to employers who take the trouble (and the money) to ask. And if that wasn't enough, she was also to discover that all those valuable (if inaccurate) files are most invariably kept secret from the people most affected – the subjects themselves.

There is, as we have noted elsewhere, no general right to privacy in Britain. In purely legislative terms, privacy is a matter for the Home Office. In the rather more important area of actually taking responsibility and acting to protect personal privacy with regard to databank information, the Home Office – mandarins and ministers alike – doesn't give a damn.

The campaign to provide some form of safeguard began in February 1967 with a private member's bill introduced by the then Labour MP Alex Lyon. Predictably, his Right of Privacy bill failed to get a second reading and was lost.

However, both the National Council for Civil Liberties and Justice, the British arm of the International Commission of Jurists, took up the issue. Justice prepared a draft bill, and, in January 1970, another backbench Labour MP, Brian Walden, introduced a

Right to Privacy bill based on its draft legislation. Walden's idea of a general and legally enforceable right of privacy began to pick up widespread support.

At which point the Home Office and government ministers began to worry. The Home Office, after all, actually pays for the largest collection of individual files, posing the biggest threat to personal privacy, anywhere in Britain: police records, immigration files and security service intelligence information.

Walden was persuaded to withdraw his Bill with the promise of a Royal Commission enquiry into the issue. True to its word, the government appointed Sir Kenneth Younger to head the enquiry. But the Home Office succeeded in insulating itself from any scrutiny: all central government activities were specifically excluded from the Commission's terms of reference.

Younger was appointed in May 1970 and reported in July 1972. He recommended legislation to control bugging and other forms of electronic eavesdropping and the urgent creation of a 'standing commission' to keep tabs on the growing practice of using computers to gather and process personal information. Alex Lyon, a member of the Commission, put forward his own minority report recommending stronger statutory safeguards for personal privacy.

As if limiting the scope of the Younger Commission hadn't been cynical enough, the Home Office then used what would become its favourite delaying tactic to avoid any action on the issue: it announced a consultation programme to 'take public reaction and the views of those interested in this matter into account before announcing our conclusions'. In short, an exercise designed to repeat whatever evidence and representation the Commission had just finished taking. It promised that a White Paper would follow.

By 1974 no such White Paper had emerged. But a general election had taken place, and Harold Wilson's Labour government had replaced Ted Heath's ailing Conservative administration. Wilson promised an early White Paper – by the summer at the latest. By January 1975 there was still no sign of it. Instead, Home Office ministers announced that they had found 'a need to re-examine certain parts [of it]'. Finally, the White Papers emerged, eighteen months late, in December 1975. And with it, owing largely to the persistence of Alex Lyon – by then a junior Home Office minister – came a supplement listing central government's own banks of computers. The list was extensive.

The White Paper itself was promisingly forthright about the threat to personal privacy posed by new technology. 'The time has come when those who use computers to handle personal information, however responsible they are, can no longer remain the sole judges of whether their own systems adequately safeguard personal privacy.'

It proposed the immediate appointment of a Data Protection Committee to produce legislation for the creation of an independent monitoring body. That body, to be known as the Data Protection Authority, should have extensive powers and be created as a matter of urgency.

In February 1976 Sir Kenneth Younger was appointed head of the new Committee. When he died shortly afterwards, Sir Norman Lindop – a quiet, thoughtful figure, then director of Hatfield Polytechnic – replaced him. Lindop began work in July 1976. His Committee's report, three years later, would offer the best ever set of safeguards for the protection of personal privacy, and still maintain a reasonable balance between the rights of the public and the legitimate activities of the police and security services.

But the Home Office again prevaricated. It promptly announced yet another new consultative exercise so that the same 'interested bodies' Lindop had spent the three previous years consulting would have another chance to give their opinions. According to the Home Office minister Lord Boston, thirteen government departments would approach more than two hundred such groups to seek their views. His boss, Home Secretary Merlyn Rees, added that the process was likely to be a long one: he 'did not think it appropriate to impose a rigid time limit upon consultation'.

In the event the process took two full years – by which time the Labour government had been defeated in a general election and replaced by the Conservative Thatcher administration. Not only was the new government the most ideologically right-wing since the War, it had absolutely no interest in protecting the privacy of its electorate.

In 1980 yet another committee examined the issue. The House of Commons Home Affairs Committee began an enquiry into the history of privacy legislation; it found the going heavy at times. One witness before the Committee was Home Office Deputy Secretary Ralph Shuffrey. When the Committee asked repeatedly, would legislation be drafted? The best answer Shuffrey would give was that it was 'under consideration'.

The climate was changing, however, and events were about to catch up with the Home Office. A special Council of Europe Convention devoted to data protection was shortly to come into effect. At first Shuffrey tried to ride out the growing pressure: 'It is not necessarily a good idea,' he told the Committee, 'to have a policy cut and dried before the Convention is ready for signature . . .'

What he actually meant was that the Home Office and government ministers were playing for time – time in which other delaying tactics could be used in Europe. As a ploy it failed miserably. The Council of Europe's Committee of Ministers approved the Convention in October 1980. Perhaps in other circumstances the British government might have been able to ignore, at least temporarily, the European edict – it had, after all, done so in the past. But the European Convention for the Protection of Individuals with Regard to Automatic Data Processing was different.

Apart from prescribing a basic human right to individual privacy, and requiring signatory nations to create their own matching legislation, it contained a penalty clause. Each signatory to the Convention agreed not to transfer personal data to or from countries lacking domestic data protection laws.

By 1980 the British information technology industry was getting into its stride. Unless the government produced data protection legislation Britain would be cut off from most of the European market. (In fact by late 1983 at least one large contract, for processing and producing Sweden's national identity cards, had been lost in this way.)

The government was cornered. It promised an early statement. When that 'early' statement finally came in March 1981 Home Secretary William Whitelaw announced that any legislation would be the minimum necessary to comply with the European Convention, and would have to wait until 'an opportunity offers'. By the start of 1982 no such opportunity had apparently offered itself. The European Convention was a year old, and had attracted several signatories; it was also fifteen years since the first attempt to get legislation passed in the UK, and still nothing had been produced.

Three quite separate political factors combined at that stage to give the campaign impetus. Labour MP Michael Meacher proposed a private member's Data Protection Bill. Like its predecessors it failed to get a second reading. But at the same time the government was facing increasing pressure from consumer groups, civil rights bodies, the medical and other professions, computer operators and above all the information technology industry. Then the *Sun* newspaper took a hand; it decided to hire private detectives to see just how much personal information it could obtain about Michael Meacher. When it published the results, the Commons was outraged and questions were asked of the Prime Minister. Mrs Thatcher, quite unexpectedly, sympathised with Meacher and announced an urgent desire to produce legislation in the very next session of Parliament. Home Office mandarins were both shocked and dismayed – it was the first they had heard of any such plans.

But what were those MPs, civil rights groups and European ministers getting so worked up about? Who knows what about you – and what do they do with the information?

Who's watching you?

There are any number of state and private organisations who keep files and/or computer records about all of us. Some of them – Gas and Electricity Boards, for example – are plainly innocuous. Others, like credit card companies and banks, although keeping potentially sensitive personal data, have an obvious need for what they keep: they are, after all, lending a good deal of their investors' money on the strength of no more than a promise to pay it back.

The real issue begins and ends with the size and nature of State databanks (and, on the fringes, those private intelligence-gathering organisations whose role overlaps those of police and security services).

The extent of State surveillance of our lives can only be guessed at: most police forces in Britain either already have or plan to buy a computer intelligence system. At best this provides local officers with quickly accesible (if often unproven) information about suspects. In addition to these local databases there is a section on the Police National Computer called simply the Suspected Persons Index. The PNC has a series of other indices with hundreds of thousands of names.

The police have other, secret, computer systems. The Metropolitan Police owns the main intelligence database used by all the 'C' divisions: Special Branch, Organised Crime, Drugs and anti-Terrorist squads. (In addition, both MI5 and MI6 maintain their own computer files.)

No one would argue that these organisations are unnecessary, nor that they shouldn't keep tabs on suspected criminals. The problems come either when, as we saw in the case of Special Branch and Mrs Madeleine Haigh, the subject of the attention is not nor ever will be a criminal or, as in Jan Martin's case, when the information is simply wrong.

Ms Martin was, in the event, extremely lucky. Her father was a former detective chief superintendent at New Scotland Yard. He began investigating his daughter's undeserved reputation as a European terrorist.

> He found out that the information had come from Holland. My husband and I had been on holiday recently and had driven through Holland. One morning we stopped at a little café for a meal; the owner thought my husband looked like a picture he had seen of one of the Baader-Meinhoff gang. He phoned the Dutch police who passed it on to the London Special Branch. We didn't know anything about it; certainly no one ever discussed it with us. The first I knew was when it was leaked to Taylor Woodrow.
>
> I think the most worrying thing about it all was that when I was taken for an interview with the Special Branch after it happened, I asked what would have been the outcome if my father hadn't been a policeman. The Branch officer just shrugged his shoulders. I would never have found out.

Demelza Val Baker also found out about inaccurate police information the hard way. In May 1983 she and a friend were driving out of Plymouth. Ms Baker was eight months pregnant. The car was stopped by police searching for drugs. They took Ms Baker to a local police station and proceeded to examine the car in minute detail. Ms Baker asked why, and was told that the registration number related to a house where a drugs raid had been carried out. This puzzled and upset Ms Baker, who had no knowledge of or involvement with any illegal drugs.

> The experience was horrifying. I was made to feel like a criminal – they didn't believe that I had nothing to do with drugs. When I

finally got home I told my father about it. He told me that the police had in fact once raided the house for drugs, but that they later admitted they had got the wrong address.

Baker had even sued the police on that occasion and received an apology and compensation. Yet the erroneous information was still on file, and used against his daughter.

These are by no means isolated examples. Early in 1986 Hertfordshire police suggested to Tayside Regional Council in Scotland that a woman it was considering appointing had a criminal record. Tayside wanted to employ Mrs Anne Trotter, of Kirriemuir, on a special fostering programme for delinquent teenagers. In line with properly recommended procedures for such jobs they wrote to the police in Hertfordshire, where Mrs Trotter had lived for a while, to check her antecedents. The police wrote back that two separate sets of 'convictions are recorded against Anne Trotter, who appears to be identical with the applicant'.

In fact, those offences involved thefts in Newcastle upon Tyne in 1942 and 1947. Quite apart from the fact that under the Rehabilitation of Offenders Act, 1974, the police had no business publicising those records, at the time Mrs Trotter was a fifteen-year-old schoolgirl in Arbroath and not unnaturally still called by her maiden name of Lawson. She has no such convictions, and was extremely upset at the allegations. What happened next made a nonsense of the government's belated attempt to protect personal information, the Data Protection Act.

The Data Protection Act

The Data Protection Act finally limped on to the statute book in 1984 – the year of Orwell's Big Brother nightmare state. Appropriately enough, then, the Act did nothing to control the power of the State, whilst managing to tie up almost every other commercial computer user in a confusion of red tape and paperwork.

The main purpose of the Act was much the same as had been suggested almost constantly since 1967: to give members of the public a right to know who held what information about them and to correct it if it turned out to be inaccurate.

But rather than fully protecting the public from the misuse of information held on them – be it accurate or not – the government had decided on the weakest possible measure that would pass

European scrutiny and allow British firms once again to apply for international data-processing contracts. To that end it introduced a series of exemptions and definitions that effectively rendered the Act worthless. For a start, only information that was wholly computerised came under its provisions – and since most sensitive data is held on a mixture of paper and computer files the vast majority of such information is excluded by the Act. Even a simple card index covering the contents of an otherwise entirely computerised set of processed files is enough to protect all that information from the people it most concerns – its subjects.

As if that wasn't enough, the government also insisted on a clever piece of semantic hair-splitting. Expressions of opinion about a living person, are – assuming they are entirely held on computer – covered by the Act. But expressions of intention are not. Thus, if an employer wrote a reference which said: 'This man is a trouble-making Communist unfit to hold a position of trust', the Act provides some form of safeguard. But if the reference said: 'This man is a trouble-making Communist, unfit to hold a position of trust and I intended to sack him anyway', the Act would be powerless.

Next came the rest of the exemptions. The government ruled out any right of access – let alone correction – in cases which involved national security, the prevention and detection of any crime and the collection of any tax or duty. In other words, almost all police, intelligence service and government financial department's computers were excluded. The only concession was the criminal records database: the public was to be allowed to know what information from the database was provided to employers and to challenge it if it proved to be wrong.

Against the background of these severe limitations, the Act divided the nation into data users and data subjects. Data users are individuals or organisations who use or control the computerised information. Data subjects are the people about whom information is so kept.

To monitor and supervise all this, the Act provided for a Data Protection Registrar. Lindop had recommended a full-blown statutory authority, but the government preferred to appoint one man to do an authority's work. Admittedly, the registrar was given a secretariat: in his first, crucial, year in office registrar Eric Howe was given just twenty civil servants.

Not the least of Howe's worries was getting data users to register. Computer experts estimate that there are roughly 400,000 such users, and the Act made it an offence for them not to have registered by May 1986. The government did not give figures for those whom it expected to register, but by the cut-off date even Eric Howe admitted that more than 100,000 known users had failed to do so. The Data Protection Registry began sending out reminders to those whom it felt should have paid the £22 registration fee.

Eric Howe knew that by November 1987 his office had to produce a Data Protection Register, to be available in all public libraries, which data subjects could consult. In the Register are the names and addresses of all those who have bothered to sign up. Also listed are the uses to which they put their computerised data. All a subject has to do, in theory at least, is write to a data user and ask for a printout of any information the user holds on computer about him or her. The fee for such a check – whether it proves positive or not – is £10.

Once again, theory dismally fails to match practice. Should a data user fail to respond, refuse to provide whatever its computers hold or correct any erroneous information, the subject has a right to complain to Howe. Anne Trotter put the theory to the test.

Mrs Trotter had abandoned her attempt to work for Tayside Regional Council after Hertfordshire police wrongly suggested that she had a criminal record. Instead, she became a teacher. When she finally learned of the Data Protection Act (of a sample of 1,000 householders in May 1987 fewer than 300 had even heard of the Act), she went about complaining and seeking compensation.

On 3 July 1987 her solicitor wrote to Hertfordshire Police claiming redress. On 8 July the police wrote back, denying any responsibility towards Mrs Trotter. The letter they had sent to Tayside Council hadn't actually said that Mrs Trotter had a criminal record, merely that the convicted Mrs Trotter from Newcastle 'appears to be identical with the applicant'. In any case, said Hertfordshire police, the Scottish Mrs Trotter wasn't covered by the Act. 'The fact of the matter is that your client is not a data subject under the terms of the Data Protection Act as it is now clear that no records are held in respect of your client . . .' In other words, because Mrs Trotter was entirely innocent while Hertfordshire Police had said she was guilty, she wasn't entitled to compensation. Which makes a mockery of the Act.

Howe, to his credit, said that he disagreed with the police interpretation of the Act. But then he could do nothing about it. Under the Act's provisions, the registrar can only instigate criminal proceedings. Mrs Trotter's case would be a civil one against the police – which Howe was powerless to help her with. Mrs Trotter was equally powerless: she couldn't afford to take civil action, and legal aid is not available to enforce those few rights granted us by the Data Protection Act.

Whether Hertfordshire Police will ever repeat its unfounded allegations against Mrs Trotter is anyone's guess. Demelza Val Baker's guess might well be that they would; as she found to her cost, inaccurate information is often not removed from police computers even when a court has fined them for their incompetence.

Why then is the government so determined to protect official computers from public scrutiny? The answer lies in something called NINO. NINO is official jargon for National Insurance Number. Almost every citizen has a national insurance number, and most of us think, if we ever spare it a thought, that it has something to do with the NHS or unemployment benefit – which, in part at least, it has. But to the government NINO is far more important. It is the key to another, rather more secret, acronym – UPI. UPI stands for Universal Personal Identifier: a vast computerised database of all State files on all citizens. If that sounds relatively innocuous, what a UPI can do is bring Orwell's Big Brother state to life.

Every government department – and many other local government or Quango-type organisations – keep files on clients. For example, the DHSS keeps records of who receives what State benefit (including child benefit), and to make these files more manageable it is creating a computerised Central Index, listing every single one of the 56 million people living in Britain. The index will be housed at the existing DHSS computer complex in Newcastle. The key to the index will be an individual's NINO.

Similarly, the Inland Revenue will shortly complete its computerisation programme. The DHSS has already passed its Central Index on to the Revenue, so the two systems contain much of the same information. Additionally, the Revenue has chosen NINO as the entry key to its system.

So far, so clever. But what can the system do? According to

former Inland Revenue officer Tony Meredith, it will be the fastest ever method of tracing anyone, anywhere.

> The National Taxpayer Tracing System will be enormously powerful. It will find anyone within a few seconds, from any one of 25,000 terminals in any one of 600 tax offices. There will be very few controls on access to the system – such as a good reason for requesting information – so it will be very, very easy for someone inside the Inland Revenue to pass information to an outsider. Frankly, you couldn't stop them.

What sort of outsider would want the sensitive, personal information held by the Inland Revenue and the DHSS? By far the biggest customer has historically (if unofficially) been the police. The government is aiming for a link-up – using NINO as the key link – between all its departments and agencies. Ultimately, the bobby on the beat will be able to find out your most personal private information with one radio call back to base.

Lindop warned in his 1978 report against allowing this to happen by stealth:

> Such linkages may or may not be desirable in the public interest. What is clear is that as the law now stands there is nothing to prevent them coming about by mere administrative fiat, without the public or their representatives in Parliament having the opportunity to debate and decide such questions, and indeed without their ever having been told about them.

By the end of 1984, the Data Protection Act notwithstanding, that position remained legally unchanged.

But then, *shouldn't* the bobby on the beat – who is after all only there to protect the public and our property – have all the information he needs to do the job, even if that means breaching the strict claims of confidentiality made by the Revenue and the DHSS? The answer is of course that the information doesn't stay with that individual bobby. It is logged on local intelligence computers, analysed and used as the basis for 'intelligence' files, and – as we shall see later – sold or passed to private detectives and commercial firms.

The police collator of records in Skelmersdale has a particularly racy style in writing his reports. The unchecked and potentially malicious gossip contained in the following extracts from a two-page document published in 1984 by the GLC illustrate how dangerous localised 'criminal intelligence' can be. (The names and addresses below have been changed to protect the people concerned.)

The right man for the job
Robert Jones, of 14 Crosby Road, Newtown – known affectionately to his CB mates as 'Tiny Tot' – paid another return visit to our fair division at 3.30 a.m. on 15.7.82 when he was stopped/checked in his nifty yellow Ford Galaxy. Gracefully reclining in the passenger seat was none other than school-breaker and suspected druggie James Richard Dack (30.3.62 – wounding, burglary, theft, damage), whose unforgettable features are pictured left. [Attached to the report is a photograph of a black man.] Dack, a state benefit subscriber, augments his hard-earned dole by working on the door at the Talk of the Town, keeping out other undesirables. Jones and Dack are well acquainted with the finer points of our division and are worth every stop/check they can get.

On a higher plane
The Ananda Vedi – a mystical meditation type set-up based in Skem – attracts seekers of the truth from some very exotic places and the latest recruit would appear to be John MacGregor, who hails from 121 Edinburgh Place – a part of Glasgow known as the Gorbals. MacGregor, who was checked on a motorbike in Connington Crescent, was apparently bound over in the Met for possessing explosives – but not convicted as such. His address in Skem is 13 Hardy Lane, the home of Rosalinda Jack.

On the face of it these two extracts might appear to contain useful information (amid the florid prose). But look closer: Jones appears not to have a criminal record, while Dack has no form for fraud or drug abuse. Yet both are implicated with a specific request for frequent stop/checks. MacGregor has not been convicted of any offence – it is impossible to be bound over for illegally possessing explosives – yet the clear implication is that he has done something unlawful. And what of Rosalinda Jack? Will she be subject to police attention simply because a man convicted of no offence whatsoever lives at her address? More worrying still, will she, like Anne Trotter, suddenly acquire a criminal record overnight?

Nor are local police intelligence computers the only state tabs kept on innocent citizens. Immigration officers (controlled, like the police, by the Home Office) will soon have access to a new computerised Suspect Index. There are some 20,000 names on this database, including wanted or convicted terrorists and drug traffickers. But the index is also used to keep an eye on British citizens whom the government dislikes or distrusts. Citizens such as the actress Vanessa Redgrave, the political activist Tariq Ali, and at least two investigative journalists: David Leigh of the *Observer* and Duncan Campbell of the *New Statesman*.

By 1988 Britain will have fallen into line with the rest of the EEC and introduced computer-readable passports. The central computers will be linked to 500 terminals at ports and airports round the country. That way, when Ms Redgrave or Messrs Ali, Leigh and Campbell travel abroad, the government can keep a more efficient eye on their movements.

The most sensitive information of all is that kept by doctors and hospitals (our medical files), school or university records and local social work files. All these categories are exempt from the Data Protection Act (and therefore legally closed to their subjects) because they are not wholly computerised. So, except in the case of a handful of education authorities, we have no right to see or challenge what a school or university says about us.

In 1985 the Campaign for Freedom of Information published a list of comments from school reports which illustrated the problem perfectly:

'A bit concerned over X's honesty, though as yet no evidence.'

'Parents are not married.' (In fact, they had been for some years.)

'This girl is a thief and a liar.' (A comment forwarded to the child's new school, where her teacher reported: 'This young lady seems honest, truthful, frank and extremely helpful.')

'Very much inclined to sulk. Wants to be liked and likes to hang around and curry favour with teacher. Very much inclined to cheat. Rather lovable in spite of all.' (This was a primary school record, written when the girl was seven and still in her secondary school folder when she was fourteen.)

Perhaps it is unsurprising, then, that education authorities and teachers often don't want to disclose such dubious and inaccurate reports to their victims – even though they routinely supply them to would-be employers, and occasionally to the police. But schools also provide writen assessments of their pupils to juvenile courts, who take these into account when sentencing, or even when deciding whether to put the child into care. Yet research by the University of East Anglia indicates that these reports may be just as damaging:

'I believe he is moving inexorably towards a life of crime and terms of imprisonment. He affects a nice side to his character but this is not genuine.'

'Mother professes an interest in his welfare, but we hear stories of drinking and late-night parties.'

'Steals from her classmates and behaves in an unfeminine manner.'

'This boy is big, black and smelly.'

'Jimmy is a cancer to the student body. If he didn't commit this offence then someone else in his family did.'

Rules of evidence in juvenile courts allow such reports to be taken into consideration by the magistrates without them being shown to the young person or his parents. In theory, the bench is supposed to pass on the general substance of the school's comments. But the 1981 East Anglia survey showed that JPs' policy on disclosure could 'vary from scrupulous adherence to total non-compliance'. In 59 per cent of cases the full report was not disclosed to parents or defendants, and a third of these benches 'seldom' or 'never' summarised or revealed any detail of the assessments. The study also checked magistrates' notes to ascertain how much importance had been attached to the school's comments: frequently it appeared that they had relied on them. Yet instead of putting the allegation to the young people in front of them and asking for their comments, magistrates had typically remarked: 'The report from your school is not very good – have you anything to say about that?'

Providing information on pupils to juvenile courts is part of a school's legal duty. Routinely passing it to the police is not. And yet all too frequently, school reports – potentially as inaccurate and subjective as those above – are handed over.

Rodney C. is a young West Indian teenager in an inner London borough. In the early hours of one morning in December 1983 he was taken from his parents' home by police investigating a burglary. Rodney has no criminal record and this was his first brush with the law. Yet the investigating officers had a school photograph of him, and his school assessment reports. Rodney was finally released without charge ten hours later.

His headmaster admitted giving the police the boy's photo, but denied handing over the school reports. And yet the police had them. Rodney hadn't given them to the police – Rodney, like most children, had not been allowed to see what was said about him. From the behaviour of the police, it appeared that not only had the school handed over either the photograph and/or the report, but had actually cooperated in selecting Rodney as a youth worthy of investigation. To this day neither Rodney nor his parents know why.

Social work files are among the most crucial and sensitive documents ever written about an individual. On the strength of them children may be removed from their parents, prison sentences rather than less severe punishments can be meted out, and old people or the mentally ill placed against their will in institutions.

In 1983 the DHSS issued a consultation paper which admitted that the information recorded on social work files cannot be guaranteed to be strictly factual: 'It is sometimes of great importance to include impressions and opinions which are of crucial significance . . . in enabling accurate impressions to be made.' According to at least one social worker, John Taylor, those 'impressions of crucial significance' can be disgracefully inaccurate. In September 1982, Taylor – then a team worker in Barnsley – wrote to *Community Care* magazine.

> I have seen the evidence for myself in educational, medical and social work practice – that people who have professional positions do make entries on files for which there is little or no evidence, entries which are personally offensive because untrue, entries which say more about that worker's insecurity or personal inadequacy than they do about the person to whom they refer.

The scope of those inaccuracies – and the effect on the subjects of the reports – is something we have considered in an earlier chapter. But some social services departments regularly pass files on their clients to police officers without telling the clients (one social services department even shares a computerised report-filing system with the police).

In 1984 both the British Association of Social Workers and the

DHSS recommended that clients should have an (albeit limited) right to see what social workers say about them on file. Despite this, the government fought tooth and nail every attempt to put these suggestions on to the statute book.

The Data Protection Act is, as we have seen, a severely watered-down version of that recommended in Lindop's original report. And it was the same story in the spring of 1987 when a private member's bill aimed at creating an individual's right of access to social work, education, employment, housing, credit, immigration and medical records was introduced.

The bill's sponsor was Liberal MP and Scottish lawyer, Archie Kirkwood. His Access to Personal Files Bill was wide-ranging and well-drafted. It was also far from being acceptable to the government, and a private member's bill has little chance of becoming law without governmental support. Kirkwood was realistic, and after the first reading did a deal with Whitehall. He agreed to drop the most contentious records – medical, immigration and employment – from his bill in return for a promise of non-opposition from the government. The amended measure swiftly received an unopposed second reading in the Commons. Next on the agenda was the committee stage to thrash out the finer points, a third reading in the Commons, a trip next door to the Lords and finally the Royal Assent.

The government reneged on the deal, however. In committee it introduced a favourite ploy: instead of *requiring* ministers to make regulations introducing the rights of access within a year, the Whitehall draughtsmen had phrased the bill so that it merely gave them the option to do so. There was to be no legal compulsion.

The trick – an old Whitehall favourite – dragged the bill through a bitter committee stage for weeks. Then, with a general election looming which would consign any unfinished bills to the parliamentary dustbin, another compromise was reached. The government promised to use 'its best endeavours' to make the necessary regulations by the end of 1988.

The government also started negotiations with the medical profession about opening its files to patients. Just in case, Kirkwood piloted another private member's bill – the Access to Medical Reports Act – on to the statute books. But that only provides a right for patients to see medical reports provided by doctors to employers and insurance companies. As yet doctors themselves seem unwilling to allow patients to see their own medical records.

In February 1987 the British Medical Association's Ethical Committee recommended that – given the right circumstances – they should. But within weeks the BMA membership – in other words the thousands of GPs and consultants who actually write out the records – voted down the idea. The prevailing opinion amongst doctors was that the records belonged to them rather than the patient, and therefore there was no general 'right' to see what was said in them. Perhaps a more honest assessment of doctors' unease at opening up their files came two years earlier in a letter from a GP to the medical paper *Pulse*: 'All GPs, I imagine, have at times in moments of pique written unfair and maybe untrue things about troublesome patients on their records. Are patients to have free access to read those things? If so doctors must be prepared for libel actions?'

But what exactly constitutes a 'troublesome patient', and what sort of unfair or true comments are recorded? Here are just a few examples.

'This lady is pregnant . . . She is married to a diabetic electronics boffin who does hush-hush work for the Admiralty, and thinks more of his cat than of Mrs B.' (A referral note from a GP to a consultant. In fact the husband does not work for the Admiralty and is not even an electronics engineer.)

A twenty-year-old university student visited his college doctor to seek treatment for a facial rash. The doctor checked the boy's medical records (supplied by his previous doctor) and asked whether he needed a repeat prescription for 'his tablets'. When the student, who took no medication whatever, asked what tablets he was supposed to need, the doctor informed him that his records showed a previous operation for the removal of a brain tumour; a history of 'grand mal' epileptic convulsions and a daily intake of anti-convulsant tablets to control the problem. None of this was true. The doctor eventually checked with the boy's former GP. Finally a terse reply arrived: 'On checking through our records I have discovered that the details regarding the temporal lobectomy relate to another patient of ours. Perhaps you would be kind enough to delete the wrong information and accept my apologies.'

Apologies are all very well, but that kind of mistake – all too common in doctors' files – can have serious consequences.

Ronald Ackerman is a laboratory technician. For more than a year he failed to get job after job when his references (notably his medical report) were taken up. In one case he had even been formally offered the job – subject to a satisfactory medical reference. Suddenly the job was pulled from under him. Ackerman began pressing to see the reference. Unusually – a tribute to his persistence – he was shown his medical report. It claimed that he suffered from depression whilst at university. The claim was completely untrue. What had happened was that Ackerman had once told his tutor that his father had suffered from bouts of depression; the information had apparently been misconstrued and ended up as a damning medical reference.

Ackerman's case illustrates the real danger of the unchecked medical gossip which makes up a substantial proportion of doctors' notes. They simply don't remain with the GP, neatly filed in a local surgery. They are fed to other GPs, consultants, schools, employers and even the police.

The case of eight-year-old Edward highlights how inaccurate reports can circulate through more than one agency – and cause chaos and heartache in the process. Edward fell over at school one day and struck his head. Three weeks later he was still suffering from serious headaches: in the end he was taken to his local hospital in no little distress. Doctors immediately noticed swollen glands and a degree of unusual brain-wave activity, but failed to reach a conclusive diagnosis of the cause of the problem. The notes recording these symptoms were not made available to his parents until much later – in fact, not until it was nearly too late.

Edward was discharged, but began to experience such severe pain that he couldn't even walk. Subsequently he spent three and a half months in a London hospital – several hundred miles away from his family home.

One of the reasons for the medical uncertainty over the cause of Edward's problems was a note included in his medical file and originating from a previous school doctor. As paraphrased in his hospital notes, this stated: 'Edward has in the past been seen by an educational psychologist . . . because of school problems when he was noted not to be getting on with other children.' Furthermore, the previous headmaster had reported that: 'He had previously attended two schools [in another county], having transferred from the first because of 'transitory emotional difficulties'. This latter remark was signed by the educational psychologist.

Unsurprisingly, perhaps, one possible symptom considered by the hospital medical staff was that Edward was suffering from a prolonged bout of school phobia. Some time later his parents received a formal warning that unless Edward was returned by them to school – and quickly – a court order would be sought to admit him forcibly to a psychiatric unit.

At this point Edward's parents began fighting to see his medical notes. When they did, they discovered that the reports about their son's alleged school problems were horribly wrong. Edward had indeed been seen by an educational psychologist – but not because he couldn't get on with other children. He had in fact a specific problem of 'laterality' – he was left-handed and the school was forcing him to write with his right hand. As to the 'transitory emotional difficulties', the original educational pyschologist had indeed recorded them – but only as part of the problem of being forced to write with his wrong hand.

It took Edward's parents more than three years to discover and enforce corrections on their son's record. Eventually the Educational Pyschology department confirmed in writing the true reasons for its involvement; admitted that the suggestion that Edward had changed schools because of some emotional difficulty was 'pure assumption' by his then headmaster – an assumption the department had added to Edward's notes; and agreed that the real reason Edward had changed schools was that his parents moved house.

They also discovered that these notes appeared to have played a major role in the confusion over Edward's diagnosis. Despite registering his medical symptoms, doctors at the first hospital had – after seeing the boy's file – recorded that his illness was 'quite likely to be psychogenic' – in other words a mental condition.

Edward was perhaps lucky: his father was a doctor, his view was that the boy had been suffering from a viral infection, and the original hospital notes even record this as a possibility. Edward should have had blood tests at a very early stage in his illness to ascertain this. His father insisted that these hadn't been done. The hospital, guardedly, said all necessary tests had been carried out – but what was 'necessary'?

At the time the hospital team had been sure – from their 'tests' – that they 'were not dealing with any physical illness'. Two and half years later, the health authority admitted that Edward's illness might *not* have been psychological in origin. 'None of the clinical and pathological findings eliminated the possibility of a physical illness.'

Finally, Edward was well enough to return to school; he had lost more than a year through illness. But his parents' problems didn't end there.

Edward's consultant had made notes about his parents. These had been forwarded to another consultant involved in the case. The notes – which only emerged later – claimed that: 'The father has continued his fruitless search for an organic basis for [Edward's] symptoms, and his wife has been reacting in a very disturbed way with many unfounded accusations about the medical and school care [he] has been given.'

The consultant concerned was not, of course, to know that the school medical reports had been false and that there were very good grounds both for distrusting the school care and for seeking a medical or organic cause of the illness. He wasn't to know because Edward's parents hadn't then been allowed to see the medical notes and have them corrected.

Nor did it end there. At one stage the parents discovered that a social worker had been invited to a meeting discussing Edward's school attendance record. Not unnaturally, they began to worry whether a social services file had been opened on them. At first the social services department denied the existence of any such file. Later it was admitted that a file did exist – but only relating to help the couple had sought when their home was flooded. Finally the truth came out that a social services file had indeed been opened on their son. The parents believe that this must have involved some breach of medical confidentiality because they at no stage consented to the passing of information between the two agencies.

Edward's parents have not been allowed to see the contents of the file (it goes without saying that Edward is also prevented from knowing what the professionals say about him). The most they could obtain from the social services department was an assurance by the director that he will keep the file in his office under his personal supervision, and that no other member of staff will have access to it.

The issue of who has access to what personal records is still in confusion more than three years after the passage of the Data

Protection Act, and more than twenty years after the first parliamentary moves were made to give the public some control over what is recorded on their files. The latest move by the Home Office, announced in July 1987, is to bring a limited right of personal access to medical files somehow within the parameters of the Data Protection Act. Quite how this will be done is not clear, since the Home Office is still drafting the necessary regulations, but one 'safeguard' has already been made clear: access will still require the approval of the GP. Judging by the vote at the BMA and the behaviour of many social services departments, that approval could be a long time in coming.

The information industry

Education, housing, social services, employment, medical, immigration, credit, police: files, files, files – all neatly stacked in council offices and government departments, and sometimes translated on to computerised records. If you can't see them – if the law still protects the 'confidentiality' of the person who wrote the reports – then surely no one else can have access to them either?

The answer, of course, is that they can – in many cases for a price. The largest computer databanks in the country belong not to the DHSS, the Inland Revenue or the police, but to two private commercial companies – CCN Systems of Nottingham, and the United Association for the Protection of Trade (UAPT) in Croydon. These two companies maintain databanks that collate information on 43 million people in this country alone – almost all the population. There are 17,500 access terminals for these systems – and an ever-growing market for the information they can provide.

Of course, neither CCN nor UAPT do anything that is downright illegal (though both shoot holes through the spirit of data protection). Both are heavily involved in providing credit references on members of the public to other commercial organisations. But additionally, both companies have – since 1982 – been collating information to index every house in the country by socio-economic groupings. In other words individual households are listed as being, for example, 'inner city', 'deprived', 'multi-ethnic', 'suburban', 'affluent', etc.

CCN's system is known as MOSAIC. The company claims that it allows for '40 million adults on the CCN database to be classified according to the area in which they live, combining financial, demographic, housing and census data'. Furthermore, the database is 'designed to distinguish areas with different consumer preferences and characteristics'.

So where does CCN get all this data from? Firstly, both it and UAPT buy lists of names on the electoral register from local councils. They pay roughly a penny a name. Then there's the information on socio-economic groupings: that's culled from information householders supplied themselves for use in the 1981 official census. The databanks are indexed by means of the Post Office postcode system, and alongside every name on file is a list of any court judgement against them, plus any other known financial information.

That financial information is itself fed back to CCN by the company's clients. For this is a two-way process: both CCN and UAPT sell their information (at between 50 pence and £1.20 a time), but CCN offers a discount to clients if they feed information into the system as well as take it out.

The people who use this information are typically interested in selling you something. So the junk mailshot that comes through your door, personally addressed and aimed at the right socio-economic consumer target group, is likely to have started life from a mailing list provided by CCN or UAPT.

The two databases are extremely powerful. CCN calls its Nationwide Consumer File 'one of the most powerful tools around for the application of "cold" direct mail'. It and UAPT's Infolink contain 43 million individual names, and they will sell those names broken down in precise analytical terms. So if a customer wants a list of all nineteen-year-old single women living in a particular area of a particular town, the computers can easily provide him with one.

But wasn't the Data Protection Act aimed at controlling just this sort of ever-growing database? And didn't it say in no uncertain terms: 'Personal data held for any purpose . . . shall not be used or disclosed in any manner incompatible with that purpose.' And what could be more incompatible than direct mailshots and the electoral register? Aren't CCN and UAPT breaking the new law?

The answer is both yes and no. Yes, they are breaking that simple clause and the entire spirit of the Act. But then there's a loophole: any information that is statutorily published can be processed, re-processed and sold in any way anyone wants. That overworked man Eric Howe queried this with the Home Office. The Home Office told the Data Protection Registrar that it wasn't interested. Howe then suggested that a warning should be attached on official information forms alerting the public to what might well happen to any data they gave. The Home Office refused the request. 'I'm disappointed,' Howe confessed in the early part of 1987.

Mailshots can be extremely irritating, and many people object to the idea of having their personal lives dissected and recorded for commercial consumption. In September 1986 the BBC commissioned a special survey on public attitudes to this type of databank. One thousand people, carefully chosen so that they were a standard sample of the population, were asked whether they approved of the information they gave when registering to vote being sold without their consent. Of these, 79 per cent disapproved or strongly disapproved of the sale of electoral registers. Only 7 per cent approved of councils selling off their lists of voters. Yet only one council in this country – Greenwich in London – has adopted a policy of refusing to sell that information. Greenwich Council describes the practice of selling the lists as 'quite immoral'.

Quite what Greenwich Council – or the thousand people polled by the BBC – would have made of what happened next is anyone's guess. The survey had been part of an investigation by journalist Duncan Campbell – one of those reporters the government wants to keep electronic tabs on at ports and airports. Campbell found that CCN also offered a computerised debt-collection system. From any one of the terminals dotted around the country, CCN's central computer can be contacted and told that you – the client – are owed money by a named individual, and that you would like it collected.

There was, as Campbell graphically showed, no checking whatsoever of this information. The computer automatically sends out harassing letters to people whom it is told owe money to its clients.

Campbell contacted the CCN computer and told it that he owed one of its clients £300. He gave his office address – the *New Statesman* magazine in London. There was of course no truth in this claim. But CCN didn't bother to check it out. Shortly afterwards, letters threatening Campbell with court action unless he paid the 'debt' within seven days began turning up at the *New Statesman*. The only check the system instituted was to ask for written confirmation from the client before a writ was actually issued. But even then the client did not have to produce any documentary proof that the debt ever existed.

CCN's debt-collection system is obviously a potential threat to everyone on its lists. After all, clients feed information into the system, with apparently no verification process before it is passed on to the next customer. Campbell also claimed to have discovered evidence that both CCN and UAPT sold information to private detectives, despite their claims to the contrary. But why, given the nature of the business, should the companies be so keen to deny this?

The answer probably lies in corporate image. The vast majority of private investigators – particularly if they belong to the professional bodies for their business – keep well within the law. But there is an underground network of private detectives who will do almost anything for money. In particular, they are happy to trade in official or officially protected information.

For example, Duncan Campbell found and secretly filmed a private detective who offered to obtain police and DHSS files on any individuals. He explained how his business worked, and how – as we showed earlier – the police already had the beginnings of a UPI, or Universal Personal Identifier: 'The chap that does my [criminal record checks] is a beat bobby. He gets on the radio and says I've seen this lad doing this that and the other. Anything known about him? Punch it into the computer.' He went on to sing the praises of NINO as the best means of getting information out of the system. 'Everybody's traceable by a National Insurance number . . . tax and National Insurance and things like that . . . are all linked together.'

Campbell gave him a mixed list of targets. Some of the first checks were unsuccessful, but then he came up with accurate details of the criminal record of an animal rights activist on the list. At this point the BBC reported him to the police and a formal enquiry began. As we write, it is still going on and the detective's name is legally protected.

Private investigations and security consultancy businesses are a growth area. Typically, the firms are staffed by ex-policemen – the more prestigious the firm, the higher the former rank or more sensitive the former department (Special Branch, for example). Gary Murray is a private detective fighting his own one-man crusade to clean up the business. He told Campbell: 'I've been in practice privately for over fifteen years and I've had contact with literally hundreds of private detectives and security consultants. Since 1968, that I can recall, most of them have had access to official records.'

Private eyes don't, however, have a monopoly on 'hot' data. There are other, more secretive organisations that collect and collate official files for re-sale to their clients. Perhaps the most prestigious of these is the Economic League.

Founded in 1919 by retired military intelligence officers, the League's declared aim is to fight what it chooses to call 'industrial subversion'. Almost 2,000 companies subscribe around £1 million a year for its services. These services are based around an estimated 250,000 files on individual men and women. In theory the League's targets are meant to be prominent political agitators known for causing trouble in the workplace. In reality this is often far from the truth.

In February 1987 the Independent Television programme *World in Action* secretly filmed an official of the Economic League offering – illegally – to supply information on a group of potential employees to a new company. The official, Alan Harvey, is the League's man in the North-East. He operates from behind heavily locked and unmarked doors in a commercial block in Skipton, North Yorkshire – one of seven League offices around the country. He offered clients a vetting service for their prospective employees: 'We can do up to ten names in three minutes over the phone, provided they're local. If they're from outside the area it will take us half an hour.'

Harvey went on to list the sort of people and organisations which the League considered dangerous. He included Labour politicians like David Blunkett, Ken Livingstone and Tony Benn (all MPs), before spreading his net wider: 'People like CND, Friends of the Earth, anti-apartheid, animal rights. They are very useful vehicles for subversives.' Next he listed exactly what sort of vetting was on offer:

> I don't want it to go outside because it's illegal. I may as well go through the whole lot: credit, criminality, number-plates, this sort of thing. You get number-plates free, but you do pay extra if you wanted to know – and it is illegal – if somebody had a criminal record.
>
> We give all our information to the police. In return they're not exactly unfriendly back. We also have the police on the [League's] press-cutting service as well; only the Special Branch so they know in parallel with us what is going on.

World in Action began checking who was actually on the League's list of subversives. It quickly emerged that people who – even by the League's own generous definition of 'subversive' – had no place on such a blacklist were routinely included for no good reason.

One such person was Eric Moonman, a former Labour MP always considered something of a moderate. Another was a highly distinguished veterinary scientist; she, it appeared, had been included simply because she had a Russian-sounding name. Subsequently she became a Dame of the British Empire – hardly the stuff of which subversives are made. And yet she was on the League's files – files which, if Harvey was to be believed, were shared with the Special Branch.

The Economic League denies that its information is inaccurate. Similarly, it denies having access to police files – despite what Alan Harvey told his clients. Nor, it claims, does it run a blacklist. Yet *World in Action* was able to show – dramatically – that it did just that. Dennis Huggins proved the point.

Huggins is a construction worker by trade. In 1981 he was building a new road in Humberside. When the contract finished he was given the firm impression that he would go on to another site. But suddenly he found it impossible to get work. So worried did Huggins become that he called his former manager, Ken Mullier, to ask if he had been blacklisted.

Mullier was shocked at the suggestion. But he knew that the company he worked for, John Mowlem, was a client of the Economic League. As such he had access to its files. He dialled the League's secret ex-directory phone number, and gave the individual company code to identify himself. He then asked about Huggins.

'They came right back and said he was politically unsuitable,' said Mullier. 'I argued that he was not. He was a first-class employee.'

Mullier was right and the League was wrong: Huggins has never been a member of any political party. Mullier decided to have the name removed from the League's blacklist. It proved a hard task.

'The only way I could do this was to supply the League with six more names to take his place. I picked out people who had either retired or left because of illness.' In other words, the League's files are potentially made up of a large number of entirely innocent names provided as a bizarre *quid pro quo* to remove other, equally innocent, names from the blacklist. This blacklist is then supplied to the League's extensive client list – a hard fact that Mullier was subsequently to find out for himself.

The programme-makers then decided to infiltrate the League's blacklist further. They supplied, through an existing League client, the names of two men which they believed had been passed on to the League as identifying active Communists. Alan Harvey quickly came up with information from his files: both men, he said, had attended Communist Party meetings. He recommended refusing them employment – despite a League claim that it never makes recommendations to employers, merely giving them 'facts' on file.

The two men in question were played a tape-recording of Harvey's allegations. Both lived in Newcastle upon Tyne; both were equally aghast.

'I've never even voted in my life,' said labourer Roy Turnbull.

Scaffolder Ken Martin said: 'It's nonsense. I've never been a member of the Communist Party. I'm more interested in football than anything else.'

But the news that he had been blacklisted at least helped explain a Martin family mystery. All five members of the family had applied for jobs at a new local factory. There were vacancies to spare, but all were turned down except for a daughter who had applied under her married name. The company running the factory was a League subscriber. Four people in Ken Martin's family may have been denied employment because of inaccurate information on the League's blacklist. If so it would certainly fit with what Harvey had said whilst being secretly filmed: he had confirmed that his system also routinely included relatives. 'It's distasteful,' he admitted. 'But who do you risk? Do you risk ninety or a hundred people, or one job?'

Ken Mullier now knows the answer to that question. He had begun looking for a new job at around the time the *World in Action* investigation began. After twenty unsuccessful interviews he asked the programme-makers to check whether a previous employer might have blacklisted him.

Once again Alan Harvey, League organiser for the North-East, was the key. 'While I still want to remain friends with Ken Mullier, I don't really want him involved in one of my companies that has a future ahead of it.'

The company Harvey was so keen to lay a personal claim to was in fact just another of the League's customers. It has 2,000 other company clients. Is Mullier's name on a blacklist supplied to them as well? He certainly thinks so. 'I feel now my career is virtually finished. I've always believed in treating people fairly and honestly, and this is the reward you get in the end.'

The government's response to all this was enlightening. Junior Employment Minister John Lee told the Commons that it was not the government's job to prescribe to companies how records should be used in recruitment. So much for the principles of data protection. At the same time the Home Secretary, Douglas Hurd, asked the police to investigate Alan Harvey's allegations that the League had access to police files. To no one's great surprise the enquiry proved fruitless.

But perhaps we should not be so surprised by the League's allegations. In the *Police Review* of 16 April 1982, a former West Midlands officer, Leslie Prince, published his views on the police and employee-vetting.

> Police officers in the United Kingdom have always been involved in the vetting of employees in the private sector. Employers who have taken ex-police officers on to their security staffs have been cognisant of the fact that, in all probability, he or she will have some form of access to criminal records. Although such checks were rarely admitted, the practice has existed for many years and in many companies it has been an integral part of security procedure.

Prince, who in addition to a lifetime spent on the beat and in CID had also served on the staff of the Police College, was by 1982 deputy chief investigator with a large electrical company and press officer for the Retail and Distributive Security Association. He viewed this type of thoroughly illegal security vetting with some concern – not for any reason of principle but rather because it put his members and ex-colleagues at an unacceptable risk of prosecution. To Leslie Prince one thing was vital: the business of running checks on employees must be legitimised and legalised.

If all this seems to shoot holes through the European-based principles of data protection, the government appears unconcerned. David Waddington, the Home Office minister charged, in 1984, with piloting the bill through the Commons, roundly abused anyone who dared question the government's motives or commitment. Waddington maintained this fantasy even when faced with a damning legal opinion by no less a person than the former European Court judge James Fawcett that the bill would be thrown out in Europe at the very first challenge. That challenge has, as we write, yet to come about: we look forward to it with interest.

This might be an appropriate point to end the section, were it not for the rather more disturbing case of Jim Smith, who achieved prominence in 1982 as Britain's first defence contracts 'whistle-blower'.

An accountant by profession, Smith worked until June 1981 for a Poole-based defence contractor called Aish, a subsidiary of the larger Horstmann Gear group. He discovered that the company was grossly overcharging the MOD – and therefore the taxpayer – for its contracts. In 1980 he began warning company directors about the consequences of this overcharging.

Matters finally came to a head at a board meeting in June 1981, when he refused to ratify Aish's accounts. The board promptly made him redundant. Smith insists that he immediately contacted the MOD and alerted them to the company's overcharging. He also applied for an industrial tribunal hearing, and made it clear to Aish that he planned to contend that the company had been making excess profits on defence contracts. At this point, according to Smith, Aish began to admit the overcharging; they subsequently repaid £412,000 in excess profits and cut a further £300,000 from three new contracts.

Aish, of course, has a slightly different perspective on the affair. It claims that it alerted the MOD to the overcharging first, and that Jim Smith lost his job as a director and financial adviser because of a need to cut costs and (ironically) falling defence contracts. The case led to an investigation by the Commons Public Accounts Committee.

When the Committee finally reported in June 1986 it had not been able to resolve the conflicting claims over who blew the whistle first. However, it gave Smith the benefit of the doubt, pointing out that the first meeting Aish asked for in March 1982 to discuss apparent overcharging had been prompted by Smith's forthcoming industrial tribunal hearing. 'It seems to us likely that the firm sought the meeting because it expected its former employees [Smith was joined by another ex-Aish man] to raise the issue of excess profits at their impending industrial tribunal hearings.'

The Committee also made it clear in its all-party report that it accepted the principle of compensation for whistle-blowers like Jim Smith who had sacrificed a good living to save the taxpayer money. Such a principle is already enshrined in working legislation in the United States.

Within a month, however, the MOD had abruptly refused any form of financial help to Smith – who by this time was in serious financial difficulties and had suffered a heart attack. 250 MPs from across the political spectrum immediately signed a motion demanding compensation for him. The MOD remained obdurate – despite the savings he had made for the department, and despite the fact that his actions led directly to a new and more cost-conscious method of controlling defence contracts.

The long running *Spycatcher* farce may be the public face of governmental attitudes towards the public and information control; the Smith case is the reality. Data Protection and Freedom of Information are dirty words to any government concerned to preserve its tawdry secrets from the scrutiny of its electors.

SIX
Citizens in Uniform

> 'Reading isn't an occupation we
> encourage among police officers . . .
> policemen, like red squirrels, must be
> protected.'
>
> Joe Orton, *Loot*

On Saturday, 4 October, 1986, Steven Shaw quietly and carefully packed up his belongings and headed for the airport. He said goodbye to friends and relatives and flew out of Britain for ever.

At twenty-four he was a little young to become an exile. He didn't leave in search of adventure, love or opportunity. He left for the good of his health. Earlier that year he had been savagely attacked in the street: his nose had been broken, his hands stamped on and his body badly bruised. A lighted cigarette had been repeatedly stubbed out on his left cheek.

There are thousands of men and women mugged and assaulted every year in Britain. Most don't feel the need to emigrate as a result. What made Steven Shaw leave was that he recognised his attackers – and that they happened to be serving police officers.

This chapter examines the relationship of the general public with the police. We write it in the knowledge that we will be attacked from both sides of the political barricades. To those in the pro-police 'law and order at all costs' lobby we will appear to be anti-police extremists. To those on the far left who fail to recognise the vital – and often difficult – job carried out by police officers, we will appear reactionary collaborators.

We have worked, over the years, with many policemen, and will continue to do so. This has not hampered us in writing what follows; in private many officers recognise the injustice enshrined in the British policing policy. The true fault lies – other than with those 'rotten apple' officers involved in individual scandals – with politicians of all parties and the senior civil servants who advise them. It is in their lap that blame for inertia, and often downright opposition, with regard to much-needed reform must rest. It was, after all, a combination of politicians and civil servants who approved a decision to prosecute Steven Shaw for attempting to pervert the course of justice.

Police accountability

We will return later to the Shaw case – and with it others equally serious. But to put them in context we must first examine the relationship between police and public. Who controls whom?

Accountability is the key: to whom are our police accountable – not just when something goes wrong, but on a day-to-day, pound-for-pound budgetary basis? And what, in any case, do we mean by accountability?

The best definition, in this context, comes from the journal of Bramshill police college: 'A person is accountable to another if he is under a duty to answer to that other person for his actions, that duty being attended by the possibility of disciplinary or similar measures if the actions are disapproved of or are irregular.' (Richard Card; 'Police Accountability', *Bramshill Journal*, Autumn 1979.)

If we take Card's definition as the yardstick, then police in England and Wales (as with much else the laws governing control of the police in Scotland and Northern Ireland are completely different) are simply not accountable – in any real sense – to anyone save themselves.

The 'police' as a concept did not, of course, exist before 1829, when Sir Robert Peel reorganised the sundry collection of JPs, parish constables and thief-takers who between them had previously kept some sort of rough order. Within a given social stratum, the entire community had a responsibility to raise 'hue and cry' in pursuit of criminals, and even had the right to keep arms for that purpose.

In addition, unpaid and part-time constables were elected from the community to oversee this responsibility. Today there are still residual common-law powers enjoyed by police which date back to these early constables. In towns, paid nightwatchmen were employed to assist the constables. With the arrival in the fourteenth century of JPs, parish constables lost a good deal of status and were responsible to the Justices, whose bidding they were required to do. In that sense the call for some form of control over the police is older even than the modern concept of police forces originated by Peel.

Gradually the system fell into disrepair and disrepute. Given that constables were unpaid, it followed that only the wealthy could afford to take on the job, and were expected to do so. And in the way of the wealthy they soon grew tired of their burden. By 1714, when Daniel Defoe wrote *Parochial Tyranny*, the office had sunk about as low as it could get.

Defoe described the 'imposition of office' as 'an unsupportable hardship; it takes up so much of a man's time that his own affairs are frequently totally neglected, too often to his ruin'. As a result a practice of paying deputies grew up; unfortunately the men picked for the job were often 'scarcely removed from idiotism'. Alternatively, it was possible to avoid office by paying a fine to parish funds – Defoe himself took advantage of this in 1721 at a cost of £10. The fines varied from place to place, but in some densely populated areas – notably London – they became an important source of parish funding. It is possible to see this as a crude precursor of the present police precept imposed by local councils – of which more shortly.

By the end of the eighteenth century the system was near to collapse. Not only were many of the deputising parish constables often illiterate and slow-witted, but they and the JPs were frequently as corrupt as the criminals they were supposed to pursue.

By the time Peel began pushing for an organised police force in London, the Napoleonic Wars were over and England began to experience what would turn out to be half a century of periodic rioting. It was the damage to property caused in these affrays and the ensuing pressure from industry that persuaded Parliament to agree to the Metropolitan Police Act of 1829. (Interestingly, no fewer than three parliamentary committees between 1816 and 1822 had rejected the notion of a police force as 'too great a sacrifice' of British liberty.)

Peel's police were put under the control of two Justices (later to be called Commissioners) specially appointed for the task. They reported directly to the Secretary of State for the Home Department, or Home Secretary (there being no local government structure which, at the time, could have taken on such a responsibility), and the force itself covered the whole of London except the City. A police rate was levied to pay for the force and to manage its property; controlling these funds was the task of a newly created receiver.

Because the Home Secretary had direct responsibility for the Metropolitan Police MPs were able to ask questions in Parliament about general policy and specific incidents. Significantly, that right to question the government on individual – and often sensitive – issues was severely restricted by later Home Secretaries.

The turbulent decades of the 1820s and 1830s led to the transfer of power – albeit gradually – from the landed gentry (the Justices' class) to the new industrial middle classes. Municipal corporations, comprising elected members of this new class, were required by the 1835 Municipal Corporations Act to set up 'watch committees' of councillors and the mayor (who had, still, to be a JP).

The Act required these new committees to appoint a 'sufficient number of fit men' to be constables, charged with preserving the peace, preventing robberies and catching offenders (such activities to be paid for by local ratepayers). Additionally, they had to make regulations to prevent 'neglect or abuse' of these duties and to make constables efficient. Finally, they had the power to dismiss any constable whom they considered to be unfit for office or negligent in his duty. Any two JPs acting in concert also held this power.

The 1835 Act determined the relationship between police, councils and the ratepayers until the 1964 Police Act reorganisation. But it was never clear from the Act exactly who was to control the new forces that sprang up across the country in the wake of Peel's Metropolitan force. It was a confusion that was to last through to the present day. What made the situation more confusing – and still does – was the fact that police constables, although subject to watch committee regulations, drew their powers not from the 1835 statute but from existing common law. To that extent they could act independently of the supervising committees.

If the relationship was unclear and the power of municipal authorities over their police forces distinctly blurred, there are signs that in some cases at least a degree of local political control was established. In Liverpool, for instance, a police force was established in 1835. For the next eleven years a sub-committee of the watch met daily to supervise police operations. Throughout that period it issued, on average, one order a week for the direct placement of officers.

At the same time, the first stirrings of the movement for an 'independent' police force could also be seen. In 1841, the then 'head constable' of Liverpool refused to obey an order from the mayor to ban a Chartist meeting. In Liverpool, as in other major cities, that tradition has died hard.

While all this was going on in the boroughs and cities, rural counties were left with the old system of unpaid and amateur constables. When rioting spread, the government found itself forced to deploy troops and divisions from the Metropolitan force to quell the uprisings. Within four years of the 1835 Act, the government pushed through a weak County Police Act allowing JPs to set up county-based forces. But because there was no compulsion to do so, many didn't bother. Finally, in 1856, the County and Borough Police Act forced them to do so, and created the first centralised control of watch committees, requiring them to report to the Home Secretary. At the same time, home inspectors were appointed to check the standards of local forces and begin to formulate national policing policies from the results of their inspections.

The years between 1856 and 1960 were characterised by clashes between chief constables and police authorities (as the new overseeing committees, made up of the watch and JPs, were called) over who had ultimate authority. Yet the law, unclear and uncertain, remained the same. It was not until a series of incidents in the late 1950s that the issue came into sharp public focus.

Two cases in particular were significant. In 1958 the Nottingham watch committee invoked its powers under the 1835 Act and suspended the Chief Constable. The committee had asked him, in the wake of a series of corruption scandals, to report on investigations he had begun into members of the council. The Chief Constable refused, arguing that it was his duty – not the watch committee's – to enforce the law. The committee then denounced him as unfit for office and suspended him.

At this point the Home Secretary intervened and reinstated the Chief Constable. He reminded the committee that although it had the power to dismiss constables unfit for duty, the police officer himself derived his powers not from the committee, nor from any Act of Parliament, but from common law. Once again the question of control over the police was blurred.

The following year the issue came to a head in the case of Garratt v. Eastmond. In December 1958 Garratt, a London civil servant, sued PC Eastmond of the Metropolitan Police for assault and false imprisonment. Neither the constable nor the Met accepted Garratt's allegations. None the less, the Commissioner of the Metropolitan police came to an out-of-court settlement with Garratt to the tune of £300. In doing so, no liability was admitted, and subsequently it was announced that no disciplinary measures would be taken against PC Eastmond. None of this would have caused much trouble had the Commissioner not seen fit to use public funds to settle the case.

By November 1959 questions were being asked in Parliament as to why public money had been spent if PC Eastmond was not at fault. Or alternatively, if he had been at fault, why hadn't he been disciplined?

The Home Secretary, R. A. Butler, was forced to admit that he had no power in the matter: the question of disciplinary proceedings was entirely a matter for the Commissioner. Nevertheless, Butler concluded that there was a need for some sort of wide-ranging enquiry: 'The case, though starting from a small incident, does have underlying it a number of questions of great importance, both to the public and the police, in which there is evidence of widespread interest and about which there is evidence of considerable anxiety.'

These questions, according to the Home Secretary, were the inability of Parliament to discuss the affairs of provincial police forces; the relationship between central government and police authorities, and that between central government and individual forces; the parallel relationships between provincial police authorities and their chief constables and between the Home Secretary and the Metropolitan Police Commissioner.

> Above all [Butler concluded], there is the relationship . . . between the police service generally and the public. I do not believe that in modern conditions the police can carry out their heavy responsibilities without adequate public cooperation and the fullest measures of public confidence. . . . The time has come to have them [the issues at stake] examined with the authority and impartiality of an independent enquiry.

What followed was the 1960 Royal Commission on the Police. Its appointment had nothing to do with the current state of crime, the efficiency of the police, the strength of their powers or the scales of their pay. The reason for its existence was the troubled question of how to control the police – particularly when things went wrong. It was a question that had been asked and not answered since the fourteenth century. In 1959 Butler's words were apposite and timely. It is a measure of how far we have yet to go that they remain so in 1987.

The Commission presented its final report in May 1962. (It had, ironically, presented an interim report in November 1960 recommending increases in police pay – an interesting indication of its priorities.)

It re-stated the legal position of police officers and pointed out that, being neither employees of the Crown nor of the police authorities, they enjoyed 'a position of exceptional independence. It follows that they are subject to little legal control in carrying out their duties.' Of course, the police had to obey the law, but as to how they enforced it, chief constables seemed to have untrammelled discretion. The chief constable, the Commission noted,

> is accountable to no one and subject to no one's orders for the way in which, for example, he settles his general policy in respect to law enforcement over the area covered by his force; the concentration of his resources on any particular type of crime or area; the manner in which he handles political demonstrations or processions, and allocates and instructs his men when preventing breaches of the peace arising from industrial disputes; the methods he employs in dealing with an outbreak of violence or of passive resistance to his authority; his policy in enforcing the traffic laws and in dealing with parked vehicles and so on. . . .

The Commission had been addressed at length by both sides: chief constables arguing for the continuation of their autonomy, and the Association of Metropolitan Authorities arguing for the right to have a say in policy decisions. In the end it decided that chief constables should not be immune from external control in making or carrying out policies which, after all, 'vitally concern the public interest'. Chief constables, it concluded, should 'be subject to more effective supervision'. But there was a problem.

> The problem is to move towards this objective without compromising the chief constable's impartiality in enforcing the law in particular cases . . . to achieve the advantage of preserving their

impartiality as regards some activities, with the advantage of placing them under a degree of external supervision as regards others: more narrowly, it is to provide effective means of redress against inefficiency or bias while not hindering the efficient and impartial chief constable.

The Commission ultimately recommended four main duties for police authorities:
1. to provide and equip an adequate police force;
2. to constitute a body able to advise chief constables on local conditions;
3. to appoint, discipline and remove senior officers from the force;
4. to play an active role in fostering good relations between the police and the public.

The Commission also decided that the legal responsibility for efficient policing in a force area should be taken away from the authorities and given instead to the Home Secretary. (The Commission had favoured all along a centralised national police force rather than the existing network of local forces.)

Following from this decision, the Commission recommended, firstly, considerably limited powers for police authorities in carrying out their duties. Those limitations were to become crucial. Police authorities should, said the Commission, be allowed to call for reports from their chief constable on matters relating to policing. But the power was not to be a means of checking or controlling a chief constable's actions – merely a forum for expressing the authority's anxiety. Furthermore, the chief constable should have the power to refuse any such report, subject only to the approval of the Home Secretary.

Secondly, authorities should have the power of hire and fire over the chief constable and his deputies (subject to the Home Secretary's agreement). But once again the Commission limited the powers, which were to have 'only a regulative effect . . . they were obviously not intended to be instruments for compelling a change of policy by a chief constable on a relatively minor matter; nor are they appropriate for that purpose'.

Finally, the authorities were to have the power to requisition moneys to cover police expenditure from their local councils.

As to who should sit on police authorities, the Commission thought that two-thirds of the members should be elected councillors, one-third magistrates. In London, of course, there were no police authorities and the Commission decided that that should not be altered; in view of the special needs of the capital, the Home Secretary was to retain overall responsibility.

The 1963 Police Bill was closely modelled on the Commission's recommendations. All the duties and responsibilities it set out were accepted and written into the statute. All except one, that is. Inevitably, the one proposal omitted in the bill turned out to be the foundation stone of the entire legal edifice of police accountability.

Instead of giving to the Home Secretary responsibility for the efficiency of each separate force, the Police Bill ensured that it remained with the police authorities. This created two enormous problems that still cause chaos today. Firstly, the Home Secretary would not be answerable in Parliament for police policies and actions – even though his department sent out (as it does today) circulars effectively telling chief constables what to do with regard to particular issues. And secondly, local police authorities did not have sufficient power to control such policies either; the Commission's suggestion to limit their powers had been made because the Home Secretary was to take responsibility. In the end, the issue was fudged and the dispute over who controls the police went unresolved. On 1 June 1965, all this became law. It remains fundamentally unchanged today.

So much, then, for the history and theory. But what has all that got to do with the average citizen, who rarely comes into contact with the police except as a victim of crime?

On 16 April 1987, the Chief Constable of the West Midlands, Geoffrey Dear, explained. 'No matter how skilfully one addresses the problem of wringing more and more operational time out of officers, the sponge must eventually run dry,' he wrote in his annual report. 'There is clearly a limit to what can be done in the future.'

The point Dear was driving at was quite simple. He hadn't enough money or officers to fulfil all his police duties in the West Midlands. Something, somewhere was going to suffer, and Dear had decided to draw up a list of priority duties – and then simply downgrade the rest. He declined, however, to list which duties – for which read crimes – would go potentially unpoliced.

Dear's announcement was the clearest-yet admission that the police can't cope with all we ask them to do. He was faced with a 10 per cent increase in crime in his area alone, and had asked the Home

Office for an extra 1,000 officers. Instead he was told to take on another 427 civilian staff, which would release 380 officers for operational duties. With this in mind, the Chief Constable issued his warning: 'It is the sheer volume of crime that leads divisional commanders to say that something has got to give.'

Dear's announcement finally lays to rest the notion that the police simply enforce the law – all of it – impartially. The very admission that only priority duties will be fully carried out involves a value judgement as to which crimes really matter – in other words a partial and subjective decision.

At this point, given the fact – as the Royal Commission noted – that these decisions will vitally affect the local population, the police authority's voice needs to be heard. In the event, the voice is either never raised, is ignored, or in some cases is silenced for ever.

If Dear was guarded about what his priorities would be, other chief constables are more forthright. In Manchester James Anderton takes a particularly hard line. Even in 1979 – before inner-city rioting became a feature of British life – Anderton was making his views clear. He appeared on television to announce that in future his policing priorities would not be 'basic crime as such' – burglary, theft and robbery, for example. 'What will be the matter of greatest concern to me,' he explained, 'will be the covert and ultimately overt attempts to overthrow democracy, to subvert the authority of the state, and . . . acts of sedition designed to destroy our parliamentary system and the democratic government in this country.'

If Anderton was keen on democracy in theory, he was less attentive in practice. The Manchester police authority, had not been given the opportunity to discuss – let alone object to – this policy shift. And yet survey after survey has shown that the crimes which worry most people (i.e. the majority of the electorate of any police authority) are theft, burglary and robbery – the very areas Anderton wished to put on the back burner. (In fairness to the men and women of Greater Manchester Police we should point out that – despite the Chief Constable's pronouncement – the force has earned considerable praise for the speed and efficiency with which it responds to attacks on old people. Anderton's comments have had an effect, however, as we shall see shortly.)

Manchester is not a unique example. The inner-city riots of the early 1980s led – largely thanks to the efforts of Lord Scarman's Brixton enquiry – to a greater realisation of the problems of policing such areas. Unemployment, dereliction and deprivation have historically turned inner-city areas into powder-kegs that can explode upon the slightest (perceived) provocation. With this in mind some forces appointed community liaison officers to work with community leaders and thus attempt to improve relations and eliminate local crime on a gradual basis. But the schemes are not regarded with any great affection within the police service itself.

The former Metropolitan police commissioner Kenneth Newman, generally viewed as an 'intellectual' policeman, gave his view of the inner-city problem in a 1983 lecture:

> Throughout London there are locations where unemployed youth – often black youths – congregate; where the sale and purchase of drugs, the exchange of stolen property and illegal drinking and gaming is not uncommon. The youths regard these locations as their territory. Police are viewed as intruders, the symbol of authority – largely white authority – in a society that is responsible for all their grievances about unemployment, prejudice and discrimination. They equate closely with the criminal 'rookeries' of Dickensian London.

Newman might have added prostitution and sundry other unpleasant features of London life to the list. And he was, of course, perfectly correct. The problem occurs in deciding what to do about the rookeries: how – and how intensively – to police them in contrast with other areas of criminal activity. That involves a value judgement, an exercise of priorities.

Typically, police response to the problem is either to have a high-profile policy, or an extremely low-profile approach. Rarely is there a successful happy medium.

Just before 1 p.m. on Saturday, 5 October 1985 Floyd Jarrett was driving his car down Rosebery Avenue, Tottenham. The tax disc was five weeks out of date – a fact quickly discovered by two police officers who stopped the car. One, a PC Casey, decided to check the car's registration number with the Police National Computer. He called up Tottenham police station and within a few minutes established that the car wasn't recorded as stolen and that the tax disc – although overdue – did relate to a car of the right make and chassis number. The only mismatch was that the computer recorded the last letter of the registration number as 'W', while Jarrett's car number plate ended with a 'U'. On the basis of this inconsistency PC Casey arrested Floyd Jarrett on suspicion of stealing the car.

It has to be said that Jarrett did not help himself when he arrived at the police station. He gave a false name and address. None the less, by 3.30 p.m. the police had established his identity and found his address in their files. According to their records he lived at 25 Thorpe Road, London N15.

In fact that was his mother's address and Floyd Jarrett lived somewhere else altogether, but, not unnaturally, he had the keys to his mother's house. These were confiscated by Tottenham police, though they failed to enter (as required) the fact on Jarrett's custody record.

According to subsequent police evidence, an off-duty officer, DC Randall, happened to be at the police station while Floyd Jarrett was being interviewed. DC Randall had apparently heard from an unidentified and never substantiated source that Jarrett was a 'major handler' of stolen goods. He proposed a raid on the house in Thorpe Road to see what might be hidden there.

Tottenham's duty officer agreed to the search – though he stressed that it must be a low-key operation. Advice from community liaison officers was that a possible riot was in the air. Not for the first time, this crucial advice was ignored.

Tottenham police were, at the time, conducting a 'dry run' of the Police and Criminal Evidence Act – a major piece of legislation affecting police and public which came into effect just over a year later. However, under its provisions – and in line with previous law – 'fishing expeditions' like those proposed by DC Randall are unlawful. Furthermore, the officers concerned must get a search warrant signed before a raid by a magistrate. Whether DC Randall and his colleagues obtained such a warrant before raiding 25 Thorpe Road was never ascertained. In his subsequent report on the independent enquiry into that afternoon's events, Lord Gifford recorded 'at least a strong case against the officers' that the warrant was signed some time later.

Perhaps it wouldn't have mattered, had the officers not proceeded to operate in what can only be described as a cavalier manner.

DC Randall, accompanied by Sergeant Parsons and PCs Casey and Allan, drove off to Thorpe Road. Inside number 25 Floyd Jarrett's mother Cynthia and his sister Patricia were watching television. The officers later claimed to have knocked three times.

The Jarretts never heard them. Perhaps significantly, none of the four policeman could remember the very distinctive shape of the Jarretts' door knocker.

The officers let themselves in with the key they had taken from Floyd Jarrett, but when they found Cynthia and Patricia in front of the television they lied and said that the door had been open already. They then began to conduct a rather cursory search of the house. Again contrary to proper procedure, they failed to provide the Jarretts with a photocopy of the warrant.

Initially, as the police acknowledged, Mrs Jarrett was extremely cooperative. Then, towards the end of the search, another of her sons arrived home and objected to the presence of the police. So much is agreed ground between the family and the police. What happened next is not.

According to the officers Mrs Jarrett – who had a heart disease – suddenly collapsed as her son argued with them. The police were then summarily pushed out of the house. Eventually they persuaded the Jarretts to let them back in and DC Randall attempted to revive Mrs Jarrett with mouth-to-mouth resuscitation. He was unsuccessful.

Patricia and Michael Jarrett told a very different story. Patricia was, apart from the police and two small children, the only eye-witness to her mother's collapse. She described how DC Randall 'took his left arm and pushed her [Cynthia Jarrett] out of the way', and then – as she lay dying – proceeded calmly to search the sideboard.

In the event the jury at the inquest into Cynthia Jarrett's death seem to have accepted Patricia's version of events. Instead of recording an open verdict they delivered one of accidental death. A subsequent investigation by the Police Complaints Authority – although characteristically cautious – felt the jury had at least accepted that DC Randall had 'inadvertently brushed past her'. (In fact the terms of the verdict, coupled with the coroner's directions, make it very clear that the jury accepted that DC Randall had laid hands on Cynthia Jarrett.)

Mrs Jarrett's death was a tragic accident. What followed – the Broadwater Farm riot and the vicious hacking to death of PC Keith Blakelock – was even worse. It is no part of our brief to defend that riot or that murder. However, the death of Mrs Jarrett, which appears to have been the spark for the riot, was avoidable. The fact that the police chose to ignore the warning they had been given indicates how little acceptance the concept of low-profile, community policing has among many individual officers.

Their testimony subsequently made it clear that they viewed the entire Broadwater Farm area as one of Sir Kenneth Newman's latter-day Dickensian rookeries, and as the Jarrett family lived on the estate they were tarred with the same brush. Yet neither suggestion is correct. The Jarretts – as recorded in *Police Review* – were crucial in defusing two potentially ugly situations outside Tottenham police station on the night of the riot, and Broadwater Farm had, in comparison with other inner-city estates, a low crime rate. In fact, in the three years leading up to the riot, reported crime on the estate had fallen by 50 per cent.

The Broadwater Farm incident demonstrates how police can behave not only in opposition to the prevailing opinion in the community, but can also ignore their own division's community liaison policy.

An even clearer example of the lack of police accountability and its effects on members of the public had already taken place – though the full implications would not emerge until October 1986. And once again it was an inner-city area trying to come to terms with the legacy of rioting that provided the setting.

On the morning of Friday, 2 August 1985 Lawrence Levey's car was broken into. Levey, a jeweller from Hale in Cheshire, lost a briefcase containing £40,000 in the robbery. He called the police immediately and a chase ensued between the gang and the police. The robbery had taken place just outside the district of Liverpool called Toxteth. Soon the car chase led the police towards Granby Street – where fifty youths armed with iron bars, stones, bricks and pieces of railing attempted to block the road.

The officers radioed Liverpool police HQ – and were told to withdraw. The city's Chief Constable, Kenneth Oxford, had drawn up a new policy for the area in the wake of the 1981 Scarman Report on inner-city riots and the police. Under Oxford's rules patrol cars, operational support units and 'outside' officers were required to obtain permission to enter the Toxteth triangle, about two-thirds of a square mile in size. Even when they were allowed in they were usually accompanied by officers from that section.

Levey was understandably annoyed that the rules had prevented the officers from chasing the gang that had robbed him. He began talking to Liverpool police officers and discovered that Oxford's policy allowed only foot patrols to operate inside Toxteth. Patrol cars, like the one giving chase to the thieves who took his money, were effectively banned from the triangle.

Mr Levey was not impressed. He took out a civil law suit against Oxford, alleging that the Chief Constable had failed to discharge his duty by allowing effective no-go areas in the city. This, said Levey, had allowed Toxteth to become a safe haven for criminals and was illegal because it breached the duty of the Chief Constable to keep the peace, detect crime and bring criminals to justice.

The case reached the Court of Appeal in October 1986 and was heard by the Master of the Rolls, Sir John Donaldson, and two other senior judges. All found against Levey. Sir John made it quite clear that Oxford had an entirely free hand: 'It is not for the courts to review his choice of methods, provided that he does not exceed the limits of his discretion which, in my judgement, is the position in this case.'

So who can review a chief constable's choice of methods? Not the courts, not the public and not, of course, the relevant police authority. A case brought before the High Court in December 1986 settled that once and for all.

Northumbria police authority had gone to court to challenge the Home Secretary's decision to allow any chief constable access to a Home Office store of teargas and plastic bullets, regardless of the views of their authorities. Home Office circular number 40, issued in May 1986 and one of its series of directives to chief constables, provided for just such access, without the need to consult police authorities. This, according to the Northumbria chairman George Gill and the Association of Metropolitan Authorities, struck at the heart of the tripartite system of police administration – the theoretical policy-making trinity of chief constable, police authority and Home Office.

Counsel for the authority, David Keene, QC, explained that it didn't object to the use of CS gas in principle and that the police under its jurisdiction had used it to quell dangerous criminals. 'What the authority is concerned about is the potential undermining of its powers and status with regard to its police force.'

George Gill added his voice: 'This case is about the principle of local accountability. We are totally opposed to plastic bullets, but that is not the reason we are going to court. We believe the Home Secretary is operating outside his remit.'

Plastic bullets have never been used in mainland Britain – though their continued use in Northern Ireland, and the resulting injuries and death, have raised vociferous protests about the need for them. None the less, fourteen of the forty-three forces on the mainland have stocks of plastic bullets; all forty-three have CS gas ready for use.

Almost inevitably, Lord Justice Watkins and Mr Justice Mann dismissed Northumbria's case. Once again chief constables were handed unlimited powers, and once again the spirit of the Royal Commission on the Police had been ignored. A year later, in November 1987, the Law Lords endorsed such judicial myopia and dismissed an appeal by Northumbria Police Authority.

If by the end of 1986 it was clear that chief constables had endless discretion in the way they chose to uphold the law (and indeed in which laws to uphold in preference to others), it had become equally clear what kind of influences and traditions informed their decisions.

In 1983 the Police Studies Institute, a well-respected research body, published the results of a survey of the attitudes and behaviour of police in London. The report, entitled 'Police and People in London', had been commissioned by the Metropolitan Police and researchers had been given access to officers at all levels in the force. The report made for often uncomfortable reading.

PSI identified a dangerous trend inside the Met. Increasingly, officers appeared to view themselves as part of a high-tech, insular machine with its own traditions and objectives to maintain against a hostile outside world. As part of that attitude the researchers pinpointed a pervasive racism, overwhelming support for one political party, rampant chauvinism, and a potentially disastrous lack of experience of life outside the police force. The attitudes revealed, and the behaviour they led to, mirrored warnings given by two eminent authorities a few years previously.

In 1979 the retiring chief constable of Devon and Cornwall, John Alderson, wrote:

> Most serving officers in this new age have become technological 'cops' who barely meet their public outside conflict or crisis . . . loss of human contact, knowledge and understanding, the very essence of democratic policing, is too high a price to pay for technology.
>
> The gulf that can arise from these conditions can open up as

police drift further into their own reactive style – a gulf which can lead to misunderstanding, suspicions, even to hostility.

Three years later Lord Scarman, in his report on the Brixton riots, went further:

> The opportunity to ignore local opinion (but not national) exists for the Metropolitan Police; and he would be a bold man (bolder than I) who would affirm that the existence of an opportunity does not breed the temptation to make use of it, especially when it is convenient or saves trouble.

The 1983 PSI report fulfils both predictions. It found racism among all classes of officer a major problem.

> There is ample evidence, within this series of studies, of the need for change in the policing of London. . . . Confidence in the police is dangerously low among sections of the population, especially young people of West Indian origin. At the same time . . . there is cause for serious concern about some aspects of police practice (rudeness, procedures affecting evidence, interpretations of power of arrest and powers to stop and search, use of force and racial prejudice).

The study went on to back up this claim. For example, in using the stop and search powers of the 1984 Police and Criminal Evidence Act, officers must first have reasonable suspicion that a person is carrying drugs, or stolen property or prohibited articles (i.e. anything which might be used for causing injury or for theft). But what, in the policeman's mind, constitutes 'reasonable suspicion'? PSI researchers asked Met officers their view. What follows are two representative verbatim responses:

> How does an experienced policeman decide who to stop? Well the one that you stop is often wearing a woolly hat, he is dark in complexion, he has thick lips and he usually has dark, fuzzy hair.

And again:

> If I saw a black man walking down Wimbledon High Street I would definitely stop him. 'Course, down here [in the officer's own division] it's a common sight so there's no point.

The report highlighted endemic racism at almost every level. Even when black people were victims rather than aggressors the history of police racism and the ensuing distrust from ethnic minorities created a new tradition of 'reactive racism'. The New Cross party fire of January 1981, in which thirteen young black people died, proved a case in point. PSI researchers noted that the police enquiry – which refused to accept the prevailing local opinion that the fire had been deliberately started by racists – was doomed from the start.

> First, at briefings, by pointing out the difficulties that investigators might face, senior officers reinforced and possibly created the expectation that black witnesses would be hostile, obstructive or untruthful.
> Secondly, senior officers found it very hard to give the impression that the theory of a racialist attack was being taken seriously. Because this was the theory of people who were unreasonably attacking them, as they saw it, they must distance themselves from it as far as possible.

The study concluded:

> Our first impression after being attached to groups of police officers in areas having a substantial ethnic minority population was that racialist language and racial prejudice were prominent and pervasive and that many individual officers and also whole groups were preoccupied with ethnic differences. . . . On the whole, further research confirmed these initial impressions.
> In some cases senior officers undoubtedly overlooked racialism or racial prejudice when it was manifest, or participated in racialist talk themselves. It was a chief inspector who (in the aftermath of the Black People's Day of Action) worked himself up into a frenzy against black people and orchestrated a session of absurd racialist talk with a large group of PCs in the canteen.

Two years after the PSI study alerted the Met to its inherent racism, the Tottenham riot fine-focused it. Steve Platt, a journalist who witnessed the riot wrote:

> A black couple trying to leave the area via William Road were turned back at the police lines to a chorus of monkey noises used to abuse black footballers by racists at soccer matches.
> 'Fuck off, niggers,' yelled one of the policemen. 'Go and live in the zoo. You can burn that down.'
> 'Get back in your rat hole, vermin,' echoed another. 'We'll be in to get you soon enough.'

By October 1986 the proportion of black police officers had risen to just 0.7 per cent of serving officers. Home Office minister Douglas Hogg blamed this on racism within the service and warned the police force to curb its racism. 'It is on the street that the image of a police force is formed,' he warned. How right he was.

The PSI report also revealed a macho tradition of chauvinism inside the Met. Once again the researchers were to be proved right. In October 1986 a secret internal report was leaked from the Metropolitan Police. It revealed that a two-year study by police officers and social workers had uncovered a devastating failure to deal with cases of wife-beating or other domestic violence.

It condemned the police for failing to take the issue seriously and for not charging husbands unless death was likely. It went on to suggest that the force laughed at wife-bashing and frequently failed to record calls for help, often imagining that the wife 'asked for it'. There was, said the report, 'a mentality that these incidents are second class. Official figures disguise rather than reveal the extent of the problem. The incidence and severity are far greater than official sources acknowledge.'

In part this was because of a failure clearly to record calls to the police alleging marital violence, and in part because officers often reported 'no cause for police action' even when they had to visit a couple to intervene in a dispute. As a result, less than 2 per cent of serious assaults recorded in the Met in 1984 were entered as marital violence. Yet a tenth of all unlawful killings are caused by wife-beating. The figures simply didn't add up.

The report concluded that there was 'a lack of empathy, understanding and commitment' over the issue of domestic violence, and repeated the view of women's groups that the police had a 'deeply-held sexist attitude'. Many officers felt unable to use police vehicles to take endangered women to refuges; the reason given was that force mileage allowance rules forbade it.

Faced with two damning reports on chauvinism in its ranks, what did Sir Kenneth Newman's office do? Nothing. The report gathered dust for nine months before it was leaked. After that the Commissioner promised to consider it – though he would have preferred to wait for the Home Office to settle national policy on the subject.

Perhaps it is not altogether surprising that individual officers display such dangerous attitudes. They live, after all, in a society which tolerates the fact that rape within marriage is entirely legal, and belong to a force which unofficially restricts its intake of women officers to 10 per cent of the total force.

Other studies have identified two further significant factors. The first is age: policemen are indeed getting younger. Before 1956 only 20 per cent of policemen were recruited before the age of twenty. By 1973 this figure had risen to 52 per cent. Most forces now aim their recruitment campaigns at school-leavers. The police force is becoming a profession staffed by young men and women with very little experience of outside life before they join 'the job'. This increases the sense of élite isolationism felt by many young officers.

The second factor is politics; unpublished studies indicate that about 80 per cent of all officers support the Conservative Party. One quoted by Robert Reiner in his 1978 report said: 'I feel with a Conservative government you can get almost anything you want.'

This support is not merely passive. In 1984, after a Labour Party debate on the police a senior member of the Police Federation asked his members to think about whether they would ever be able to serve a future Labour government loyally. The Police Federation is the trade union for rank-and-file officers.

It perhaps came as no surprise, then, when in April 1987 yet another leaked document from Scotland Yard included an extensive attack on left-wing councils. To Chris Smith, Labour MP for Islington South, the leaked briefing paper revealed 'a supposedly independent police force taking political stands'. As he knew only too well, there are no statutory police authorities in London to monitor the performance and priorities of the Metropolitan Police – a force of 27,000 officers (many of them armed) and 10,000 civilians, with a budget of more than £727 million annually. Smith knew that of that £727 million roughly £323 million comes from ratepayers. Yet neither he nor they have any say in which policing priorities the Commissioner chooses to take. It all seems a far cry from the recommendations of the Royal Commission in 1962. The reality of the situation was expressed by Leon Brittan, then Home Secretary, in 1980.

> I have emphasised that chief constables are operationally independent. The Home Secretary cannot give them instructions . . . about the deployment of their officers. Nor may a police authority issue such instructions. That is the key element in our policing arrangements. The reason is sound. It has always been true that the police must act in the name and with the support of the community as a whole. The impartiality and independence of chief constables in their force is therefore vital.

Brittan was right in at least one respect: chief constables are entirely independent of any control whatsoever. None the less, a clause in the Police and Criminal Evidence Act of 1984 requires that: 'Arrangements shall be made in each police area for obtaining the views of the people in that area about matters concerning the policing of that area and for obtaining their cooperation with the police in preventing crime in the area.'

As a result, liaison committees have been set up across the country. The committees have no power, however, and the police no duty, to pay any attention to what they might say. Both they, and the Act that spawned them, merely perpetuate the myth of local accountability. The reality is starkly different. Sir Robert Mark, a former Commissioner of the Metropolitan Police, summed up the force's attitude in his memoirs:

> These then are the two great problems for the next generation of policemen. Resistance to political encroachment on their operational freedom, and exposure to the brunt of social change. By comparison with these two, crime is never likely to be more than the conventional costly nuisance it is today and terrorism, as today, in reality a comparatively insignificant issue. [*In the Office of Constable*, Collins, 1978.]

The story doesn't end there, however. It is a combination of this lack of genuine accountability and the development of police insularity, coupled with gross underfunding, that leads to cutting corners and bending the rules. Whilst there is no excuse for either – just as there was no excuse for rioting – it is possible to understand how they come about, and to have sympathy for forces overstretched in a constant battle against rising crime.

Confessions

When one is talking about bending the rules there is one key word: confession. The manner in which police officers obtain confessions from suspects has long been a cause of friction. In 1977 an official enquiry was held into the case of three South London youths jailed for the murder of Maxwell Confait. The enquiry was held because all the youths were clearly innocent, yet all had signed statements admitting their guilt after rough treatment under interrogation. The three were subsequently freed and awarded large sums in compensation.

(The payment of compensation is a more regular occurrence than is generally realised. In 1986, for example, the Metropolitan Police quietly settled fifty-two cases brought against it – the majority for false or malicious imprisonment – with a series of out-of-court payments totalling £376,000. The figure was never put to any monitoring body, since there is no such organisation covering the Met.)

The Confait case led to a separate Royal Commission on Criminal Procedure in 1978. The Police and Criminal Evidence Act of 1984 made sweeping changes to the rules governing confessions, but they were not an improvement.

Before examining the way in which some officers 'encourage' suspects to sign confessions, let us consider the Case of the Phantom Criminals. On 6 January 1986, Police Constable Ron Walker did something extremely brave – he rang Scotland Yard. In itself that was not particularly courageous, nor anything out of the ordinary. Scotland Yard frequently receives phone calls from officers in PC Walker's Kent division. But this call was different.

Walker asked to be put through to CIB2 – the Yard's anti-corruption department. It was the end of a lengthy and secret investigation he had carried out into his colleagues; it was also the beginning of the end of his career.

Seven years previously Walker, then a new detective constable, had sat in the CID room as a detective inspector read the riot act. The inspector had just been shown the latest official figures showing the clear-up rate for crimes in each area served by a Kent police division. He was not pleased. 'They're crooked. They're ridiculous. Anybody can see they're crooked.' He then turned to the junior CID officers and warned: 'There'll be none of that here. There'll be no dodgy write-offs here. No way.'

Walker was impressed; but the dodgy write-offs didn't end. As he moved from one Kent station to another the young DC came across the same dishonest fiddle – the writing off of scores of unsolved crimes in phoney confessions.

The concept of write-offs had originated in the Home Office during the 1970s as a legitimate way of clearing up crime. The idea was that convicted criminals would make statements whilst in prison admitting their involvement in other offences. In return the Attorney General agreed not to prosecute them uless there was a real advantage to society to be gained.

The scheme had no safeguards, however. There were no checks on confessions to ensure that they were genuine. In no time at all the system was being abused. For detectives under pressure and attempting to achieve good results for public consumption, and for habitual criminals eager to earn risk-free favours from the police, the write-off scheme was a godsend. Walker found Kent detectives quite unashamed of their fiddle.

> On one occasion I was in the office with another detective constable – a very experienced man who I had always thought was an excellent policeman. He was on the phone to someone in the statistics office at the force HQ.
>
> He was making a list of unsolved burglaries, checking that they were still outstanding. I wandered over to his desk and it was covered in blank statement forms. When he came off the phone, he just sat there and started writing out this statement – a completely phoney confession writing off all these burglaries.

Walker was horrified. But that detective wasn't the only one bending the rules.

There was another occasion when one of the senior detectives came into the office waving this little bundle of write-offs, laughing about it and complaining that he had so many crimes written off that he could clear up every offence in his patch for the rest of the year. He was saying he would have to feed them into the system slowly over the months so that the figures didn't go over the top.

It was a bad joke the way things were being run. There was this change of direction coming about: junior officers just wanted promotion; the senior officers just wanted good clear-up rates. Helping the public became less and less important.

Two events then persuaded Walker that the situation had got too far out of hand. A lengthy investigation he had been running into two particularly assiduous local burglars was sabotaged by a senior officer worried that if they were arrested they weren't the type to admit a series of other bogus offences – and that in turn would take the force clear-up rate down.

Almost simultaneously he came across another fiddle – phantom crimes. Detectives were inventing offences which were then admitted to by criminals willing to go along with the abuse. As a result crime figures were artificially improved.

A detective had nicked this young lad who was prepared to play ball with him. I saw him get on to a PC from this lad's area and tell him to go out and get some vehicle numbers, so that he could get the names and addresses off the computer and put them down as stolen cars. The next thing you know the lad is confessing to stealing them.

Not all Walker's colleagues were on the fiddle. Some, like him, objected strongly to what was going on. Others, though, either turned a blind eye or were actively engaged in massaging the clear-up rates.

In the end he decided to quit CID, go back into uniform, and start his own investigation. The first point of call was the statistics department. Here the clear-up rates provided a strong pointer to what was going on. In 1978, before the fiddles started, a typical Kent police division solved 24.4 per cent of the burglaries on its books. Within a year that figure had risen to 69.5 per cent. The difference was too big to be explained away.

In fact no one was trying to do any explaining. Nor was this an isolated phenomenon affecting a few detectives in the south-east corner of England. Official statistics for divisions and sub-divisions across the country showed an extraordinary variation in clear-up rates. In some areas they were as high as 90 per cent. Yet in others – and for no apparent reason – the figure would be less than 10 per cent. But although senior officers and chief constables were either unaware or unworried, the Home Office had begun to take an interest. Its Inspector of Constabulary had begun monitoring the system.

Meanwhile, Ron Walker was busy about his own investigation. He had come across the names of two criminals who appeared suspiciously often in the write-off logs. One, Robert H. had written off eighty-seven offences, including seventy-three burglaries, during a visit by Kent detectives to his Borstal institution. The confession was lengthy and contained a good deal of convincing detail. Yet it was pure fantasy.

The offences were real enough, but there was no way that Robert H. could have committed them all. For example, he had admitted a string of nine burglaries which occurred on dates when he was safely locked up in prison. In all, seven of his confessions proved to be undoubtedly bogus and a further eighteen were distinctly suspect. Robert H. had given the detectives a degree of detail known only to three parties: the victim, the real offender – and the police. If he hadn't committed the crimes the only explanation was that he had been given the information by the Kent detectives.

The second man, Ernie C., provided yet more evidence. In all, he had admitted committing fifty-four burglaries within six months. In one case he had confessed to stealing money from a householder's electricity meter. Yet when Walker checked back he found that the householder had, in the meantime, admitted committing the crime himself, and alone. Ernie C. could not have done it. There was also something implausible about the confession itself. It was a lengthy hand-written document that would have taken at least an hour merely to write down. Walker's research proved that, although the detectives in question had had almost an hour with Ernie C. in prison, it would have been physically impossible to question the man, persuade him to recall old offences and confess to them, as well as to write the statement down.

Walker began to do some arithmetic. The sub-division had a declared clear-up rate of 49 per cent for the period, including the bogus write-offs; of 375 burglaries recorded, 185 were shown as detected. But Walker knew that 127 of those offences were fraudulently written off, which left a detection figure of just 58 and a genuine clear-up rate of 15.5 per cent. The implications were quite clear. 'It meant the detectives could afford to spend plenty of time taking it easy. In just a couple of days' work they could get enough crimes written off to keep the crime figures looking right for the next six months.'

Matters came to a head when the area's most active juvenile burglar was given bail while on a charge of house-breaking. Walker was amazed – until he discovered that a deal had been done. The boy agreed to confess to thirty other offences provided that the police didn't oppose bail when he came up before magistrates on remand. A few weeks later he was arrested again for burglary carried out while on bail. Walker was stunned at the behaviour of his colleagues.

> They knew that if they didn't oppose bail he would go out and commit more offences, but they didn't mind as long as he agreed to ask for a lot of other offences to be taken into consideration. It didn't matter that the people of Kent were burgled as long as the books looked good.

The phantom crime department was also active at the time. Walker looked through one sheet of offences prepared for a suspect to admit, and found a series of suspect crimes. All were thefts of rear-foglamps worth £5 each, yet none had a crime report number – the identifying numeral given to each complaint by a member of the public. When Walker later showed this log to the *Observer* the newspaper was able to prove that none of those named had ever lost a rear-foglamp, let alone reported the 'theft' to the police.

So, on 6 January 1986, Walker made his phone call. He was told that he would have to lodge his complaint first with his own force. Walker was nervous – he knew what could happen to him – but he decided to go through with it.

It took two weeks for an investigation to be launched. Then he was interviewed by an officer from Scotland Yard's Serious Crime Squad (C1). He warned the Yard that it would have to move quickly or key documents would disappear. Within four days two events had taken place. Walker's wife was already being snubbed by other police wives, and Walker had been put on sick leave. Of swift action by C1 there was no sign.

In the event it took six months before the Yard took the unprecedented step of raiding thirteen Kent police stations. By then it was too late. All the handwritten originals of the phoney confession had vanished; many had been shredded, and it was impossible to tell whether the criminals concerned had actually signed their own confessions. Of more than a hundred documents vital to the enquiry only one remained intact.

Nonetheless, a 450-page report from C1 to the Director of Public Prosecutions and the Police Complaints Authority confirmed that the write-offs were indeed bogus, as Walker alleged.

Confession is not habitual for most suspects arrested by the police, yet it can provide vital – occasionally the only – evidence in their trial.

The pressure put on the three innocent youths in the Confait case should have provided a lesson to be learned. Instead, the law governing confessions was loosened rather than tightened when the Police and Criminal Evidence Act (which we shall henceforth refer to as PACE) came before the Commons in 1984, and came into effect a year later.

Before we examine what PACE did and did not do to provide safeguards with regard to confession evidence, the way in which confessions are physically recorded needs to be understood.

Confessions are taken in the form of statements. When a typed version of such a statement reaches the court it appears to be a continuous narrative – a sort of coherent unburdening of the soul. Yet it rarely happens that it started that way. Typically, police officers will put questions (and frequently leading questions) to the suspect. The suspect's replies are then written down as if spontaneously uttered; there is no record of any intervening questions.

To make things potentially even more dangerous it is the police who actually write the statement down. The only physical contact a suspect has with his or her 'confession' is to put a signature at the bottom of each sheet, agreeing that the words above are truthful. Where a suspect is illiterate or semi-literate the police officer concerned is supposed to read the confession out loud before the suspect makes his or her mark on the statement

In many cases the suspect signs the confession after hours, even days, on his own. Occasionally he does so in fear of physical violence or as a result of menacing behaviour from the police interrogator. Sometimes that threat of physical violence is a reality, and suspects are beaten into signing a confession. The Home Secretary agreed in the summer of 1987 to re-examine the case of the so-called Birmingham pub bombers, after evidence came to light that their 1974 confessions had been encouraged by violence in the police cells.

In the Birmingham case the confessions and now disputed forensic tests were the only evidence against the accused. Police officers are well aware that a suspect's confession may be the only thing they have to go on: yet if the 1983 PSI study is to be believed, they are not overly scrupulous in the way they obtain such evidence.

> They [the interrogating officers] do not themselves believe that it is wrong to offer inducements or make threats in order to get someone to talk, and also they do not believe that their supervising officers seriously expect them to refrain from using threats and inducements . . . officers have good opportunities to make threats and inducements without this appearing in the official report. [*Police and People in London*, 1983.]

Sometimes the offer of an inducement – typically the granting of police bail – is more effective then threats of physical violence. A study for the Welsh Council for Civil Liberties in 1984 included the following all-too-familiar comment from a suspect:

> I just wanted to get out of there really – [to accept] the offer of bail they kept making all the time. I didn't even, as I was signing the confession statements admitting all, I didn't even then think they were going to put me in prison or anything. I thought this is all going to be very nasty in the future, but if I can get out now I can sort it out, and it was an easy way out. At that time I had been shut up for fifteen-odd hours or something, and I was totally shattered, and I didn't know where the hell I was, or what I was doing, and I just agreed . . . I had no one with me on my side . . . I was totally in their power. [*Political Policing in Wales*, WCCL, 1984.]

Prior to the introduction of PACE, the obtainment and subsequent use of confessions was governed by the Judges' Rules – a series of guidelines (they did not have the force of law) laid down at a meeting of all judges.

The guidelines said, in general, that any evidence improperly obtained could not be put before a jury, and that if during the course of a trial the defence alleged a breach of Judges' Rules in obtaining the confession, it was up to the police to convince the trial judge that no such breach had occurred.

There was also a limit to the time in which a suspect could be kept in custody without being charged, and the following impressive edict:

> Every person at any stage of an investigation should be able to communicate and consult privately with a solicitor. This is so even if he is in custody, provided in such a case no unreasonable delay or hindrance is caused to the process of investigation or the administration of justice by his doing so.

The Home Office had even added its own directions, to the effect that people in custody should be informed of their rights both by notices pinned up in the police station and by having them spelled out verbally by a police officer.

If that was the theory, once again reality proved very different. The Confait case enquiry report included this telling evidence from a Deputy Assistant Commissioner of the Metropolitan Police: 'All I can say in all honesty is that if there is a duty to inform every person in custody orally that he has a right to consult a solicitor before we commence the interview, then in practice we do not do it.'

At least, however, the Judges' Rules provided that evidence improperly obtained could not be used against a defendant in court. In 1980 Derek Pascall had been interviewed at Stoke Newington police station. In the course of an attempt to encourage a confession from him, Pascall had been punched in the stomach, the chest and the face, pushed on to a bed and burned repeatedly with cigarettes.

Two officers had been responsible for this; one, Detective Constable Rex Sargeant, had held Pascall while his colleague applied the third degree. The confession Pascall signed was later quashed in court, and in March 1986 a jury at Shoreditch County Court awarded him £3,500 damages. The case was to haunt DC Sargeant later that same year.

The introduction of PACE changed the old reliance on Judges' Rules. Since it was now statute law it was an opportunity to enshrine once and for all the good points of the old system. It turned out to be an opportunity not so much missed as never even aimed at.

The Act retains the old criterion of ruling out statements that were made under threat 'of oppression' – though a code of practice attached to it allows the use of inducements which are 'proper and warranted'. It does so by creating an entirely new, and nebulous, category of confession.

Under the old rules confessions had to be made voluntarily to be admissible in evidence. PACE changes that; now statements have to be 'reliable'. A statement may not be used in evidence if it was made in consequence of anything said or done likely to render it unreliable. But any evidence unearthed as a result of an unlawfully obtained confession is admissible in evidence – an interesting notion which came to court in October 1986.

PACE also contained another anomaly with regards to conditions governing confessions. Although it included the definition of oppression laid down by the European Convention on Human Rights ('torture, inhuman or degrading treatment') and even added to it ('and the use or threat of violence'), it failed to deal with the use of 'reasonable force' with regard to a confession. Reasonable force is a traditional fall-back for police officers who are alleged to have assaulted suspects in custody, and PACE specifically empowers a police officer to use reasonable force, where necessary, in the exercise of *any* power in the Act not qualified by the need for consent. Confessions are not so qualified.

It is this power provided by PACE which marks the greatest change in the law relating to the police force since its inception. Previously a policeman was no more than a 'citizen in uniform' upholding the law. PACE gives individual officers more power than their fellow men and lifts them into a new class of citizenship.

In promoting PACE in Parliament the government set great store by its procedural requirements and codes of practice as safeguards for the suspect. But in doing so it overlooked two crucial factors: a theoretical safeguard only has any value if it is both operated and seen to be operated; and if the safeguards don't prevent unfairly obtained evidence being put before a jury, they are of fairly minimal importance.

So even though police officers may in theory be disciplined for failing to abide by the new codes of practice, unless they are disciplined the public can have no confidence in them. The Home Office does not, as a matter of course, issue details of any such disciplinary cases. So it's left to straw-polling by concerned bodies to test how – if at all – the system is working. The NCCL is just such an organisation: after the introduction of PACE it asked the Metropolitan Police solicitor when an officer had last been disciplined for a breach of the rules. To no one's great surprise he was unable to remember a single instance.

Yet, as the PSI report noted in 1983 (and it's worth reminding ourselves that the Met commissioned that study): '. . . our findings suggest that departure from rules and procedure affecting evidence are far more common than outright fabrication and have a far more significant effect on the quality of evidence that goes before the courts.'

The only real safeguard is to do as other Westen countries do: rule out the use of any evidence improperly obtained. Yet PACE established a general presumption that unfairly obtained evidence *should* be admissible unless the defendant can show that to admit it would make his trial so unfair that it ought to be excluded.

This is not only vague and unclear, but it actually shifts the burden of proof to the defence – a rare and disreputable principle in most areas of English law.

It was against this background that the trial of Hassan Muller took place at the Old Bailey in October 1986. Muller, a seventeen-year-old white youth, was charged with affray. The circumstances of the alleged offence were the events on the Broadwater Farm estate on the night following Mrs Cynthia Jarrett's death. The sole evidence against him was a long signed confession made at 1 p.m. on 1 November 1985 in Enfield police station.

There were, as Muller's defence counsel noted during the trial, special circumstances surrounding the police investigation into the Broadwater Farm riot. PC Keith Blakelock had been savagely killed and many officers had suffered injuries from the hail of bottles and bricks thrown by the crowd. The police were under pressure from their own ranks, and from the general public, to get results.

Riots are difficult places to collect forensic evidence against those involved. In the absence of any forensic clues, the case against Muller rested on confession. He had been arrested on the basis of a fifty-page confession signed by another youth, Howard Kerr. Kerr had also been charged in connection with the riot and had named nineteen other people – Muller included – in his statement to the police.

So much the jury was told. It was also told that Muller had been held incommunicado on the instructions of a senior officer. He was interrogated over a two-day period without access to a solicitor or his family. In fact, when his family asked his whereabouts they were given the address of a completely different police station. This, it emerged, was 'general policy' in the riot investigation.

PACE allows all of this. It says that the police may delay access to a solicitor for up to thirty-six hours (or forty-eight hours in the case of detention under the Prevention of Terrorism Act), and even where a suspect is allowed to see his legal adviser the police can demand to be present provided that:

(1) The suspected offence is 'serious' (and the qualifications and definitions of 'serious' under the Act make virtually anything other than traffic violations potentially serious).

(2) The police have reasonable grounds to believe that access would cause interference with or harm to evidence; or physical injury to other persons; or might lead to the alerting of anyone else suspected of a serious offence; or might hinder the recovery of any property obtained as a result of a serious offence.

In any case – whether serious or not – the police have a legal duty only to grant access to a solicitor 'as soon as it is practicable'. Furthermore, the right to legal advice only exists when a detained person actually requests it. Nor does the Act require the police to inform the suspect of this right; that duty is laid down in the code of practice – which doesn't have the force of law. The family and friends of a suspect are similarly allowed to be denied access to him or her for up to thirty-six hours.

The choice of this time period of thirty-six hours is, perhaps, a little strange. Research shows that suspects are at their most vulnerable in the early stages of detention, and most confess – if they are going to – before twenty-four hours have elapsed. Yet PACE allows a thirty-six-hour breathing space for the police before a suspect has the right to legal advice.

It took less than that thirty-six hours to induce Hassan Muller to confess, and he was not given access to his solicitor before signing his statement. At the trial his counsel, David Mitchell, cross-examined one of the officers involved in that decision, Detective Constable Brendan McAllister. McAllister admitted that he didn't 'trust all solicitors'. Mitchell then asked him whether a solicitor would have impeded the investigation. 'I can only surmise,' McAllister replied. 'Not all solicitors are reputable. Some do things which may impede arrests of other individuals for worse offences.'

So the case against Hassan Muller rested on the statement of Howard Kerr and his own confession. At this point the jury was sent out and the judge, Mr Justice Dennison, began to hear more of Howard Kerr and his fifty-page confession.

Kerr had insisted at the start of his interrogation that he had been in Windsor during the riot at Broadwater Farm, visiting a girlfriend. Like Muller, however, Kerr had been held incommunicado – in his case for two and a half days.

In the end he confessed to involvement in the riot and was charged. But when a senior officer checked Kerr's alibi he found six separate witnesses who supported it. As a result the police offered no evidence against Howard Kerr when the case came before committal magistrates.

Judge Dennison was unimpressed by the defence argument. Even if, he said, the police had withdrawn the charges against Kerr, it didn't 'necessarily mean that all the material in his confession was untrue'. The judge didn't explain how if, as the police apparently accepted, Kerr had been in Windsor during the riot he could have identified Muller as one of those involved. The Kerr case was, he said, 'irrelevant', and the jury was recalled.

Mitchell then cross-examined Muller's chief interrogator, Detective Constable Rex Sargeant. Sargeant denied Muller's allegations that he had threatened him, or that he had warned the youth he would get what he wanted 'the easy way or the hard way'.

At this point Mitchell reminded the constable of the Shoreditch case and the little matter of £3,500 damages awarded to Pascall for assaulting Derek Pascall in pursuit of a confession. Sargeant recalled the incident and admitted that the allegations had been made in court. But despite the jury's verdict and the damages, the constable still maintained that he had done nothing wrong.

The jury in the Muller case were less certain. It took them just forty minutes to acquit him, unanimously, on all counts. They accepted that his confession had not been genuine, and therefore by implication that it had been improperly obtained. Muller had endured eleven months in custody as a result of the abuse of police power.

Confait, Pascall, Kerr, Muller: all cases which prove that police can and do make up or induce false confessions. Yet ten years after the report of Sir Henry Fisher's enquiry into the Confait scandal highlighted the dangers of using confessions as the sole evidence in criminal prosecutions, the lessons are still unlearned.

PACE, preceded by the Royal Commision on Criminal Procedure, has not merely failed to safeguard the rights of the suspect – and all suspects are innocent until proved otherwise to the satisfaction of a jury – but actually managed to make the potential for abuse greater still. Which, in itself, is no mean feat.

What about the point implicit in all this, that there should be some way of dealing with errant police officers – some complaints procedure to remove rotten apples from the police barrel and satisfy their victim? Enter the Police Complaints Authority.

Complaints against the police

'The police are a disciplined body and proper leadership requires that the administration of discipline should be in the hands of the chief constable.'

So said the Royal Commission on the Police in 1962. The majority of its members found no cause for concern with regard to the process of disciplining officers and no need for anyone outside the force to be involved in the investigation of complaints against the police. The Commission's reason for saying this was that it found no evidence to the contrary and felt that relations between police and public were 'not bad'. The Police Act of 1964 enshrined this cosy view and ensured that only policemen could investigate or discipline other policemen. It was an unfortunate legacy, to say the least.

Within a dozen years pressure on the Home Office for some measure of change in the system had proved irresistible, and eventually, in 1976, the Police Complaints Board was created. It had little real power, however, being unable to enquire into complaints from the public, though it had limited powers to direct that internal disciplinary proceedings should be taken against errant officers.

Once again only the police were allowed to investigate allegations against their colleagues, and the Director of Public Prosecutions had sole discretion over whether or not to prosecute. Nevertheless, the Police Federation viewed the PCB as such a threat that it advised its members not to cooperate with it. Even the Board began to have doubts about its own efficacy. In its first report it admitted a degree of powerlessness in cases where policemen were accused of violent assault because, it felt, the investigating officer was too likely to accept the mere word of the policeman under suspicion and would not push the enquiry to the limit as a result.

By 1979 the Board was calling for new powers and a new semi-independent way of handling investigations – though one which still relied on police investigators. Stung by criticism of the PCB's performance, its chairman, Sir Cyril Phillips, promised more action (within the distinctly narrow limits of his remit) and admitted: 'The existing Board has kept so low a profile that it has climbed into a ditch.'

Even Sir Cyril's modest proposals (he had chaired the Royal Commission on Criminal Procedure a year earlier) ran into stubborn opposition from a Home Office working party. Since the members of that committee were on it to represent police organisations, no one was unduly surprised. Sir Cyril's recommendations were shelved, and the system carried on as before. But Phillips's Royal Commission had left its mark: the majority of its proposals, giving widespread new powers to the police, were embodied in the Police and Criminal Evidence Act. In return for these powers, the Commission had said, new safeguards in the policing of complaints should be introduced to maintain the balance.

Apart from the obvious potential for investigating officers to go lightly on their colleagues, critics of the system had identified two major (and a host of minor) defects. In deciding whether or not to prosecute officers for alleged criminal offences revealed by internal investigations, the DPP required a higher standard of proof than when dealing with cases against ordinary members of the public. In both cases he only sent for trial those cases where there was a 50 per cent chance of conviction. But in assessing that percentage chance he took into account an apparent reluctance by juries to convict policemen.

'I feel very strongly that it's not part of the business of any prosecutor, and in particular the Director of Public Prosecutions, to prosecute people whom one believes are going to be found innocent at the end of the day,' the DPP, Sir Thomas Hetherington, explained in 1981. He had the grace to admit, though, that this policy allowed many guilty policemen to go free. In 1979, for example, there had been more than 8,000 complaints; only thirty had gone to court.

Under the PCB system there was a sort of safety-net. In cases where the DPP didn't prosecute officers could still be subject to internal disciplinary measures, assuming that evidence was found. By the time Sir Thomas was justifying his prosecution policy, however, it had become clear that the disciplinary safety-net had a huge hole in it. It was called double-jeopardy.

This meant that if the alleged disciplinary offence was substantially the same as that which the DPP had rejected for prosecution, no disciplinary action could be taken. Why? Because, according to the police, this would mean their officers being 'tried' twice for the same offence. Since the whole point of the DPP's refusal was to rule out any trial, the argument seemed tortuous at best; but it held sway and disciplinary hearings were by 1982 a rare commodity.

On the few occasions when a hearing did take place an extremely high standard of proof was required to make out a case. Allegations that officers had broken the force's own disciplinary code had to be proved beyond reasonable doubt – the same standard of proof as in court cases. This might at first seem only fair. But, as critics were quick to point out, not only was the investigation, prosecution and judging of such hearings controlled by the police (and held behind closed doors), but no other professional body required such a high standard of proof in disciplinary matters. In 1983 16,231 complaints were filed against the police; only 10 per cent led to disciplinary measures.

This, then, was the position prior to PACE. The Act took account of the Royal Commission's proposals and abolished the PCB. In its place was created the PCA – the Police Complaints Authority.

The PCA consists of a chairman, currently the former Ombudsman Sir Cecil Clothier, appointed by the Queen – in reality the Prime Minister makes the appointment, then obtains royal approval. In addition, the Home Office appoints at least eight other members for a three-year term of (paid) office. Police officers past and present are excluded from appointment, though not from the Authority's staff of around seventy men and women. PACE did give the PCA more muscle than its predecessor – but only in a supervisory role. Once again, police officers were being left to investigate their colleagues.

In terms of supervision the PCA is legally bound to oversee all investigations into complaints involving death or serious injury – and for once that word 'serious' is well defined and errs on the side of the complainant. It also has the right to approve the investigating officer and set out conditions relating to the conduct of his enquiry – for example, the Authority can insist that the investigating officer be drawn from a different force to that of the accused policeman. There is also provision for the Authority to demand that it supervises any complaint enquiry where it considers that this would be in the public interest. Finally, PACE included a conciliation scheme that allows less serious complaints to be ironed out between the aggrieved party and the accused officer.

All of this is a welcome step forward, but is it enough? The major complaints that dogged the old PCB system remain unresolved, and the only concession to the principle of independence has been the setting up of a special unit inside the Metropolitan Police to investigate complaints.

The Complaints Investigation Bureau is housed away from the main Scotland Yard HQ in Tintagel House on the Albert Embankment. It has three sections. CIB1 is in charge of administration – logging complaints and liaising with the other sections of the Bureau, the DPP and the PCA. CIB2 is the investigation arm; it deals with all serious allegations and its operations are subject to PCA supervision. CIB2 has nineteen investigating officers (detective superintendents and detective chief inspectors) plus thirty-eight sergeants.

CIB3 handles internal disciplinary cases. It spends much of its time trying to find a way round the double-jeopardy rule. The best method it has managed to date is to look for a slightly different violation also involved in the alleged incident. So, for example, in 1986 when an officer was acquitted of burglary, CIB3 managed to charge him with the disciplinary offence of failing to book out the Panda car he had allegedly used in the burglary. He was fined by a disciplinary board and later resigned from the force.

Inevitably it is CIB2 which falls under the harshest spotlight. Its investigators don't have any great affection for their jobs; one candidly told the *Guardian* in March 1986:

You don't enjoy it too much because you're nicking policemen. It gives you a dirty feeling because it reflects on you and spreads over into the whole force. There is an undercurrent of distaste for anyone who deals with a bad case because you wish it had never happened. All we can do is sweep up the debris.

At the time CIB2 was investigating just such a bad case. On 6 August 1983, five young schoolboys were attacked in Holloway Road, North London. Their assailants were the five occupants of Mobile Police Unit 'November 33' – one of three District Support Units driving around the area that night.

The concept of District Support Units – in some ways successors to the Special Patrol Groups, involved, for example, in the death of Blair Peach in 1979 – was that a team of eight officers should set off from base in a police van, be dropped off on route to patrol their individual beats, but still be ready and trained to regroup in the van for swift response to an incident in their own or any other area. The practice worked out rather differently in this case.

The eight young officers in November 33 had only been together for three weeks. Yet already they had dropped into the habit of driving round the streets together, hunting as a pack and looking for trouble rather than doing beat duty. Moreover, as Scotland Yard was later to admit, DSU officers in general had more interest in getting on with their colleagues than priding themselves on developing into a professional support unit. Internal camaraderie had become dominant.

On the evening of 6 August 1983, the occupants of November 33 had already been on the streets together for a double shift when they were taunted by a group of youths at a local fair. Unable to catch that group, the unit went looking for trouble. In Holloway Road it found some.

The five schoolboys walking down the road knew nothing about what had happened previously. They were what they seemed: five young lads walking innocently down a North London street. There was no reason why three of the officers in November 33 – PCs Edward Main, Nicholas Wise and Michael Gavin – should attack them. But they did. The youths were brutally beaten before the van drove off towards its base. It was to take four years, three separate police investigations and two separate PCB and PCA enquiries before the officers could be brought to court. All eight of the occupants of Mobile Police Unit November 33 agreed to cover each other's backs. They also secured some measure of cooperation from the fourteen other officers in the two other DSU vans on patrol that night. A conspiracy of silence began.

An exhaustive police enquiry was launched the day after the assaults occurred. The five youngsters were able to give descriptions of the men who attacked them and the three officers were asked to take part in a standard identity parade. All three refused after taking legal advice. The other officers on patrol that night steadfastly refused to help identify the guilty policemen.

The best that Scotland Yard could manage was an inferior sort of identification process called a confrontation: each of the suspects was shown, one at a time, to the boys. They were unable positively to identify any of the officers – a fact one of the boys put down to an attempt to alter their appearance. One was wearing facial powder, another had changed his hair and the third had altered his moustache.

Yard officers investigating the assaults sent a report to the DPP in March 1984. He decided one month later not to prosecute. The case became another unresolved file in the offices of the Police Complaints Board – a file inherited by the Police Complaints Authority when it took over in 1985. Because of the serious implications of the case the PCA ordered another enquiry. In January 1986 the Authority was forced to concede that it too had been unable to identify the officers involved. The announcement caused a storm of protest inside Parliament and in the press.

None the less, the Home Secretary, Douglas Hurd ruled out any further investigations by either the PCA or the police. 'I am forced to conclude that no further investigation or enquiry could lead anywhere,' he told the Commons in February that year. The reason was simple enough. Without cooperation from the officers on patrol that night CIB2 was simply unable to get enough evidence.

In the end it was neither the Home Office, the Police Complaints Authority nor CIB2 that cracked the wall of silence. It was a journalist. Brian Hilliard, editor of *Police Review*, ran a strongly worded editorial on the affair. The article, headlined simply 'Bastards', provoked three of the officers in November 33 on the night of 6 August to come forward.

Their testimony in court in July 1987 was enough to send their guilty colleagues to prison for up to four years. Mr Justice Kenneth

Jones told the convicted men that they had 'behaved like vicious hooligans' and 'lied like common criminals'.

> To be called upon to sentence five police officers is about as heavy a burden as a judge can be expected to bear, but I have a duty to perform. All right-thinking people in this country have a deep sympathy and respect for our police.
> We know that there are evil elements in our society who are concerned to undermine the authority of the police and provoke them, but none of this applies in your case. This was a brutal, bullying and unprovoked attack upon innocent schoolboys who had given you no particular provocation and no particular trouble. Yet you turned upon them and beat them brutally.
> By these assaults you have betrayed your manhood and been false to the high traditions of the Metropolitan Police. Perhaps worst of all you have done much to undermine the respect which right-thinking citizens should, and do, have for our police. If that was not enough, in order to save your skins you all conspired to lie and lie again, and you did nothing to repair that damage that you had done.

Scotland Yard set about repairing what damage it could. It reached out-of-court settlements with the boys to pay compensation for their injuries. Meanwhile, the three policemen who had assaulted them and two of their colleagues who had shielded them began their jail sentences.

The PCA claimed that the convictions were a great endorsement of its efficiency. Yet not only had it taken four years to bring the officers before a court, not only had the PCB, PCA and the CIB2 all in reality failed to get anywhere near the truth, but there were three other officers in November 33 on the night of the attacks. What had happened to them?

All three readily accepted that they had been involved in the cover-up. They could hardly do otherwise. They and their five colleagues had all been paraded before Deputy Assistant Commissioner Bob Innes in December 1985. They, like their subsequently jailed colleagues, had chosen to remain silent rather than assist the enquiry.

When they agreed to testify in court all three negotiated a deal which granted them immunity from the charges of conspiracy to pervert the cause of justice levelled against their colleagues. Such deals are almost unheard of in normal criminal prosecutions: police officers are empowered only to indicate to a court that a man has proved helpful by turning Queen's evidence – certainly not to offer him immunity from charges arising from his own guilt.

Worse, it transpired that no disciplinary action was to be taken against the three. The Metropolitan Police announced that it had no plans to hold a disciplinary tribunal – a decision backed by PCA chairman Sir Cecil Clothier. Neither body would discuss the terms of the deal agreed with the officers, but Brian Hilliard confirmed that the PCA had guaranteed no disciplinary charges as well as immunity from prosecution.

It all rather made a mockery of the PCA's publicity boasting: 'Independent, powerful, thorough, fair, immediate and public.' The Holloway Road case was about as far removed from any of those claims as can be imagined. Nor was this the only case.

In the PCA's review of its first eight months' work the case of Cynthia Jarrett was reported. The coroner's jury had clearly indicated in its verdict that it did not accept the testimony of DC Randall and his colleagues. Yet the Authority completely exonerated the officers from any blame, other than mildly rebuking one of the officers for lying about using Floyd Jarrett's key to enter the house.

Lord Gifford's report on the (unofficial) enquiry into the case – the Home Secretary had ruled out any public enquiry – pinpointed thirteen separate and specific instances of police misconduct in relation to Cynthia and Floyd Jarrett. Each of those thirteen could have been grounds for any one of six disciplinary offences ranging from abuse of authority through discreditable conduct and racially discriminating behaviour to falsehood or prevarication. Gifford's report concluded that:

> The members of the Authority, although lay people, appear to have no idea what standards of conduct are expected by reasonable members of the public. They expect that a police officer conducting a search who so carelessly pushes past a woman standing peacefully in a doorway of her house, that she falls and dies, will be disciplined. . . . The case of Mrs Jarrett's death in our view calls into question whether the members of the Authority who were party to the decision should continue to hold their responsible public office.

Both the Jarrett and the Holloway Road cases have an even more fundamental point to make. They shattered once and for all the myth enshrined in practice and legislation since 1964 that 'only a copper can nail a bent copper'. Brian Hilliard is a civilian. It was his intervention that brought the Holloway officers to court. Lord Gifford is a barrister: he was easily able to identify disciplinary offences in the Jarrett case that the PCA apparently overlooked.

In fact it is only police who are allowed this transparent fiction. Bent businessmen are investigated by specialist teams from the Inland Revenue and Customs and Excise (as well as police fraud squads): there is a system of Ombudsmen in Britain which, while far from perfect, manages to investigate governmental misdeeds. Solicitors are disciplined by a panel partly made up of lay people, and the actions of their Society's disciplinary department are subject to scrutiny from a non-lawyer, the Lay Observer.

The truth is that, as most policemen will admit, they would be unwilling to cooperate with a fully independent enquiry. They would simply remain silent. They are evidently unaware of the irony of this attitude; it is their own organisations which have been actively campaigning for several years to remove the historic right of silence from suspects being held for questioning.

If the provisions of PACE had left the major loopholes in the complaints system untouched, and the Jarrett and Holloway Road cases thrown them into sharp relief, there are other, more insidious, flaws in the system.

One of these – so-called 'cross-fertilisation' – is a direct result of allowing policemen to investigate their fellow officers. Unlike the situation in most criminal matters, police investigating allegations against other officers actually give the accused most if not all the details of the case against them.

On the surface this appears to be eminently fair. And, of course, it would be were English criminal procedure universally based on the same principle. But ours is not an inquisitorial system of justice – it is instead an accusatorial process. In other words, rather than being there to assist the court in determining the truth, barristers get on their feet to win an argument; to do so they habitually attempt to trick a witness with unseen evidence. All this is well within the rules.

Yet when it comes to investigating complaints against the police, the process somehow reverts back to the principles of natural justice.

Thus, once an investigating officer has taken a statement from the aggrieved party, he almost invariably puts the minute details of it (sometimes even reads it verbatim) to the accused officer – who then knows precisely what to expect in any court cross-examination.

Cross-fertilisation is an in-built danger of the complaints mechanism, according to Sir Cecil Clothier: 'Cross-fertilisation is inherent in the process. There's no way of preventing it or knowing if it's happening. . . . I can understand the caution which prompts some lawyers to warn clients not to say anything to us until their court action is over.'

The issue of privileged information is another problem area. The majority of serious complaints against the police involve allegations of assault or brutality. The evidence of police surgeons can therefore be crucial to both sides. Most doctors will answer specific questions from solicitors acting for complainants or their families, but some refuse to provide vital evidence on the advice of officers ostensibly investigating the complaint. The case of Trevor Monerville is an example.

On 31 December 1986, Monerville, a young black man, had been celebrating the New Year at his aunt's house in North London. He left in the early hours of the following morning. Some twenty hours later he was discovered by police in the back of a car in Stoke Newington. The car had a broken window. Trevor Monerville was arrested for criminal damage and taken to Stoke Newington's fortress-like police station. In the course of the next two days he was twice taken to a local hospital, and his father twice visited the police station to ask if anyone there knew where his son might be.

It was to take Mr Monerville senior until 3 January to track down his son – in Brixton prison. By then he had sustained injuries requiring an emergency brain operation. Trevor Monerville is now partially paralysed down one side and sufers severe headaches and double-vision. It is unclear how he came by his injuries.

Meanwhile, Stoke Newington police have dropped all charges against him. The Monerville family initially lodged a complaint with the PCA, but they dropped it when it became clear that the PCA enquiry was actually hampering their own progress towards a civil action against the police.

The most vital piece of evidence in the Monerville case was the bag containing clothes he was wearing that New Year's Eve. Whether or not they were bloodstained would have been crucial in determining whether he had received any injuries at the (known) time he changed his clothes in the police station. Bloodstains, however, have a limited useful life as evidence – they decay. Yet four weeks after the incident the clothes were still in Stoke Newington police station, untouched by the PCA investigators. When the Monerville's solicitor, Jane Deighton, asked for them they were quickly whipped away to police forensic laboratories. It took her until 13 February to get them back.

The evidence of those doctors who examined Trevor Monerville would also have been decisive in establishing exactly when he came by his injuries. Deighton wrote to all three doctors involved. All three refused to answer her questions. Dr K. Gupta explained: 'I have been advised by the officer in charge of the case that it is not in the public interest to make the statement you ask for.'

Dr Hanna Steisow wrote: 'I cannot supply you with the information you require as I have made a statement to the Complaints Authority and this statement is subject to public interest privilege.'

The third doctor, James Henry, told Deighton over the phone that the officer investigating the Monerville case had told him not to speak. The right to silence claimed by these doctors under public interest privilege only applies, under the law relating to complaints, to the actual statements made to the PCA – not to the information contained in them. In the end, two of the three doctors did agree to supply the necessary data, but it is not surprising that some solicitors advise clients to forgo the PCA's investigations altogether.

Gareth Peirce admits that she advises clients alleging assault by the police to go straight for civil action. 'A solicitor would be negligent who didn't advise a client that there is a grave risk involved in making a complaint.' She should know. She acts for a young student called Sarah Hollis who became caught up in a nightmare on the night of 1 March 1985.

Several months earlier, Manchester University Conservative Association had invited the then Home Secretary, Leon Brittan, to address them. The visit was planned for 1 March. Understandably, Greater Manchester police began careful security preparations. Among those they spoke to was the manager of the students' union where Mr Brittan was due to speak. It was apparent to the police that there was likely to be a demonstration by students opposing Conservative policies. Plans to cope with this were also discussed.

On the night of the visit about 400 students turned up and stood on the steps of the union building. The crowd was noisy but good-natured. Among them were a twenty-three-year-old politics undergraduate, Steven Shaw, and his girlfriend Olivia. Inside the building a third-year medical student and union council member was helping to issue tickets. Her name was Sarah Hollis.

Shortly before the Home Secretary was due to arrive, twenty members of a police support unit walked towards the building. Suddenly they ploughed into the demonstrators in a 'flying wedge' format. Other officers quickly joined in. Between them the two groups forcibly cleared the steps. The students were taken completely by surprise. Most had assumed – as had many union officials – that the Home Secretary would be discreetly brought in via another door, leaving the demonstrators to pose on the steps for an attendant media. Hundreds of statements given by the students subsequently alleged that the police had issued no warning and had brutally manhandled many people during the incident. Equally, there is little doubt that many students fought back.

In the midst of the mêlée Steven Shaw was dragged from the crowd by his leg. Olivia was punched. After the Home Secretary left the building, Sarah Hollis protested to the police about a student she had seen dragged away the hair. 'Suddenly I was grabbed by the back of the head. I was pushed and fell. I was got in the back and went down. The next thing I remember is the ambulance. My neck was seriously damaged although my head was only bruised. I had to wear a collar for three and a half weeks.' Before reaching the safety of the ambulance Sarah Hollis had tumbled down the union steps. Her picture, lying crumpled at the bottom of them, appeared widely in the next day's papers.

The following Monday, 5 March, Steven Shaw went to a students' union meeting which decided to form a defence committee for those arrested and to press for a public enquiry. Shaw was writing a thesis on police technology and had been in contact with Manchester City Council police monitoring unit. He offered to liaise with the Council and to collect witnesses' statements and photographs of the demonstration.

Tuesday, 5 March. Shaw's rented cottage in nearby Oldham was broken into. A file containing his research for the police technology thesis was stolen. It was to be the first of a remarkable series of coincidental burglaries.

Wednesday, 6 March. Shaw was driving his 1966 Morris Minor to the students' union. *En route* he was stopped by two uniformed police officers – ostensibly for the unlikely offence of speeding. It was the first time he had ever been stopped by the police, and with the demonstration and burglary fresh in his mind he refused to accept the standard road traffic offence documentation the officers thrust at him. He was asked to accompany them to a nearby police station. When he produced his documents the desk sergeant remarked: 'You're the chap making allegations about your thesis.' At that stage the only people Shaw had told about the burglary were his professor, the head of the Council's police monitoring unit and the student union executive. Nine days later Shaw was stopped again for speeding. After the Easter vacation he was stopped again – twice.

Meanwhile, Sarah Hollis's injuries sustained during the Brittan fracas had prompted her father to take action. The Reverend Peter Hollis is the rector of Sudbury in Suffolk. He complained to his MP, Tim Yeo, Conservative member for Suffolk South. Yeo in turn wrote to the Home Secretary expressing his concern. On 12 March his involvement in the growing row was made public in the *Guardian*.

Greater Manchester Chief Constable James Anderton had also moved swiftly, inviting a team of outside officers to investigate the students' complaints under the old PCB procedure. John Reddington, deputy Chief Constable of Avon and Somerset, was appointed to lead the team. Among the complaints received was one from Sarah Hollis.

Thursday, 9 May, 3 a.m. The phone rang in Hollis's house. The line went dead as she picked it up. The same thing happened at 10.30 p.m. the next night.

Saturday, 11 May. Two uniformed motorcycle officers stopped Hollis while she was riding her bicycle. They gave the pretext that it appeared unsafe, and asked her name and address.

That night her house on the crumbling Hulme estate was broken into. The thieves removed more than £700-worth of her property – but strangely left her cheque book. Also missing were her membership cards for Amnesty International, CND, Christians in Politics and the British Holistic Medical Association. Stranger still, two brief statements of witnesses who had seen her thrown down the union steps on 1 March were also taken. One of the witnesses, student Jean Entwhistle, would be burgled herself seven months later, and vital documents stolen.

The clear-up rate for burglaries in Hulme is very low – perhaps a reflection of Chief Constable Anderton's announced priorities for policing. But within six weeks two professional criminals, Frank Logan and Amanda Hughes, were charged with the break-in. Both pleaded guilty and Logan went on to serve six months in prison. Later he would tell a very strange story indeed.

Steven Shaw was, all this time, experiencing an extremely frightening series of events. On 14 May he was again driving his Morris Minor when two men in a red Cortina stopped him. The car had a 'W' registration plate – Shaw made a note of the full number but the note to his solicitor containing the information never arrived. The men explained that they were police officers, and asked Shaw to accompany them to Bootle Street police station to answer questions about the Brittan demonstration. Shaw was later able to describe both men in considerable detail to John Reddington and the Avon and Somerset enquiry team.

He certainly had good cause to remember what happened. For about an hour they questioned him about the events of 1 March, and about his politics. He was denied access to a solicitor on the spurious grounds that he had not been arrested, but was at the station voluntarily. He was then given an intimate internal body search, slapped across the face and punched in the chest. He subsequently needed surgery as a result of the search.

Shaw formed a strong impression that the officers had seen his research notes; the giveaway was some confidential information they referred to about police activity during the previous inner-city riots. Before they allowed him to leave, the officers warned him that he could be picked up at any time. To stress the point they reminded him of the dates of two of his final examinations.

Two days later, on 16 May, Sarah Hollis had her first meeting with deputy Chief Constable Reddington. Her solicitor went too, having earlier passed on Hollis's allegations of harassment and suspicions about the burglary. At first, Reddington seemed unconcerned about the injuries she had received after the Brittan demonstration. His mood was to change very quickly. 'I told him about the harassment and the burglary. He started shouting at me, saying, 'Are you accusing the police?'

Friday, 17 May. Sarah Hollis stopped her bike at a set of traffic lights. Two casually dressed men got out of a car, walked up to her and warned: 'Just remember we can pick you up any time we like and we know the date of your exams.'

Both Hollis and Shaw took advice from their lawyers, and they both went into hiding away from Manchester for two weeks. But the anonymous phone calls to Hollis's flat continued. There was one at 6.30 p.m. on 24 May, two on 25 May, at 10.15 a.m. and 6 p.m.

May also saw the first magistrates' hearings of cases against those arrested at the demonstrations. It was at these hearings that their solicitors saw confidential complaints enquiry statements being used by police prosecutors. It turned out that the DPP had ordered the enquiry team to hand them over.

In the absence of any public enquiry, and in view of the problems of the Avon and Somerset investigation, Manchester City Council decided to hold its own hearings under the chairmanship of John Platts-Mills, QC. When Shaw and Hollis returned to the university they gave evidence to the Council enquiry. Sarah Hollis gave evidence on 11 June and 15 June. On the evening of 11 June she was stopped by two men in a red car. She thought she recognised one of them from the incident at the traffic lights. One of the men said:

> We have been told that you paid a visit to the enquiry at the town hall today – been telling them some of your lies, have you? Well, you can just go back and tell them not to take any notice of what you have said because you were lying. Tell them none of it is true, and just remember we know if you do what we say or not – and if you don't we'll pay you a little visit in hospital next week.

Hollis did indeed have a hospital appointment coming up for some routine checks. She tried to protest that the hospital staff wouldn't let the men in. 'Listen to the clever bitch,' one of the men said. 'If we want to we can just walk into the ward, Ms Female, and really give the doctors something to sort out.'

The next day she confided the story to a barrister at the enquiry, James Wood. 'She was obviously terrified,' he recalled later.

Then, at the end of July, both Hollis's and Shaw's allegations were made public for the first time. The *Guardian* ran the harassment story under the headline 'Policemen "persecute students who protested against Brittan"'. The report included a telling quote from deputy Chief Constable Reddington, the officer heading the complaints enquiry: 'We have not received any complaints of this nature. They should be sent to the Chief Constable of Manchester, who I am sure will take them seriously. But I cannot imagine why any policeman would want to do these things. It will certainly have no effect on my enquiry.'

No complaints of harassment? What about the interview Reddington had had with Sarah Hollis on 16 May – the interview in which she had first raised her fears of harassment and the deputy Chief Constable had responded by shouting at her: 'Are you accusing the police?'? And then again, why should such serious allegations, which were obviously connected in some way with the Brittan demonstration enquiry, be excluded from Reddington's brief?

In the event, the issue was forced on Reddington's team. Manchester Police quite properly referred the article to the Police Complaints Authority, who in turn instructed the enquiry team to look into it.

At roughly the same time the two burglars charged with breaking into Sarah Hollis's flat came up before committal magistrates. Both Frank Logan and Amanda Hughes were well-established professional thieves. Logan specialised in car theft and was already on a six-month suspended sentence for theft; Hughes's speciality was house burglary. Both lived in separate flats in John Nash Crescent, the same block as Sarah Hollis.

Hughes had been the first to be arrested, six weeks after the break-in. Local CID officers told her that they had found her fingerprints in the flat; she confessed and named Logan as her associate. But she was surprised that the officers seemed particularly anxious to examine every piece of paper in her flat. Both she and Logan insist that they took no documents from Hollis's flat.

At their subsequent trial on 16 September, Logan was jailed for six months and Hughes was put on probation. Subsequently, however, Logan swore an affidavit with his solicitor claiming that two detectives, whom he knew from a previous arrest, had encouraged him to burgle Sarah Hollis's flat.

> One of them said to me that if I was going to do anything I should do Sarah Hollis's place. I thought it was 'Hollin's place'. I asked them where she lived. The detectives said she lived on the

same crescent as me, John Nash. I was surprised and thought at first it was a joke. But then there was something about the flat having a picture of Maggie Thatcher in the window.

A week later Logan identified the flat and the burglary went ahead.

Logan made a statement when he emerged from prison. He says that what prompted him was a series of strange incidents over a two-week period: a series of knocks on his flat door with no one there when he went to answer them, and unmarked police cars following him. (Logan, like many professional criminals, claims to know the registration numbers of all unmarked police cars in his area.)

How much weight can be attached to Logan's allegations? He is, after all, a convicted thief. But there is a ring of authenticity in his claims, and they dovetail with Hollis's own – and quite independent – complaints about harassment. Equally, Logan knew that by making the statement, and by swearing it in front of his solicitor, he was putting himself at risk of prosecution should his allegations not be upheld. That risk has now been realised.

Reddington's investigations and the separate Platts-Mills enquiry continued through the summer. Shaw, meanwhile, graduated and began work in London with a GLC-funded research unit examining police technology. Hollis came back to Manchester at the beginning of the autumn term to continue her course in medicine.

Then, at the beginning of November 1985, the Platts-Mills enquiry issued its report. Amongst other findings it reported that there had been 'a deliberate attempt by unknown police officers to frighten and harass key witnesses'. But the harassment did not end there. Hollis and Shaw were both preparing to give interviews for a BBC programme investigating the case. On 15 November Sarah Hollis noticed two men following her round Manchester. She recognised one from the incidents earlier in the year. Finally, the men, who she believes to be police officers, approached her and made further threats. Unsurprisingly, perhaps, Sarah Hollis broke down and cried in front of the BBC cameras when giving her interview.

The then deputy Chief Constable of the Greater Manchester police force, John Stalker, declined to appear in the programme. But he sent an abrasive letter refuting the Platts-Mills report and threatening prosecution of those witnesses whom he alleged had made false statements.

By the end of 1985 the complaints enquiry had taken more than 400 statements and run up costs of around £250,000. John Reddington had resigned – he took over the UK Atomic Energy Police instead – and had been replaced by Alan Vickers, Deputy Chief Constable of South Wales.

Sarah Hollis, meanwhile, had declined to speak to the complaints team again. Mindful of what had happened to her in the previous nine months she decided to let her statements to the Platts-Mills enquiry do the talking for her. If she had hoped to avoid more trouble this way she was to be disappointed.

On 15 January she again recognised one of the officers who had threatened her. This time he appeared to be waiting for her outside a friend's house. Two days later she was followed on her bike by a marked police car. As she rode away she overheard a uniformed officer speaking into his radio: 'She's just passed now,' he said. And then, on 22 January 1986 in Manchester city centre, she was attacked. She suddenly found herself held from behind and the man she had recognised previously verbally abused her. He then punched her in the face, giving her a black eye.

At around the same time two officers were travelling to Steven Shaw's parents' house in London. It was to be his first statement to the complaints enquiry. On the advice of his solicitor he agreed to cooperate and gave a full account of the incident at Bootle Street police station the previous May. He was also able to provide a detailed description of the two officers who had attacked him.

Sarah Hollis, too, had had a change of heart and on 30 January had an informal talk with one of the enquiry team. The following day, Friday, 31 January 1986, Steven Shaw made one of his regular visits to Manchester to see his girlfriend Olivia. Shaw was worried – a few day before making his statement to the complaints team a note had been pushed under the door of his office in London. It read: 'We'll kill you, you bastard.' He had later received a telephone call at the office, the caller, a man, repeated the same words.

Friday and Saturday passed off without incident. Then, at Sunday lunchtime, Olivia went to a local pub with friends. Shaw stayed in the house. At around 2 p.m. he walked to a nearby shop to buy cigarettes. His subsequent statement to the police complaints enquiry described what happened next.

> I was not paying particular attention to what was going on around me, but the next thing I recall is the taller of two men barging into my left shoulder; the same man then punched me in the area of my stomach with a clenched fist. I can then recall being pushed towards an alleyway. By now I had a chance to see the faces of both men and I immediately recognised them as being the same two policemen who took me to Bootle Street police station on the 14th of May.

Shaw went on to allege that the officers had punched and kicked him, struck him in the chest with a bottle, and burned him on the cheek with a cigarette.

He managed to stagger back to Olivia's house, where he was found slumped against the wall with his nose and mouth caked with blood. Photographs of him show very ugly bruising around the eyes and mouth.

Shaw later discharged himself from Manchester Royal Infirmary and went into hiding. He and Sarah Hollis took advice from lawyers, friends and local councillors on what to do next. They decided that the best protection was through publicity; they also hoped this might help identify their attackers. But at some point during the week beginning 10 March Sarah Hollis was persuaded to change her mind.

During that week she received an anonymous phone call. She has since declined to go into detail, but the gist of the caller's message was that if she withdrew her complaints of harassment and assault, and withdrew from any publicity, she would be left alone.

Within weeks Sarah Hollis withdrew all complaints against the police except that referring to her original injury at the Brittan demonstration. She simultaneously stopped giving interviews and refused to discuss her decision. By the end of the month Alan Vickers's complaints enquiry had made no progress in identifying the attackers. None the less, the Police Complaints Authority announced that its £250,000 investigation was almost complete. Papers were shortly to be passed to the DPP for consideration.

It was to take a year for any results to be made public. Three police officers were charged with criminal offences arising out of the Brittan demonstration: two were accused of assault, one of perjury. All were acquitted. The PCA report which led to the charges concluded that there were several other genuine cases of assault against Manchester students, but the police investigation had failed to identify the officers concerned. However, another eleven policemen were to be subject to internal disciplinary warnings about entries of events in their notebooks.

The PCA had wanted to publish a full account of the enquiry and its findings, but the DPP instructed them only to print a brief summary in case the trials of the three policemen were adversely affected. It was clear, however, that the complaints team had been unable to identify the officers allegedly involved in persecuting and attacking Steven Shaw and Sarah Hollis. Worse still, Shaw and Frank Logan were to be charged with perverting the course of justice. But by then Steven Shaw had packed up his belongings and left England.

The PCA report and the DPP's decision provoked widely differing reactions. Sarah Hollis was stunned.

> Enquiries should still be held into the eight assaults. There were a limited number of police on duty. Are the police in Manchester not to be held accountable for their actions? I never believed this type of thing could happen, but the experience of a policeman throwing me downstairs has irreversibly damaged my confidence in the police. Until they eradicate those men from the police who are prepared to go out and assault people we can't be comforted by this enquiry.

Daniel Scott, a student also present at the demonstration said:

> I spent many hours carefully giving evidence to the Police Complaints Authority, specifically identifying individual officers in photographs whom I had witnessed hitting people. Perhaps I and all the other students and lecturers who cooperated with the enquiry made the whole thing up? Or perhaps we just wasted our time.

Professor John Griffiths, Emeritus Professor of Public Law at London University, analysed the implications:

> In eight cases where the evidence clearly showed an assault had occurred it had not been possible to identify the individual officer responsible. This indicates that the police is not a disci-

plined force in the sense that wrongdoing is discoverable through the hierarchy of command. It means that police officers can act illegally and in contravention of what one assumes their orders are and can do so with impunity because discipline is slack. . . .

However faultless the supervision and however thorough the investigation, the police have shown once again that they can effectively close ranks and prevent the full discovery of facts.

The chairman of the PCA decided to explain. On 17 April 1987, in a signed article in the *Guardian*, he wrote:

What those who have not been involved in war or public disorder do not understand is the unutterable confusion which exists when opposed parties of struggling people clash with one another. . . . Let us suppose that among the officers present on that night [of the Brittan visit] there were some who saw, or thought they saw, a colleague using quite unnecessary force amounting therefore to violence on some unoffending student; and let us suppose that such officers decided to keep that knowledge or belief to themselves rather than denounce a colleague for a wrong action done in a moment of stress and about which they might be mistaken anyway.

That would be wrong, reprehensible and, technically, itself a breach of discipline. But would a lawyer be the first to stand forward and denounce a fellow lawyer for a questionable action done in the heat of courtroom battle?

Failure to denounce one's friends and relations has never been a subject for discipline in any civilised body of people. . . . In fact when conduct is bad enough, police officers do come forward and offer evidence against fellow-officers as soon as they realise there is no other way in which offenders are going to be brought to book.

There can be no clearer indication to police officers up and down the country that should they choose loyalty to an erring colleague over and above telling tales to those investigating the misdemeanour, the Police Complaints Authority will quite understand.

The reality of the Manchester affair, as discovered by three separate investigations – one by the BBC, one by author Martin Walker and one by John Platts-Mills, QC – was that not only had police officers used excessive force and failed properly to plan the policing of the Brittan visit; not only had other officers then covered up the assaults on students that night by refusing to identify the guilty men, but there had been what Walker described as 'an unofficial firm within a firm' inside the Manchester police force which set out to victimise and intimidate the two most 'troublesome' complainants, Steven Shaw and Sarah Hollis.

All of this might appear sufficient to justify the warning by Hollis's solicitor, Gareth Peirce, that going to the Police Complaints Authority can involve a very grave risk. After all, those responsible for attacking Hollis and Shaw have still not been identified and Shaw himself faces criminal proceedings should he ever set foot in England again, even though Frank Logan was eventually acquitted.

The case against the PCA doesn't end there, however. There are two other glaring inadequacies in its powers and policies.

The first is that it has no power to investigate complaints against police officers officially off-duty when they make an arrest. The Authority made the admission in March 1986 with regard to the case of Mr Gerald Farrelley. In August 1985, Mr Farrelley was hit on the head with a truncheon by PC Frank Gerachty of the Metropolitan Police. He was hit so hard that the truncheon split in two and knocked him unconscious. He later had six stitches in his head. PC Gerachty claimed in court later that he was off-duty at the time and that Farrelley had attacked him with an exhaust pipe. Some time after the alleged attack he had returned to the scene and found the very exhaust pipe lying on the ground. He admitted, though, that he had failed to record this significant discovery in his notebook.

Worse still for PC Gerachty, the only injury discovered by police surgeons was a slight graze to his little finger. Perhaps unsurprisingly a jury at Southwark Crown Court threw out his attempted prosecution of Gerald Farrelley for assault. During the case PC Gerachty had admitted hitting Farrelley with his truncheon.

The PCA then explained its position. Because PC Gerachty was off-duty at the time he assaulted Farrelley, the Authority could not intervene because the policeman had no more official status than any ordinary citizen at the time. However, the Authority said, the officer's Chief Constable could look into the case.

Whether or not the Metropolitan Police ever disciplined PC Gerachty is anyone's guess. It remains so because of the second main inadequacy of the PCA – the way disciplinary procedure, nominally under its control, is handled. The punishment meted out to wayward officers in disciplinary hearings is never publicised. According to John Steele, the civilian head of CIB1, this is because it is an 'essentially private matter. . . . It's always been held to be something the public is not entitled to know, and not even the complainant is told.'

It's all a far cry from the grandiose claims of the Police Complaints Authority (which has now taken to dubbing itself the *Independent* Police Complaints Authority). Even its chairman, Sir Cecil Clothier, admits that it is far from powerful enough. In his annual report presented in April 1987 he called for a simpler procedure for sacking 'unsuitable' police officers, and admitted that the Metropolitan Police had proved adept at frustrating his enquiries. Perhaps the entire process is most accurately summed up by John Stalker, deputy Chief Constable of Manchester at the time of the Brittan visit. A fortnight after Clothier issued his report, Stalker described the PCA as 'comically irrelevant'.

Stalker, of course, was only one of a long line of senior policemen to dismiss the concept of complaints against the police. Perhaps that is how the Hollis/Shaw cases of this world come about. It is certain, however, that the issue won't go away. In 1986 15,865 complaints were made to the PCA (a figure which doesn't include those petty complaints dealt with by conciliation between the police and complainant).

Of those 15,865, 3,003 were allegations of assault or actual bodily harm, 381 of death or serious injury, and 36 of corruption. By the end of the year 48 criminal prosecutions had been brought as a result; 40 were for assault, 1 for corruption, 3 for traffic irregularities; and 1 for irregularity of evidence.

The figures are a mere fraction of the total complaints. Clothier insists that is is unfair to judge the PCA on prosecuted cases alone, since they represent the instances of solid evidence. Look instead, he has urged, at our general aims and principles. But it is precisely these which account for so little public confidence in the system. Even the Police Federation – the voice of the accused officer – now accepts the need for fully independent investigators completely unconnected with the police service. It is a call that most people find hard to resist – except, apparently, for politicians.

SEVEN

And Justice For All

> 'Justice is open to everybody in the same way as the Ritz Hotel.'
>
> Judge Sturgess, quoted in the *Observer*, 22.7.22.

Is it all, in the end, too late? Have the centuries of fudge and nudge, the litany of broken promises and failed legislation made it impossible to repair and reform our system? We hope not. If we thought so we wouldn't do the work we do, nor would we have written this book. Despite it all we believe that reform can be made – albeit over a lengthy period.

To that end, bearing in mind all that has gone before, this brief chapter will set out a programme of major legislation which could start the ball rolling.

The first and most crucial law must be a written constitution or bill of rights. Until we have some legal yardstick against which the rights and responsibilities of citizen and State alike can be measured, there can be no progress towards a universal appeal against injustice in whatever area it occurs. Nor, we believe, is it simply enough somehow to incorporate into UK law the European Convention on Human Rights. The Convention talks a good fight, but whether it could stand the strain of exposure to English judges is doubtful; it is too vague. A constitution along the lines of the American one – warts, amendments and all – is never going to be perfect, but it's the closest we'll ever get.

The next logical (and disgracefully long overdue) piece of legislation must be a genuine Freedom of Information Act, combined with the abandonment of section 2 of the Official Secrets Act, and the introduction of a Sunshine Act requiring all governmental business at national and local level to be carried out in public. There would, of course, be exceptions to this rule – as there are already in similar laws relating to local authority business – for the protection of national security and of legitimately private matters (parental rights resolutions, individual housing benefit subsidies and the like). But national security would be decided by an all-party Commons select committee, which would also oversee the work of the security services. The services themselves would be statutorily defined, with a written charter of responsibilities and rights.

Individual privacy needs protection, from safeguarding people's right to a quiet life free from interference to a comprehensive Data Protection Act backed by a watchdog with real power.

These are basic reforms; implementing them in good faith would bring a spirit of natural justice back into our contact with the State. But a 'spirit' isn't enough – legislation is only as good as the legal machine that enforces it. To this end legal aid must be made available for both civil and criminal cases and tribunals, and open to all. There can be no excuse for a legal system which endows its citizens with rights but at the same time deprives them of the right to invoke them.

The creation and maintenance of all this would be extremely expensive; yet the whole business of law and government is expensive. Surely there can be no more important priority than ensuring a just deal for the people who pay for it.

In addition, the legal system we have to date relied on must be reformed, which in itself will potentially save money. As a priority a new cadre of professional judges must be trained gradually to replace the existing network. The new judges should not be drawn from the ranks of barristers, as at present, but should instead form a separate profession without the absurd traditions, loyalties and trappings of our present judiciary.

At the same time our network of amateur magistrates must be phased out, to be replaced with another professional cadre of investigating magistrates, whose job is to discover the truth, rather than merely hear it argued over by lawyers. Overseeing all this must be a fully fledged Ministry of Justice.

Finally, the legal profession itself should be streamlined and the old barriers between solicitor and barrister – together with their accompanying restrictive practices – abolished. A unified profession, open to all, stands a better chance of acting both in its clients' and the public interest.

All too expensive? Not cheap, certainly, but then no one ever suggested that justice can be obtained at cut-price rates. Unrealistic idealism, irrelevant to the ordinary person? Idealism, without question, but balanced and rational, we hope. As for the ordinary person isn't that precisely who this book has been both for and about?

Index

absconding, 142, 143, 144, 149
Access to Medical Reports Bill (1987), 211
Access to Personal Files Bill (1987), 211
Accident Compensation Corporation, New Zealand, 157–8
accommodation: agencies, 86–7; bed-and-breakfast, 75, 77; council housing, 75–7, 88–90; for the homeless, 74–7; privately rented, 86–8; *see also* householders
Accommodation Act (1953), 86–7
Ackerman, Ronald, 213
Acres, Dr Douglas, 20
Action for the Victims of Medical Accidents (AVMA), 156, 157
Advisory Committee on Legal Aid, 15
Advisory Committee on Pesticides (ACP), 182
Afan Valley council tenants, 88
Aish, defence contractor, 224–5
Alderson, John, 99, 241–2
Allan, PC, 237–8
Allen, Major John, 69–70
Allen, Sir Phillip, 186–7
Ananda Vedi, 207
Anderton, Chief Constable James, 235, 271, 272
Angry Brigade trial, 35
animals rights activitists, 110–11, 219, 220
Argyle, Judge Michael, 8
Armstrong, Sir Robert, 164, 176, 177, 178, 192
Arnold, Elizabeth, 151
assessment centres, juvenile, 142, 145
Assistant Masters' and Mistresses' Association, 159–60
Association of Chief Police Officers (ACPO), 44–5
Association of Directors of Social Services, 152
Association of Metropolitan Authorities, 232, 240
Athenaeum club, judges' membership of, 6–7
Atkins, Sir Humphrey, 177
Attorney General, 13, 20, 37, 43–4, 106, 107, 170, 188, 248
Attwell, Leslie, 79–80

Baader-Meinhoff gang, 196, 201
bail, application for, 21, 22–3

Bail Act (1976), 22
Baker, Demelza Val, 201–2, 205
Baker, Kenneth, 159, 160
Bar Council, 13, 58
Barber, David, 153, 154
'Barraclough, Miss B.', 132, 133, 134, 135
barristers, 6, 7, 12, 14, 72–3; challenging of jurors, 35–7; and vetting of jurors, 42–3; *see also* lawyers, solicitors
Bartletts de Reya, solicitors, 63, 65
BBC, 104, 119, 275, 279
Beckford, Jasmine, 139, 152
bed-and-breakfast accommodation, 75, 77
Bedford Hill, Balham, prostitution in, 117
behaviour modification programme, 146–8, 149, 151
Benn, Tony, 184, 220
Bentham, Jeremy, 34
Berkeley, Taxing Master, 67
Bernstein, Lord, 81
Birmingham: council tenants, 88; social services, 138–9
Birmingham Daily Argus, 108–9
Birmingham Children's Hospital, 153, 154
Birmingham pub bombers, 253
Black People's Day of Action, 243
Blakelock, PC Keith, 238, 156
Blunkett, David, 220
Blunt, Sir Anthony, 169
Blyth v. Birmingham Waterworks Co. (1856), 156
Borenden, Rex Morley-Morley, Vicomte de, 2–5, 60, 71
Borrie, Sir Gordon, 86
Boston, Lord, 198
Bowe, Colette, 176, 177
Bowman, Barry, 64
Boy George, 96
Boyne, Harry, 184
Boyson, Dr Rhodes, 166
Bradford Teacher Training College, Miss Ward expelled from, 7
Bradford University demonstration (1986), 105

Bramshill Journal, 227
breach of confidence, 106–7, 178
Brighton bombing, (1984), 12–13, 14
British Association of Social Workers (BASW), 139–40, 210–11
British Medical Association, Ethical Committee, 212
British Nuclear Police, 167
British Nutrition Foundation, 179
British Steel Corporation (BSC), 106
Brittan, Leon, 94, 97, 98, 99, 166, 175, 176, 177, 246, 269–70, 274, 277, 280
Brixton riots, 23, 235, 242
Broadwater Farm riot (1985), 238–9, 256–9
'Brooks, Paddy, Claire and Patricia', 131–7, 138
brothels, 117
'Brown, Ann', 128
Buckley, Kevin, 189
Buckmaster, Lord, 6
building and repairs: council housing, 88–90; and the householder, 83–6; school, 159–60
Burgess and Maclean, defection of, 169
Busy Bees agency, Islington, 87
Butler, R. A., 231, 232

Cabinet, 164; responsibility, 173, 175–8; secrecy, 105–6
Cabinet committees, 169, 173–4
Calderdale Council, 160, 193
Callaghan, James, 173–4, 180, 183, 184
Cambridge 'Kite' building development, 194
Cambridge University Institute of Criminology, 140
Cameron, John and Lynette, 160–1
Campaign for Freedom of Information, 208
Campbell, Duncan, 208, 218–19
Cannon, Geoffrey, 179–80
Cantley, Mr Justice, 191
Card, Richard, 227
Cargill, Ian, inquest on, 28–9
Cargill, John, 28–9
Carlisle, John, MP, 105
'Carole' and 'Gemma', 119, 120–4, 126, 138
Carr, Robert, 37
Carroll, Lewis, 163
Casey, PC, 236–8
CCN Systems of Nottingham, 216–17, 218–19; debt-collection, 218–19; MOSAIC databank, 216; Nationwide Consumer File, 217
Centre for Studies on Integration in Education (CSIE), 161
challenging jurors, 35–7; for cause, 35–6; peremptory, 36–7; 'stand by for the crown', 37
Chapel-en-le-Frith infant school, 159
Chernobyl disaster, 195
Chief Constable(s), 230, 232, 233, 234–5, 239–41, 246, 271

child abuse, 125, 129, 130, 139, 151
Child Benefit Act, 161
Child Care Act (1980), 126–7, 141
child labour, 129
children: behaviour therapy and drug therapy for, 146–7, 148; and care system, 119–52; delinquent, 125–6, 130–1, 141–4; and education, 158–62; endangered, 130–1; and health rights, 153; in law, 127–31; parents' access to, 121–2, 127–8, 132, 133, 135; at risk, 120, 130; voluntary care, 126–8
Children Act (1948), 126
Children & Young Persons Act (1969), 125, 131
Children's Legal Centre, 144, 145, 147–8
Chrysler car company, rescue of, 170
circuit judges, 6, 7, 9, 12
civil liberties and human rights, 93–112
civil servants, 169, 170, 180, 191, 203, 227; and Clive Ponting, 41, 171–3; and ESTACODE, 186–7, 189; and Sarah Tisdall, 189–91 and Westland affair, 176–8
Clothier, Sir Cecil, 261, 266, 268, 281
CND, 93, 95–6, 97–8, 101, 102, 190–1, 220
Cockburn, Sir Alexander, 113
Cockfield, Lord, 180
Coke, Sir Edward, 37, 74
Coldshield Windows Ltd, 83
Colwell, Maria, 139, 152
Communist Party, British, 98, 222
Community Care magazine, 210
community liaison officers, 236, 237
Community Rights Project, 193
compensation, 5, 69, 71, 73, 91, 204, 225; medical negligence claims, 156–7; no-fault, 157–8; by police, 247, 265
Complaints Investigation Bureau (CIB), 262–6, 281
complaints tribunal on telephone tapping, 100–1
compulsory care orders, 125–6, 127, 143
Comyn, Mr Justice, 30
Conegate Ltd, 114
Confait, Maxwell, murder of, 247, 252, 254, 259
confessions, police methods of obtaining, 247–59
Conservative Party/Government, 198, 269–70; Brighton bombing (1984), 12–13; education policy, 160; and the Lobby, 184–5; and Parliament, 166–78; police officers' support for, 245; *Spycatcher* case, 163–4; trade union 'reform' by, 112; Westland affair, 175–8, 180
constables, 227–8, 229, 230; see also police
contempt of court, 107–9
Contempt of Court Act (1981), 45
Control of Pollution Act, (1984), 193

Conway, Russell, 60, 71
coroners, 24–32
Coroners Act (1887), 30
coroner's jury, 24, 27, 28, 29–30, 31
council housing, 78, 88–90; waiting lists, 75–6, 120, 122
Council of Europe Convention on data protection (1980), 199
County and Borough Police Act (1856), 230
County Police Act (1839), 230
court clerks, 14
Court of Appeal, 55, 106, 110, 240
Courts Act (1971), 15, 36
Courts of Justice, Strand, 163
Cox, John, 98, 99, 101
Cozens-Hardy, Lord, 6
Criminal Justice Act (1967), 34
Criminal Law Act, (1977), 36, 37, 38, 39
Criminal Legal Aid Committees, 22
criminal records database, 203
'cross-fertilisation' (in police force), 267–8
Crossman, Richard, *Diaries*, 105–6
Crown courts, 37–9, 48
Crown Prosecution Service, 46
CS gas, police use of, 240–1
CS Windows plc, 85
Cunnell, Chris, 83
Curzon Street House, MI5 HQ, 99
Customs and Excise, 114–15, 267
Customs and Excise Act, 102

Dack, James Richard, 207
Daily Express, 106–7
Daily Telegraph, 102, 184
Dalyell, Tam, 105, 172, 191
Darling, Mr Justice, 108–9
databanks, private commercial, 216–19
Data protection/information, 196–225
Data Protection Act (1984), 202–3, 204–5, 206, 208, 211, 215–16, 217, 223–4
Data Protection Authority, 198
Data Protection Committee, 198
Data Protection Registrar, 203–5, 217–18
Davies, Glanville, 66, 67–9, 70
Davy, Brian, 26
Davy, James, inquest of, 25–7
Davy, Marie, 26
Dear, Chief Constable Geoffrey, 234–5
Dearing, Sir Ronald, 101
debt-collection systems, CCN's, 218–19
Defoe, Daniel, *Parochial Tyranny*, 228
Deighton, Jane, 269
Denning, Lord, 4–5, 6, 7, 45, 60, 71, 180
Dennison, Mr Justice, 258
Deptford fire case (1981), 27
Devlin, Lord, 32, 41
Devonport naval dockyards, plans to privatise, 180
Dewsbury parents affair (1987), 160
DHSS (Department of Health and Social Security), 75, 77, 128, 145, 148, 152, 153, 161, 166, 179; computerised Central Index, 205, 206, 216; and legal aid, 50; and social work files, 210–11
Director of Public Prosecutions (DPP), 25–6, 44–5, 46, 170, 176, 252, 260–1, 262, 264, 273, 277, 278
Distillers company and Thalidomide, 107–8
District Support Units (DSUs), 263–6
divorce or separation, statutory charge for, 52–5
'dock briefs', 46
doctors: medical records of, 208, 211–16; negligence claims against, 156–8; overworked junior hospital, 155–6
domestic violence and the police, 244–5
double-jeopardy rule, 262
Donaldson, Sir John, 10–11, 240
drug therapy, 146, 148
drugs, 201–2, 236

Economic League, 220–3
Edmands, Trevor, 96
education, 119, 166; cut-backs in, 159–60, 161, 162; and the family, 158–62; and parental choice, 160; and private tuition, 160–1; and school data information, 208–10, 216; and 'special needs' children, 161–2; sponsored teaching materials, 162
Education Act (1944), 158, 160, 161; (1981), 160, 161, 162; (1986), 105
'Edward', medical reports of, 213–15
Edwards, David, 56, 58
EEG brain scan, 148
electoral registers, sale of, 217, 218
Elizabeth II, Queen, 9, 79
Ely Report, 68–9, 71
Entwhistle, Jean, 272
'episodic discontrol syndrome', 148
'Ernie C.', 250
ESTACODE, 186–7, 189
European Convention on Human Rights, x, 255, 282
European Court of Human Rights, 94–5, 100, 107–8, 111, 114, 137–8, 161
Evans, Richard, 185, 186
Executive, 164–5

Fagan, Michael, 79
family rights, 119–62; children in care system, 119–52; and education, 158–62; health rights, 152–8; *see also* children; local authorities
Family Rights Group, (FRG), 127–8, 135
Farley, Margaret, 154
Farrelley, Gerald, 280
Fatal Accident Enquiries (in Scotland), 31, 168
Fawcett, James, 224

Feldman, Anthony S., 3-5, 60, 71
filibuster technique, 105
fire safety in multi-occupation houses, 77
firearms, registration of, 166
Fisher, Sir Henry, 259
food industry and NACNE Report, 179-80
The Food Scandal, 179-80
Foot, Michael, 169
Forster, Stewart, 159
fostering, 121-2, 128, 131-2, 133, 202
Franks Committee (1971), 183, 186-7, 188, 190
Fraser, Lord, 91
fraud, 2-5, 267
Fraud Squad, 3
freedom of assembly, 109-11
freedom of expression, 101-9
freedom of thought, 96-101
Friends of the Earth, 99, 220

Garratt v. Eastmond (1959), 230-1
Gates, Lucy, 139
Gateshead, legal aid refusal rate, 21
Gavin, PC Michael, 263-6
Gay News, 115
'Gay's the Word' bookshop, 1984 trial, 115
GCHQ case (1984), 91-2, 111
Geard, Graham, 82
Geffen, Ivan, 48-9, 56-7
GEN groups, 174
General Belgrano, sinking of, 170-2
Genet, Jean, 115
Gerachty, PC Frank, 280
Gibbens, Judge Brian, 8
Gifford, Andrew, 180
Gifford, Lord Tony, QC, 10, 15-16, 266, 267
Gill, George, 240
GJW, lobbying firm, 180
Glidewell, Lord Justice, 111, 116
Goldstein, Recorder Simon, 8
Good Relations Public Affairs Ltd, 181
Goddison, Corey and Lucy, 162
Goodison, Valerie, 76
Graham-Green, Taxing Master, 67
government, 163-92; and the media, 183-6; and official secrets, 186-92; and Parliament, 165-78; and the people, 178-83; theory of, 164-5; *see also* information; local authorities
Granada Television, 106
Greater Manchester Police, 235; and Hollis/Shaw cases, 269-80
Greenwich Council, 218
Griffith-Jones, Mervyn, 112, 113
Griffiths, Professor John, 278-9
Grunwick dispute, (1977), 38
guarantees, builders' long-term, 83, 85-6
Guardian, 190-1, 262-3, 273-4, 279
Gupta, Dr K., 269

Haigh, Mrs Madeleine, 93-5, 96, 201
Hailsham, Lord, 1, 8-9, 10, 12, 13-14, 15, 16-17, 19, 24, 36, 37, 72, 102-3, 104, 108
Halligey, Peter and Sylvia, 64-5, 66
Hanlon, Mrs Mary, 54-5
Hansard, 166, 169
Hansen, Ole, 18, 55, 56
Harman, Harriet, MP, 99, 108
Harrison, Dennis, 90
Hart, Judith, 173
Harvey, Alan, 220, 221, 222, 223
Havers, Sir Michael, 43-5, 170, 176
Hayward, Betty Burke, 2-5, 60-1, 71-2
health care/rights, 119, 152-8
Health Education Council, NACNE Report published by, 179
Heath, Edward, 10, 180, 181, 197
Hell's Angels, 82
Henriques, Steven E., 63-4, 65, 69
Henry, Dr James, 269
Hereford Hospital, 156, 157
Hermon, Sir John, Chief Constable, 104
Hertfordshire Police, 202, 204-5
Heseltine, Michael, 171, 172, 173, 175-6, 180, 190, 191
Hetherington, Sir Thomas, 261
Hewitt, Patricia, 99
Highland Regional Council, 131-7
Hilliard, Brian, 264, 267
Hirst and Agu v. Chief Constable of West Yorkshire Police (1986), 110-11
Hodgkin, Rachel, 147-8
Hogg, Douglas, 244
Hollis, Sarah, case of, 269-80, 281
Holloway Road case, (1983), 263-6, 267
home, the right to a, 74-7
Home Office, 39, 40, 42, 99, 100-1, 108, 114, 148, 248, 259, 260, 261, 264; and data protection, 197, 198, 199-200, 208, 217-18; Inspector of Constabulary, 250
Home Secretary, 167, 195, 198, 199, 223; and the police, 94, 228, 230, 231, 233, 234-5, 240, 246, 253, 264, 269-70
homeless, 74-7, 87-8; bed-and-breakfast accommodation for, 75, 77; local councils' obligations towards, 74-5; priority needs, 75, 76; privately-run hostel for, 87-8
homosexuality, 115, 116
hospitals, NHS, 153-6
House of Commons, 9, 164, 196-7; filibuster, 105; and governments, 165-78; and the Lobby, 183; Questions, 165-8; register of MPs' interests, 185-6; select committees, 169-72; Social Services Committee hearings (1983), 141-4; Table Office, 168
House of Commons committees: Environment, 185, 194-5; Foreign Affairs, 170-2; Home Affairs, 170, 198-9; Privileges, 85; public Accounts, 224-5

House of Lords, 6, 9, 10, 76, 91–2, 105, 107, 115, 126, 164, 183
house repairs and improvements, 82, 83–6, 88–90
householders, rights of, 77–86
Housing Act (1980), 77
Housing Defects Act (1984), 89
Housing (Homeless Persons) Act (1977), 74–5, 76
Howe, Eric, Data Protection Registrar, 203–4, 205, 217–18
Hoyle, Doug, MP, 21
Hoyle, Michael, 65–6
Huggins, Dennis, 221–2
Hughes, Amanda, 272, 274
Humberside County Council v. DPR, 125
Humble-Smith, Roger, 65
Hurd, Douglas, 195, 223, 264
Hutchinson, Lord, QX, 43

Ian Greer Associates, 180
immigration: computerised Suspect Index, 208
Incitement to Disaffection Act, 102
indecency see obscenity
Industrial Relations Act (1971), 10
industrial schools, 130–1
industrial tribunals, 51, 224
information, government communication of, 165–92; *Belgrano* affair, 170–2; briefing, 183; and Cabinet committees, 173–4; and data protection, 196–225; leaking, 172, 176–7, 179, 183, 185; and the Lobby, 183–5; official secrets, 163–4, 169, 170–2, 178–80, 183, 186–92; Parliamentary Questions, 165–9; public enquiries, 194–6; and secrecy in local government, 193–4; and select committees, 169–72; *Spycatcher* case, 163–4, 192; and Table Office, 168; and Westland affair, 175–8
information industry, 199, 203, 216–25
Inland Revenue, 267; computerised Central Index, 205–6, 216
Ingham, Bernard, 176, 177, 184
inner city riots, 235–6, 237–40; Brixton, 23, 235, 242; Broadwater Farm, 238–9, 244, 256–9; 1981 trials, 22; Scarman Report on (1981), 235, 239; Toxteth, 239–40
Innes, DAC Bob, 265
Inns of Court, 7
'Inquest', 27–8
inquests, coroners', 24–31
Interception of Communications Act (1985), 100–1
International Paint, 181
intoximeters, 106–7
Inverness Procurator Fiscal, 136
Inverness sheriff's court, 134–5
Isherwood, Christopher, 115
Islington Council housing problems, 77

Jack, Rosalinda, 207–8
James, Professor Phillip, 179
James, Professor William, 179
James Committee, 37–8
Jarrett, Cynthia, death of, 237–8, 239, 256, 266–7
Jarrett, Floyd, 236–8, 239, 266
Jarrett, Patricia, 237–8, 239
Jeger, Jenny, 180
Jones, Graham, 88
Jones, Mr Justice Kenneth, 264–5
Jones, Robert, 207
JPs see magistrates
judges, judiciary, 5–16, 86; circuit, 6, 7, 9, 12; freedom of expression of, 102–4; High Court, 6, 9, 28, 91; Kilmuir rules, 103–4; 'practice direction' to, 35; recorders, 6, 8, 9, 11–14; short working-day of, 39
judges' lodgings, 7
Judges' Rules, 254, 255
judicial appointments, 11–15
judicial misbehaviour, 102–3
judicial review, 91–2
Judiciary, 164, 165; see also law
juries, 2, 32–45; acquittal rate in trials by, 40–2; challenging, 35–7; coroner's, 24, 27, 28, 29–30; 'perverse', 33, 40; 'special', 34; vetting of, 34, 42–5
Juries Act (1949), 34; (1984), 44
Justice, 196
Justice of the Peace (magazine), 22
Justices of the Peace Act (1361), 18
juvenile offenders/courts, 125–6, 130–1, 141–4, 145, 209

Kartun, Derek, 156
Kaufman, Gerald, 110
Kay, Brian, 152
Keene, David QC, 240
Kelly, Jimmy, 26
Kent, Monsignor Bruce, 98, 99
Kent police, 247–52
Kerr, Howard, 257, 258, 259
Kilmartin, Mrs, 48
Kilmuir, Lord, 104
Kilmuir rules, 103–4
King-Hamilton, Judge Alan, 40
Kinnear, Johnnie, test case of, 51–2
Kinnock, Neil, 99, 184–5
Kirkwood, Archie, MP, 167–8, 211
Krafft, Alan, 82

Labour Party/Government, 163, 173–4, 197–8, 245–6
Lacey, Ron, 140, 149–50
Lady Chatterley's Lover (Lawrence) trial, 112–13, 115
land ownership, legal concept of, 86
Latey, Mr Justice, 122, 123–4

law, legal system, ix–x, xi, 1–73; breach of confidence, 106–7, 178; and children in care, 119–140, 144–5; common law, 6, 79, 86, 102, 178, 227, 229, 230; compensation, 5, 69, 71, 73, 91, 156–8, 204, 225, 247, 265; contempt of court, 107–9; coroners, 24–32; and education, 159, 161–2; and freedom of assembly, 109–111; and freedom of expression, 102, 106–9; and health rights, 152–3, 156–8; and homosexuality, 115, 116; and householders' rights, 79–86; judges, 6–16; judicial review, 91–2; jury, 32–45; juvenile offenders, 125–6, 130–1; lawyers, 61–73; legal aid, 45–61; magistrates, 16–24; need for Ministry of Justice, 10–11, 15–16; no written constitution, x, 164, 178; obscenity cases, 112–13; and the Ombudsman, 90–1; pornography, 113; and prostitution, 116–17; Rent Act legislation, 86; Scottish, 131–7; and tenants' rights, 86–92; and trade unions, 111–12
Law Lords, 6, 54, 76, 104, 106, 114, 241
Law Society, 5, 23; and compensation, 69, 71; and complaints about solicitors, 61–72; and Ely Report, 68–9, 71; and Glanville Davies case, 66–9; and Lay Observer's enquiries, 68, 69–70; and legal aid, 49–50, 53–61 *passim*, 65, 66; Negligence Panel, 63, 65–6; Remuneration Certificate (assessment scheme), 64
Lawrence, D. H., 112, 113
Lawton, Kathleen, 53–4
lawyers, 61–73; complaints about, 61–72; suing, 66; *see also* barristers; solicitors
Lay Observer, 68, 69–70
Layfield, Sir Frank, 195
Leach, Edmund, 119
Leaf, Malcolm, 64
leaking information, 172, 176–7, 179, 183, 185, 201, 244, 245
LEAs (local education authorities), 158, 160, 161–2
Lee, John, 223
Legal Action Group, 18, 55
legal aid, 5, 26, 45–61, 65, 66, 72, 91, 92, 133; civil, 46, 49–56; contribution by defendants, 47–9; and coroner's inquest, 26, 27, 28; criminal, 46–9; emergency applications, 50; in magistrates' courts, 21–2, 46, 47; refusal rate, 20, 21–2; solicitors' payments, 56–8; statutory charge, 52–6; 24-hour duty solicitor scheme, 47
Legal Aid Act (1974), 21, 26
Legal Aid Practitioners Group (LAPG), 48–9, 57, 72
Legg, Thomas, 11–12
Legge, Michael, 170–1, 172, 173
Legislature, 164, 165; *see also* Parliament

Leigh, David, 208
Lemon, Dennis, 115
'Len' and 'Christine', 128
Leonard, John, QC, 43
letters, interception of, 101
Lever, Harold, 170
Levey, Lawrence, 239–40
Levitt, Richard, 96
Lewenden, Mike, 149
Lewton, Karen, 101
Libel Act (1792), 34
light, householder's right to, 80–1
Lincoln Green Primary School, Leeds, 159
'Linda', 150
Lindop, Sir Norman, 198
Lindop Committee report, (1979), 198, 203, 211
Lion Laboratories Ltd, 106–7
Liverpool police, 229–30; and Toxteth riots, 239–40
Livingstone, Ken, 220
Lobby, 165, 183–5
lobbying, poitical, 179–83, 185
local byelaws, 193
local councils/authorities: child care system, 120–52 *passim*; compulsory care orders, 125–6; and education, 158–62; environmental health services, 87, 88, 89; and homeless, 74–7; and housing repairs, 88–90; and judicial review, 91–2; meetings open to the public, 175, 193–4; and the Ombudsman, 90–1; and parental rights resolution, 127, 133, 135; and the police, 229, 233, 245–6; reorganisation of (1974), 89; sale of electoral registers by, 217, 218; secrecy of, 193–4; voluntary care, 126–8
Local Government (Access to Information) Act (1985), 194
Local Government Act (1972), 193
lock-ups for children in care, 145, 150
Logan, Frank, 272, 274–5, 278
London, rented accommodation in, 86–8; *see also* metropolitan Police
London Criminal Court Solicitors' Association, 72
London Reform Societies trials (1794), 33
Long Ashton (Avon), legal aid refusal rate, 21
Lord Advocate, Scottish, 31
Lord Chancellor, 6, 8–15, 36, 40, 72, 108; and judges, 8–15, 102–4; and legal aid, 26, 51, 55–6; and magistrates, 16–17, 24
Lord Chancellor's Department (LCD), 9, 10, 11, 20, 21, 26, 39, 40, 50, 57–8; Lay Observer, 68, 69–70; legal aid advisory committee, 26, 51, 54
Luff, Peter, 180–1
Luscombe, Victor, 159–60
Lyon, Alex, MP, 196, 197

McAllister, DC Brendan, 2, 258
McClusky, Lord, Scottish Law Lord, 104

INDEX

McCowan, Mr Justice, 67–8, 191
McGahey, Mick, 99
MacGregor, John, 207
McHugh, Dr Mary, coroner, 30
McKay, Lord, 103
McNaith, Corrie, 95
McRae, Willie, death of, 167–8
McSorley, Ronald and Patricia, 82
magistrates (JPs), 16–24, 37; advisory committee's recommendations, 19–20; and bail applications, 21, 22–3; and children in care, 121, 122–4, 127; compulsory care orders, 125–6, 127; and juvenile offenders, 125–6, 130–1, 141, 209; lay, 9, 16; 'place of safety' order, 121; and the police, 227–8, 229, 230, 234, 273; stipendiary, 9, 16, 134
Magistrates Association, 19, 20, 21, 23
Main, PC Edward, 263–6
Malim, Christopher John, 66–7
Mann, Mr Justice, 241
Mark, Sir Robert, 40, 246
Martin, Jan, 196, 201
Martin, Ken, 222
Massiter, Cathy, 96–8, 99, 101
Mather & Platt Ltd, 66–7
Maxwell-Fyfe, Sir David, 97
May, Lord Justice, 162
Mayhew, Sir Patrick, 176, 177
Meacher, Michael, MP, 199–200
Mead, William, trial of (1690), 33
media, and governments, 183–6
Medical Defence Union (MDU), 156–7
Medical Protection Society (MPS), 156
medical records/reports, 208, 211–16
Megarry, Sir Robert, 74, 79
Mental Health Commission, 146
Metropolitan Police, 228–9, 230, 231, 242–6, 281; CIB, 262–3; compensation paid by, 247; Confait case, 247, 252, 254, 259; Garratt v. Eastmond (1959), 230–1; Gerald Farrelley case, 280; Holloway Road case, 263–6, 267; Jarrett case and Broadwater Farm riot, 236–9, 256–9, 266–7; intelligence database of, 200–1; PSI Report (1983), 241, 242–4, 253, 256; Trevor Monerville case, 268–9; see also inner-city riots; police
Metropolitan Police Act (1829), 228
MI5: 167, 201; and Spycatcher case, 163–4, 192; surveillance and telephone-tapping by, 96–9, 100–1, 163
MI6: 167, 201
MIND, 140–1, 144, 149–50; In Whose Best Interests?, 140–1
miners' strike (1984–5), 110
ministerial responsibility, 168–9, 173, 175–8
Minsitry of Justice, need for, 10–11, 15–16
Mitchell, David, 258
Moben plc, 83–6
Mogg, John, 177

Molesworth cruise missile site, 95
Monerville, Trevor, 268–9
Monopolies and Mergers Commission, 180
Moonman, Eric, 221
Mowlem, John, 221
MPs: private members' bills, 196–7, 199–200, 211; register of interests of, 185–6; see also House of Commons
Mulberry Home Extensions Ltd, 83, 84–5
Muller, Hassan, 256–9
Mullier, Ken, 221, 222–3
Municipal Corporations Act (1835), 229, 230
Murray, Garry, 219

Nabney, Dr Jack, 59
NACNE (National Advisory Committee on Nutritional Education), report (1981), 179–80
NALGO, 140
National Audit Commission, 153
National Children's Home, 141
National Consumer Council, 162
National Council for Civil Liberties (NCCL), 99, 108, 111, 196, 256; Justice Deserted, 38–9
National Farmers Union, 80
National Health Service (NHS), 152–6; hospital delays, 153, 155; overworked junior hospital doctors, 155–6; shortage of nurses, 153–4; underfunding, 154, 155, 166
National Health Service Act (1946), 16, 152; (1977), 152
National House Building Council, 89
National Industrial Relations Court, 10
National Insurance inspectors, 78
National Taxpayer Tracing System, 206
NAYPIC (National Association of Young People in Care), 144, 145
negligence, 159; medical profession's, 156–8
Neville, Mrs Esther, 80, 90
Neville-Jones and Howie of Poole, 65
Newcastle, legal aid refusal rate, 21
New Cross party fire (1981), 243
New Zealand, no-fault compensation scheme in, 157–8
Newman, Sir Kenneth, 236, 239, 245
NINO (National Insurance Number), 205–6, 219
no-fault compensation scheme, 157–8
Northern Ireland Police Federation, 104–5
Northumbria police authority, 240–1
nuclear power, danger of, 195
nuisance, 82
Nunan, Manus, recorder, 11–14
nurses, 153–4

Obscene Publications Act (1959), 102, 113
obscenity and indecency, 102, 108–9,

obscenity and indecency – *cont.*
  112–15; and homosexuality, 115; *Lady Chatterley's Lover* trial, 112–13, 115; and pornography, 113–14; Williams Report on (1979), 114
Observer, 30, 251
Office of Fair Trading, 85–6, 180
official secrets, 163–4, 169, 170–2, 178–80, 183, 186–92
Official Secrets Act, 42, 102, 105, 106, 172–3, 186, 187–92, 282; Franks Report on (1971), 183, 186, 188, 190
official secrets trials, 41, 42–3, 44
Old Bailey (Central Criminal Court), 33, 41, 112–13, 163, 19, 256–9
Ombudsman (Commissioner for Local Administration), 90–1, 261, 267
Orton, Joe, *Loot*, 226
Osmond, Grant and Rose, solicitors, 64
Otton, Mr Justice, 111
Oulton, Sir Derek, 102
Oxford, Chief Constable Kenneth, 239–40
Oxfordshire Education Authority, 161–2
Oz magazine, 113

parens patriae, legal doctrine of, 129
parental rights resolution, 127, 133, 135
Park House assessment centre, Salford, 145
Parliament, x, xi, 6, 164; and government, 165–78; and the Lobby, 183–5; MPs' right to free speech in, 105; sovereignty of, 168
Parliamentary Questions, 165–9
Parsons, Leslie, 66–9, 71
Parsons, PC, 237–8
Pascall, Derek, 254, 258, 259
passports, computer-readable, 208
peace movement, 93, 95–6, 97–8
Peach, Blair, death of, 26, 31, 263
Peirce, Gareth, 23, 27, 269, 280
Peel, Sir Robert, 227, 228, 229
Penguin Books and *Lady Chatterley* trial, 112–13
Penn, William, trial of, (1690), 33
personal freedom, 112–18; and pornography, 113–14; right to read, 112–13, 115; sexual rights, 115–17
'Persons Unknown' anarchist trial (1979), 40–1
pesticides lobby, 181–3
Pesticides Safety Precautions Scheme (PSPS), 181–2
phantom crimes, 249, 251
Phillips, Sir Cyril, 260
Pickles, Judge James, 11, 14–15; article in *Daily Telegraph* on prisons, 102–4
place of safety order, 121
plastic bullets, police use of, 240–1
Platt, Steve, 244
Platt-Mills Enquiry, 273, 275, 276, 279
poaching, 41

police, police officers, 142–3, 226–81; accountability of, 227–47; age of, 245; British Nuclear Police, 167; complaints against, 259–81; confessions obtained by, 247–59; confidentiality of, 167–8, 170; and coroners' inquests, 26–7; cross-fertilisation among, 267–8; and data protection, 200–9, 216, 219; and domestic violence, 244–5; and Economic League, 220–1, 223; and employee-vetting, 223; expenditure and income, 233, 246; and freedom of assembly, 109–11; and freedom of expression, 104–5; history of, 227–34; and inner-city riots, 237–40, 256–9; phantom crimes, 249, 251; politics of, 245–6; priority duties of, 234–5; and prostitution, 117; and Public Order Act (1986), 110–11; and racism, 241, 243–4; Royal Commission report on (1962), 231–4, 235; search warrants, 78; stop and search powers, 242; and subversives, 99–100; surveillance by, 93–101; write-offs of unsolved crimes, 248–51, 252; *see also* Metropolitan Police; MI5; MI6; Special Branch
Police Act (1964), 229, 234, 259
Police and Criminal Evidence Act (PACE: 1984), 78, 237, 242, 246, 247, 252, 254, 255–6, 257, 259, 260, 261–2, 267
police authorities, 230, 231, 232–4, 235–6, 240, 246
Police Complaints Authority (PCA), 238, 252, 259, 261–2, 263, 264, 265, 266, 269, 274, 277–9, 280–1
Police Complaints Board (PCB), 259–61, 262, 263, 264, 265, 271
Police Federation, 26, 245, 260, 281
Police National Computer (PNC), 44, 45, 236; Suspected Persons Index, 200
Police Review, 223, 239, 264
Police Studies Institute (PSI): *Police and People in London* report (1983), 241, 242–4, 253, 256
police surgeons, evidence of, 268, 269
Ponting, Clive, 41, 171–3, 191
Poor Prisoners' Defence Act (1903), 46
pornography, 113–14
post-mortems, 26
Powell, Enoch, 185
Powell, Mr Justice, 192
PRC Homes, 89–90
pressure groups, 195; *see also* lobbying
Prevention of Cruelty to Children Act (1879), 129–30
Prevention of Terrorism Act, 257
Prince, Leslie, 223
Prince's Lodge hostel, Tower Hamlets, 87–8, 90
prisons: Judge Pickles' article on, 102–4; remand, 22, 37, 39; special secret isolation cells, 108

private investigators, 219–20
privileged information, issue of, 268, 269
Profumo scandal, 8
prostitution, 116–17, 236; juvenile, 129
Provisional IRA, 12
public enquiries, 194–6
Public Order Act (1986), 80, 110, 111
Puhlhofer v. London Borough of Hillingdon (1986), 76–8

R. v. Aubrey, Berry and Campbell, 42–3
R. v. Bingham Justices, 18
Race Relations Act, 41–2
Ramblers' Association, 80
Randall, DC, 237–8, 266
rape, 8
read, the right to, 112–13, 115
recorders, 6, 8, 9, 11–14
Reddington, John, 271, 272, 274, 275, 276
Redgrave, Vanessa, 208
Reed, Mrs Ann, 58–60, 61
Rees, Caroline, 158–9
Rees, Mark, 116
Rees, Merlyn, 198
reformatories, 130–1
Rehabilitation of Offenders Act (1974), 202
Reid, Lord, 106
Reiner, Robert, 245
remand prisoners, 22, 37, 39; eight-day rule, 39
Remuneration Certificate, 64
Rent Acts, 86
Richards, Judge Bertie, 8
Right of Privacy Bills, 196–7
Rimmington, Eric, 96
'Robert H.', 250
Robertson, Geoffrey, 24, 31
'Rodney C.', 209–10
Rossi, Sir Hugh, 195
Royal Commission on Criminal Procedure (1978), 247, 260, 261
Royal Commision on Legal Services (1979), 46, 54, 56
Royal Commission on the Police (1962), 231–4, 235, 241, 246, 259
Royal Ulster Constabulary, 104
Ruddock, Joan, 98, 99
'Run the World' charity fund-raising event, 96
Russell-Davies, Dr Derek, 147

St Andrew's hospital, Northampton, 146–51
Salford City Council, 145, 193
Salisbury, Harold, 99–100
Samaritans, 120
Samuel Rhodes School, 162
Sargeant, DC Rex, 254–5, 258
Scargill, Arthur, 99
Scarman Report, (1981), 235, 239, 242

school building and repairs, 159–60
Scotland Yard, 201, 245, 247, 263, 264, 265; CIB2: 247–8; Serious Crime Squad (CI), 252
Scott, Daniel, 278
Scott, Peter, QC, 15
secure units for children in care, 142, 143, 144, 145, 146
security consultants, 219
Seeley, Major General J. E. B., 187–8
select committees, parliamentary, 165, 169–72, 173, 174, 177–8, 185
separation of powers, theory of, 164, 173
Severn, Alan, 90–1
sex offences, 8, 113
Sexual Offences Act (1985), 117
sexual rights, 115–18
Shaw, Steven, 226, 227, 270–80, 281
Sheffield Peace Action Network, 96
sheriff's court, 134–5, 136
Sherwell, David, 145
Shipley, Peter, 181
shoplifting, 8, 48
Shrimpton, Dr Trevor, 179
Shuffrey, Ralph, 198–9
Silkin, Sam, Attorney General, 43
Simmons, Mrs June, 55
'Simpson, Denise', 141–4
Sizewell B enquiry (1987), 195
Skinner, Dennis, 30
Smith, Chris, MP, 245–6
Smith, Jim, accountant, 224–5
Smith, John, social worker, 151
Smith, Mandy, social worker, 139
social services: 'At Risk Register', 120; child care system, 120–40; information in files, 210–11; Scottish, 131–7; underfunding, 139; voluntary care, 126–8; see also local authorities
Social Work (Scotland) Act (1968), 131, 132, 133
social workers, 120, 121, 123, 127, 128, 151–2; attacks on, 139–40; power of, 131–9
solicitors, 61–72, 88, 267; complaints about, 61–72; and judicial review, 91; and legal aid work, 47, 56–8; negligence by, 61–6, 69–70; overcharging by, 64–5, 67–8, 71; and the police, 257, 258, 268, 269, 272, 273; professional misconduct by, 61, 63
Solicitors' Complaints Bureau (Law Society), 61, 63, 70–1
Spastics Society, 161
Special Branch, 42, 43, 44, 93–4, 99–100, 196, 200, 201, 219, 220, 221
Special Patrol Groups (SPGs), 263
'special juries', 34
'special verdicts', 34
Speed, Acting Sergeant Ian, 25
Spring, Derek, 84, 85
spies, 169, 188

Spycatcher, case, 163-4, 192, 225
Spyway private hospital, 146-51
Stalker, John, 275-6, 281
'stand by for the crown', 37
standing committees, 169, 174
Stanley, John, 170, 171, 172, 173
statutory charge (legal aid), 52-6
Steel, David, 180
Steele, John, 281
Steisow, Dr Hanna, 269
Stevenson, Sir Melford, 8
Stoke Newington police, 268-9
stop and search powers, 242-3
Sturgess, Judge, 282
subversives, 97, 98, 99-100, 101, 102, 220-2
Sun Book of Page 3 Girls, 114
Sunday Times, 105-6, 107-8, 167, 179
Sunshine Act, US, 175
surveillance, police, 93-101; see also data protection

Table Office, 168
Tariq Ali, 208
taxing masters, 54, 67
Taylor, Mr Justice, 101
Taylor, John, 210
Tayside Regional Council, 202, 204
telephone-tapping, 94, 95-6, 98-9, 100-1, 167
tenants' rights, 86-92
Tennant, Dr Gavin, 146, 147, 148, 149, 150, 151
terrorist trials, 44
Thalidomide scandal, 107-8
Thatcher, Mrs Margaret, 12-13, 39-40, 112, 168-9, 175, 176-7, 184-5, 191, 198, 200
theft, burglary and robbery, 38, 235, 236, 242, 250-1, 262, 270, 271-2, 274-5
Thomas, Jimmy, 192
Thomas, Linda, 157
Thompson, Jean, 16-17, 24
'Tinkerbell', 98-9
Tisdall, Sarah, 189-91
Tish, Roberta, 49, 56
Tottenham police and Broadwater Farm riot, 236-9
Toxteth, police policy in, 239-40
trade unions, 99, 111-12
transsexuals, 116
trespass, 79-80, 81
'trial by newspaper', 107
Trotter, Mrs Anne, 202, 204-5
Turnbull, Roy, 222
Twist, Miss Pauline, 64-5
Tyler, Paul, 181

UAPT (United Association for the Protection of Trade), 216-17, 219
UK Immigrants Advisory Service, 51

UPI (Universal Personal Identifier), 205, 219
US Freedom of Information Act, 182
Ustinov, Peter, 74

Vagrancy Act, 102
'the value element', 64
verdicts: majority, 34; 'special', 34
vetting of jurors, 34, 42-5
Vickers, Alan, 276, 277
Vidal, Gore, 115
Vinelott, Mr Justice, 68, 69
Vives, Mrs Margaret, 84-5
Voice (monthly), 188-9
voluntary care, 125, 126-8, 131-2, 141

Waddington, David, 223-4
Waldegrave, William, 181
Walden, Brian, 196-7
Walker, Caroline, 179-80
Walker, Martin, 279, 280
Walker, Peter, 181, 182
Walker, PC Ron, 247-52
Wallace, John, Teresa and Allan, 161-2
Wallguard Ltd, 83, 84, 86
Wallis, Tim and Bridie, 95-6, 99
Ward, Miss, expelled from Bradford College, 7
Ward, Tony, 27-8
Warrington bench, 20-1
watch committees, 229, 230
Watkins, Lord Justice, 241
Weeks, Wilf, 180
Welsh Council for Civil Liberties, *Political Policing in Wales*, 253
welfare of the child, concept of, 129
Westland affair, 175-8, 180
Whiskin, Fred, 61-4, 69-70
White Papers, 165, 197-8
Whitehouse, Mrs Mary, 115
Whitelaw, William, 199
Wicks, Nigel, 177
Widgery, Lord, 125
Williams, David, 188
Williams, June, 51
Williams, Michael, 108
Williams, Tennessee, 115
Williams Committee Report (1979), 114
Willis, Mr Justice, 43
Wilson, Harold, 163, 170, 184, 197
Wise, PC Nicholas, 263-6
Witham, Margaret, 99
Wood, James, 273
Woodhouse, David, 156-7
World in Action (ITV), 220-2
Wright, Peter, *Spycatcher*, 163-4, 192
write-offs (of unsolved crimes), 248-51, 252

Younger, Sir Kenneth, 197, 198
Younger Report (1972), 197
Youth Treatment Centres, 143, 144